The Larousse Guide to
Birds of Britain and Europe

by Bertel Bruun

Illustrated by Arthur Singer

Consultant editor Bruce Campbell

Revised edition in collaboration with
Lars Svensson and Håkan Delin

Larousse and Co. Inc.

New York

Preface

Creating a field guide to the birds of Europe is a major undertaking
This book would not have been possible without extensive help from
many ornithologists, amateur as well as professional. Field orni
thologists have been particularly helpful, and much that we have
learned from this ever-growing group has been incorporated in this book

The author and artist would particularly like to thank Dean Amadon
Oliver L. Austin Jr., Jeffery Boswall, John Bull, Erik Hansen, Max E
Hodge, Charles O'Brien, Allen O'Connell, Niels O. Preuss, Chandler S
Robbins, Ole Schelde, Peter Scott, José A. Valverde, Charles Vaurie
Sven Wahlberg, Herbert S. Zim, and especially Bruce Campbell, whose
detailed knowledge has been a great contribution to the book and whe
has assisted and advised most valuably in its preparation.

The author and artist would also like to thank the staff of the
American Museum of Natural History for their assistance.

B.B., A.S

Preface to revised edition

Since first published in 1970 the original guide has experienced eigh
reprintings and translations into ten foreign languages. As the interest i
birds has grown the fund of knowledge has increased enormously an
with increasing speed. It has, therefore, been deemed necessary an
beneficial to incorporate this new knowledge as well as the change
status of some species in the form of this completely updated and revise
edition. A multitude of bird-watchers using the guide has offere
suggestions and changes which in many cases are incorporated in th
present edition. A special thanks for such help goes to Lars Svensson an
Håkan Delin and also Iain Robertson for their assistance in the revisior
and to Erik A. Bruun for his enthusiastic suggestions for improvemen
The editors of the foreign editions have also contributed greatly, addin
information as it pertains to their specific geographical areas. We want t
express our gratitude to these many enthusiasts. Again our special thank
to Lars Svensson who has also contributed many new line drawings.

B.B., A.S

First published in Great Britain by
The Hamlyn Publishing Group Limited

Published in the United States by
Larousse and Co. Inc.,
572 Fifth Avenue,
New York, N.Y. 10036

1978, 1979

ISBN 0–88332–152–1 (cased edition)
ISBN 0–88332–153–X (paperback edition)

Library of Congress Catalog Card No. 78–50996

Printed in Italy by Officine Grafiche A. Mondadori, Verona.

Contents

How to use this book

This guide covers the continent of Europe bordered by the Atlantic, the Mediterranean, the Bosphorus, the Black Sea, the Caucasus Mountains, the Caspian Sea, the Ural River and Mountains and the Arctic Ocean. This is a land mass of 3,900,000 square miles. The geographic and climatic environment varies from the Arctic areas in the far north to the Mediterranean in the south with its subtropical climate. In the east the zones merge into those of the Asian continent. Europe, most of Asia, and northernmost Africa form the *Palaearctic* region.

The major natural vegetative regions are mapped on the opposite page. The distribution of birds tends to correspond with these natural regions even though agricultural activities have changed them greatly.

The book covers the breeding birds, the regular visitors, and the casual visitors which have been recorded at least five times in this century. A list of more accidental visitors is found in the back of the book. Among the breeding birds are counted introduced species which are well-established in a feral state.

At the present time there is a tendency for eastern and south-eastern birds to extend their range further west and north-west and new species are continually added to the list. The present list gives the status as known in December 1976.

The English names in this guide are those in common use. Local or foreign names are not as a rule included, though a number of common alternate names have been included in the index. The scientific name follows the English name. The scientific name consists of two parts: the genus, followed by the specific name.

Closely related birds are grouped together in genera, closely related genera into subfamilies, subfamilies into families and families into orders. Within species several subspecies may be recognized. Only where subspecies are easily identifiable are they included in this book. Different colour phases may also occur; unlike subspecies these are not usually geographically separated, though their proportion in the population may vary in different regions. Where distinctive phases occur these have been mentioned.

The sequence is that of an evolutionary order, progressing from the least to the most advanced families of birds. Exceptions are made where they are deemed practical for identification. For instance, the white herons are grouped together, and the Hemipode put next to the closely similar but unrelated Quail.

Text, map and illustration of each bird are placed together.

The text gives the English name, the scientific name, the total length (and in some cases the wing span) in centimetres (unless otherwise stated), the abundance, habitat, characteristic features of plumage and silhouette, behavioural characteristics, and songs and calls of each bird.

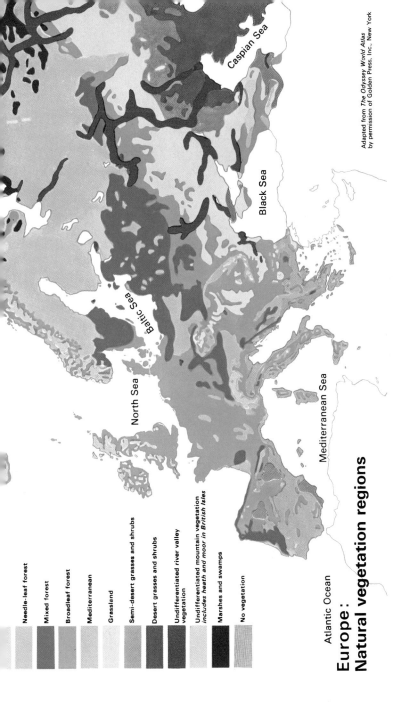

Europe:
Natural vegetation regions

Needle-leaf forest

Mixed forest

Broadleaf forest

Mediterranean

Grassland

Semi-desert grasses and shrubs

Desert grasses and shrubs

Undifferentiated river valley vegetation

Undifferentiated mountain vegetation includes heath and moor in British Isles

Marshes and swamps

No vegetation

Atlantic Ocean

Mediterranean Sea

Black Sea

Caspian Sea

Baltic Sea

North Sea

Adapted from *The Odyssey World Atlas* by permission of Golden Press, Inc., New York

There are introductions to each order and family. In some cases smaller groups are also furnished with introductory notes where this is of value. Furthermore the status of each species in the British Isles and Ireland is given in abbreviated form:

R: resident S: summer visitor W: winter visitor P: passage visitor V: vagrant

A species may belong to several of these categories.

The illustrations feature the adult male in breeding plumage. If the plumage in winter differs, this is also shown. Females differing from males are shown. Immatures differing from adult birds are shown. If different colour phases occur, these are shown. Birds often seen in flight are also shown on the wing. In a few cases comparative illustrations are used to call attention to similar species on different pages. On the illustrations ♂ means male, ♀ means female, imm. means immature and juv. means juvenile.

In some cases whole spreads are used to illustrate particularly difficult groups.

The distribution maps have been carefully compiled from the most recent references and in order that as much detail as possible can be represented four colours have been used. The purple areas represent the residential range of the species. The red areas represent the summer breeding range only. Blue areas are the winter ranges and the yellow represents those areas where the species occurs on migration. Broken lines in the appropriate colour represent the irregular limits in the range of the species; for example, a broken blue line indicates the irregular winter limits. A solid yellow line represents the irregular migration limits of the species.

Neighbouring areas outside Europe are included although this book does not comprehensively cover the birds of these areas. The small size of the maps clearly limits the amount of detail which can be incorporated and readers are referred to more local guides and lists for such details.

The distribution maps give wintering areas in blue, breeding areas in red and where the bird occurs all year round in purple. Migration areas are shown in yellow. The irregular winter and summer limits are shown as broken blue or red lines. The irregular migration limits are shown as a solid yellow line.

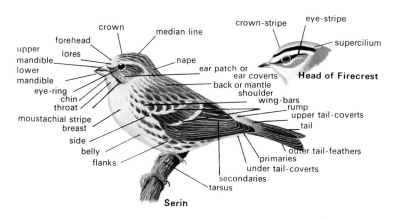

Head of Firecrest

Serin

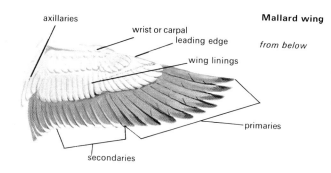

Mallard wing

from below

axillaries

wrist or carpal

leading edge

wing linings

primaries

secondaries

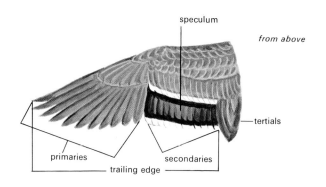

speculum

from above

tertials

primaries

secondaries

trailing edge

Identifying birds

When you see a bird and want to identify it, there are certain points you should look for. If you cannot identify the species, you should write these down on the spot.

Whooper Swan   Bewick's Swan

The size of a bird is important. Often two species vary so little in colour and other respects that you cannot use these features at a distance and have to rely on size, for instance in the case of the Whooper Swan and Bewick's Swan. Sometimes it is difficult to tell the size exactly and it is always valuable to have other objects, particularly other known birds to compare with. It should also be kept in mind that under certain conditions, for instance in foggy weather, birds look bigger than in sunshine.

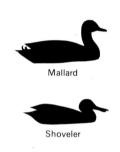

Mallard

Shoveler

The shape of a bird is likewise of importance, particularly at long distances or against the sun when other features are obscured. The illustration of the Mallard and the Shoveler shows the great difference in shape in otherwise quite similar species. In flight, shape is also important, particularly in the case of birds of prey and other species which are most often seen on the wing. The differently shaped wings of the Sparrowhawk and Merlin tell the two apart at a glance even under the worst conditions for seeing other details. In general you should try to note the proportions and shape of bill, head and neck, wings, legs and tail.

Sparrowhawk

Merlin

The colours of birds are important, in many cases diagnostic, but they are not always easy to see and different light may change them considerably. Often the coloured parts in which you are particularly interested are not visible, such as the speculum of a duck when the bird is sitting. You then have to rely on other features for identification.

In describing the colours and plumage patterns of a bird, it is important to know the terminology of the anatomy. The illustration on page 9 shows the position of important named areas.

Examples of different parts of the plumage being essential for identification are innumerable. Here only two are illustrated: that of the pattern of stripes on the head distinguishing the Sedge Warbler from the Reed Warbler; and the much wider, white rear-edge of the wing distinguishing the Calandra Lark from the Skylark, which only has a narrow white edge. The main things to note are general pattern (spotted, striped, etc.), tail and rump colours, wings (stripes, patches) and facial pattern. In some cases eye, bill and leg colour will confirm the identification.

Many birds have characteristic movements which are helpful in identifying them. Experienced birdwatchers can often tell a bird at a glance by its movements. The Starling walks upright on the ground whereas the Blackbird runs with a crouch. The Chaffinch hops from branch to branch whereas the Great Tit climbs about with great dexterity, one moment hanging upside down, the next sitting upright. On the water the Moorhen swims with constantly bobbing movements of head and tail while the Coot laboriously but smoothly

Reed Warbler

Sedge Warbler

Skylark   Calandra Lark

Starling   Blackbird

Tit   Finch

Coot   Moorhen

works its way forward. The pattern of flight differs greatly, the woodpeckers flying in great undulations, the Starling in a straight line. The wing action likewise differs, the Swallow gracefully gliding back and forth with a few relaxed wing-beats interspersed, the Swift speeding ahead on stiff wings, which move very rapidly.

Swift   Swallow

Song

Bird songs and calls are very valuable in identification. In fact they are often the only safe means by which to separate closely related species of warblers. Experienced birdwatchers use songs and calls for identification as much as they do other features like colour and shape.

Most birds sing only in spring and early summer. Most species have a characteristic way of delivering their songs, usually from a special song post. This may be hidden like the Nightingale's or exposed like the Icterine Warbler's. Some, like the Garden Warbler, sing while they move about. Others like the Whitethroat, have characteristic song-flights.

Besides the song, birds utter many other sounds; flight calls, alarm calls and contact notes. Often the calls are as characteristic as the songs and you can, for instance, identify many night migrants by their calls alone.

Describing songs and calls is very difficult and no truly satisfactory way has been found. An interesting new method is that of showing the song of a bird on an audiospectrogram or sonagram;

Garden Warbler

Whitethroat

Icterine Warbler

two of these are illustrated here. They require much practice to be useful. The best way to learn the songs and calls of birds is to find an experienced observer who can take you out into the field and show you what to listen for. Next best is the use of recordings, which can be played at home but cannot be used in the field. A list of useful records commercially available is given in the back of this book.

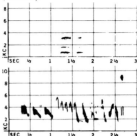

The sonagram is a graph of pitch (in kilocycles) against time (in seconds). Those shown here are for the Pheasant (above) *and the Skylark* (below).

Miscellaneous factors in identification

Besides the physical features and behaviour characteristic of each species, other factors play a role in identification; although they are not and cannot be diagnostic, they are nevertheless of great help. Identification usually involves a process of exclusion; few birds are identified on positive evidence alone. The place where a bird is seen is important. In this book all birds which have not previously been recorded in Europe are excluded. Likewise, within Europe the species vary greatly in their distribution, and although for instance the Pintail Snipe and the Snipe are very similar, few British birdwatchers would even in their wildest dreams consider checking every Snipe to make sure it was not a Pintail Snipe.

Besides the geographical area, the habitat is of importance, although any given bird may occur exceptionally in almost any habitat. When you see a pipit on a shore you immediately think of the Rock Pipit; if you see it in a wood, the chances are that it will be a Tree Pipit. If a brown warbler is seen among reeds, you think of all the different *Acrocephali;* if you see it in a wood, you think first of a Garden Warbler and probably the *Acrocephali* do not enter your mind, unless something unusual about the bird arouses your suspicions.

The time of year a bird is seen also plays an important part in narrowing down the choice of species you consider before identity is established. You do not see warblers in the northern Scandinavian forests in the midst of winter and Bramblings are rare enough in southern Europe in summer. So, with experience you automatically discard a large number of theoretical possibilities. The range maps used in this book should help you in this respect as well as in deciding the geographical possibilities.

The abundance of a species is also of great importance. Remember, if faced with a choice, you are always most likely to have seen the most abundant of the possible species.

Although one theoretically should try to identify all birds, it is very difficult in practice to do this. On the other hand, it is imperative that all rare and unusual observations be substantiated by definite and positive identification, preferably by more than one observer. If in doubt write down all the facts about the observed bird — and only what you have observed — on the spot so you can later consult more experienced friends and/or the literature.

Migration

Although by no means all birds migrate, the phenomenom is so wide-spread and plays such a part in field ornithology that an introduction to this phenomenon is justified even in a book on identification.

Some birds are resident throughout their range all the year round. This does not necessarily mean that individual birds do not travel at all, but only that their travels do not take them outside their breeding range. Others are partial migrants, which means that part of a population or some populations migrate while others stay within their breeding range. In Europe it is usually the north-easternmost populations which migrate, due to the more severe weather conditions in these regions. True migrants leave their breeding range entirely.

Many birds move south long before food and weather conditions force them to do so (for instance, the warblers) whereas others do not move until forced to do so by snow and ice (for instance, many ducks).

The physiological basis for migration is not known in its entirety but experiments have proved that day-length is of importance and influences the hormonal production of the pituitary gland. Before migration birds store energy in the form of fat to be able to sustain the strenuous effort of travelling.

Birds are also known to find their way on migration with the help of stars and the sun but recognition of the local geography also plays a role, explaining how some individuals are able to return to the same garden year after year.

In Europe most migratory species move toward the south-west through Europe in autumn. As can be seen from the range maps there are several exceptions to this general rule — for instance, the Black-headed Bunting, which moves almost due east in autumn. In spring, when the migrants return, they usually arrive earlier in the west of Europe than in the east and centre. The speed of migration varies greatly but generally spring migration progresses more rapidly than autumn migration and late spring migrants travel faster than earlier travellers.

Although the breeding birds of Europe move toward the south in winter, we also have some birds which nest in the southern hemisphere and winter here, for instance the Great Shearwater and Wilson's Petrel, both of which spend their 'winter' (our summer) in the North Atlantic.

Some of the most important sites in Europe for observing migratory birds

1 Reykjanes	14 Portland Bill	26 Biarritz
2 Fair Isle	15 Dungeness	27 Camargue
3 Revtangen	16 Cley	28 Col de Bretolet
4 Skagen	17 Gibraltar Point	29 Sempach
5 Skatudden	18 Spurn Head	30 Neusiedlersee
6 Signilskär	19 Texel	31 Danube Delta
7 Puhtu	20 Heligoland	32 Volga Delta
8 Cape Clear	21 Blåvands Huk	33 Marismas du
9 Bardsey	22 Falsterbo	Guadalquivir
10 Skokholm	23 Ottenby	34 Gibraltar
11 Lundy	24 Kalmarsund	35 Capri
12 Slimbridge	25 Rybatschii	36 Malta
13 Isles of Scilly		37 Bosporus

Another common type of migration is the vertical movement displayed by mountain birds which move down into the valleys in winter.

Different from migration are the mass occurrences (invasions) of certain species like the Crossbill, which appears in large numbers in western Europe after years of good fir seed production in Russia. Another phenomenon is the dispersal of young birds immediately after the breeding season and before the true migration. This is particularly characteristic of herons.

Birds usually migrate over a rather wide front but many show a ten-

Unlike most European birds, the Black-headed Bunting, which breeds in Italy and the Balkans, migrates eastward in autumn.

dency to concentrate in certain areas where they can easily be observed. Night migrants are sometimes forced down in certain areas when they meet adverse weather conditions. Many migrating land birds will follow coastlines, and at places where they are forced to cross water to continue their migration they may concentrate in large numbers. Such places are Falsterbo in southern Sweden, the Bosporus and the southern part of Spain. When land birds have to cross mountains they concentrate in the valleys.

Sea and water birds likewise may be concentrated along certain coastlines and may rest in vast numbers on especially favourable feeding grounds.

During migration, birds are very vulnerable to displacement due to adverse weather and wind conditions, and spring and particularly autumn are the most likely times to see rarities from far-off places. Particularly good places to find these rarities are islands and promontories attracting birds from large areas.

A map of some of the bird observatories and localities which are particularly good for the observation of bird migration is given on page 15.

Studying birds

This book is intended to be a guide to help in the identification of birds. The identification is not an end in itself, but only a tool by which further studies can be made and further pleasure gained. Identification in itself carries a certain pleasure but 'species-collecting' serves very little purpose unless it is an integrated part of more advanced study.

Birds can be studied wherever you are at all times of the year. You need little equipment; in most cases a pair of binoculars, a pencil and a note-book will suffice.

The Great Tit is easily attracted to feed at bird tables.

In spring, when the weather improves, a tremendous change takes place in the world of birds. The migrants arrive from the south; the wintering birds disappear, heading north. Data on arrivals and departures are important and interesting. Some arrive at the same spot on the same date year after year; others vary much more. Some arrive by day, some by night, some singly, some in pairs, some in flocks; some are very much influenced by the weather, some less so. For the departing birds and those only passing through, the same sort of information can be collected and compared. The permanent residents also change their behaviour in spring, and songs, which have not been heard for a long time, again ring through the air. The birds take up territories where they intend to nest. Some have small territories, some large ones; some defend them only against members of their own species, some against other species as well. Some prefer gardens, some fields, some woods. The opportunity to study these different phenomena is shared by all observers and in a very short time many interesting facts can be learned.

As the birds start singing a new field of study is opened up. Why does the bird sing? Are there individual differences in song? When does it sing? How often? What influences the singing? If a tape recorder is available, recordings can be made and compared. When the male has attracted a female to his territory by his song, a new phase starts. Selection of nest site, nest building, egg laying, incubation, hatching, and care of the young, follow in sequence.

At this stage the opportunities for interesting studies and observations are innumerable. The behaviour of birds in different situations is almost infinitely varied. What makes the bird decide to choose one branch for the nest site? How is the nest built? With what? How long does it take? Is it the male, the female, or both which do the building? And the eggs: When are they laid? How big is the clutch? Who incubates them and for how long? How does the bird react to enemies threatening its nest? How many young are hatched? In what order? When do the parents start feeding them? How often? How much?

The nesting habits of the Pied Flycatcher have been extensively studied by means of nest boxes.

What sort of food? How many of the young survive to leave the nest? When do they leave? How long do they stay with the parent birds? Is the species double-brooded, starting the whole sequence all over again?

All these questions may be answered by watching the birds, sometimes even from inside a house. Another aspect of breeding biology is the number of birds present in a given area. If carried on for some years much information can be gained by regular counts and eventually it may be possible to see what factors influence the numbers of birds present. Nest boxes can be put up and will be readily used by a number of species, making the study of almost all aspects of breeding biology much easier.

For closer study, coloured rings can be used, marking each bird with different combinations of coloured rings on its legs, so that it can be recognized as an individual even at a distance. This sort of study should only be undertaken by the more seriously-inclined birdwatchers and in many countries the use of coloured rings is now regulated and permits have to be obtained.

Regular marking with numbered rings stamped with the address of the institution sponsoring the scheme is also for the more advanced and is regulated to avoid misuse and confusion. Although many young are still ringed, the emphasis is now more on trapping adult birds. Bird-ringing is a very important tool for learning many different things about birds: if the bird migrates, where, when and how; it also throws light on life span, mortality and population composition, if enough birds are ringed.

When the next generation has been reared, a new phase occurs, the autumn migration. This again offers a multitude of subjects for study. The composition of a population changes, species disappear and others arrive. As with the spring migration, the questions of when, how and where arise. What influences the departure? How does the migration take place?

There are many places where diurnal migration can be observed as it takes place and here a new set of questions arises: What time of day? How many species and individuals are involved? How high do they fly? How fast? In what direction? When the migratory season has passed, the resident birds are faced with the task of surviving the winter with its cold, snow and ice. Many change their ways completely and there is much to be studied. What do they eat? Where? When? How and where do they sleep? Do they have special roosts and when do they arrive at them and how long do they use them?

At this time of year many birds are attracted to feed at bird-tables, particularly if the weather is unseasonably bad. Not only will you see many unfamiliar birds at close range, but their behaviour and food choice can be observed and studied. Do any individuals rank over others? Does this change? When do they eat? How much? What influence does the weather have on feeding behaviour?

These bird-tables also offer golden opportunities for photographing birds, but specialized and somewhat expensive equipment is needed to obtain good results. A telescopic lens and a tripod are essential, but the results certainly warrant the expense and the troubles.

Then it is spring and the cycle begins again.

When you start watching birds it is a good idea to contact more experienced birdwatchers in the neighbourhood as soon as possible. They will be very helpful and can give many hints as to where to go, when, and what to look for. They will know other birdwatchers and will know about clubs, meetings etc., all of which make the first steps easier and more rewarding.

Practically every country has its own ornithological societies and in many areas there are local groups which can be very helpful, not only to the beginner, but also to the more advanced student. Many publish journals and bulletins from which valuable information can be gained.

Divers

(order *Gaviiformes*, family *Gaviidae*) are specialized for swimming and diving. Divers come ashore only to breed. Usually silent in winter. In flight, head is held lower than body. The wing-beats are fast, uninterrupted by gliding. When diving, the swimming bird springs up and forward to begin the plunge, but it can also submerge stealthily. Clutch, 1–3 eggs.

BLACK-THROATED DIVER *Gavia arctica* L 64 W 119
Common. Breeds on deep lakes, usually in secluded places in mountains or tundras; sometimes on seashores. In winter along seashores, sometimes in small, loose flocks with Red-throated Diver. In summer, black throat and light grey crown are diagnostic. In winter, back is grey with scaly white spots visible only at close range, crown and nape paler. Bill thin and straight, proportionately more slender than Great Northern's. In flight, with difficulty told from Red-throated by shorter upstroke of wings. Call on breeding grounds is low wailing cry; in flight sometimes utters rapid quack like Red-throated Diver's.   RWP

RED-THROATED DIVER *Gavia stellata* L 56 W 112
Common in breeding range on fresh and salt water; winters mainly along the coast, often in company with Black-throated Divers. Often migrates in small flocks. Much slimmer than Black-throated and thin, light-coloured bill slightly upturned. Habitually holds head and bill pointing slightly upward. In summer, red throat diagnostic. Winter colour is lighter than Black-throated, with tiny white spots on back. Usual call a rapid goose-like quacking. Wailing call rarer.   RWP

Great Northern Diver

GREAT NORTHERN DIVER *Gavia immer* L76 W147
Rare except on breeding grounds on inland lakes in Iceland. Otherwise along seashores. Although varying in size, it is considerably larger than Red-throated and Black-throated Divers, with a proportionately much heavier, straight bill. Colours in winter resemble those of Black-throated. In summer all-black head and back with bands of white spots are characteristic. In winter told from White-billed by shape and colour of bill and darker sides of head. Immature birds have pale bill with dark culmen. Flight heavy, almost goose-like. Calls in breeding season include loud wail and yodelling; quacks in flight like other divers.   W

WHITE-BILLED DIVER *Gavia adamsii* L 76 W 152
Rare along seashores. The largest diver, almost identical to Great Northern but with light-coloured, slightly upturned bill. The maxillary feathering extends further above nostrils than on Great Northern and shafts of primaries are white; dark in Great Northern. In summer plumage, head is slightly darker and white spots on back slightly larger and fewer than Great Northern's. Both species have similar calls.   V

cormorant sea duck merganser diver grebe

Black-throated Diver

winter

summer

Red-throated Diver

winter

summer

mm.

winter

Great Northern Diver

summer

mm.

White-billed Diver

winter

summer

21

Grebes

(order *Podicipediformes,* family *Podicipedidae*) are diving birds, smaller than divers, with lobed toes. Short legs far back on the body; tail very short; wings short. Flight hurried. Head held low in flight. Courtship displays are often elaborate. Nest in floating vegetation. 2–7 eggs.

GREAT CRESTED GREBE *Podiceps cristatus* L 46 Common in lakes and sheltered bays with reed cover. In winter also along shores. Sometimes breeds colonially; often encountered in small flocks in winter. Largest of our grebes, best told by long, straight neck. In winter loses prominent ear tufts and can be confused with Red-necked Grebe, but notice pale line above the eye, greyer back, longer neck, longer pink bill. Mutual display includes diving for waterweed and standing breast to breast on the water. R

RED-NECKED GREBE *Podiceps grisegena* L 43 W 81 Common in marshy lakes and ponds; in winter mainly on salt water, scarce on inland water. In summer unmistakable. In winter, can be confused with Great Crested, but notice shorter neck, shorter black and yellow bill. Dark wing always has two white patches, like Great Crested Grebe, but forward patch (shoulder) much less pronounced. It has no pale line above the eye. Sharp call note: 'kell-kell'; squealing note in breeding season. W

SLAVONIAN GREBE *Podiceps auritus* L 36 W 59 Uncommon. In summer almost exclusively found in inland lakes; in winter on sheltered sea coasts, scarce inland. In summer unmistakable. In winter told from Black-necked by pure white front of neck, and straight bill; also seems heavier. Rippling trill in breeding season. RWP

BLACK-NECKED GREBE *Podiceps nigricollis* L 30 W 59 Sometimes common in lakes with heavily reed-fringed shores where it nests in colonies. In winter found along seashores and in larger ice-free lakes. In summer plumage, black neck diagnostic. In winter similar to Slavonian Grebe, but has greyer neck and slim, slightly upturned bill. At a distance, straighter neck helpful as field mark. Usually forms small flocks in winter, while Slavonian is seen singly. Rippling call and other notes in breeding season. RWP

LITTLE GREBE *Tachybaptus ruficollis* L 25 Common in lakes with dense vegetation. In winter also found along rivers, in harbours and other sheltered places, singly or in small parties. Very elusive. Rather uniform brownish plumage characteristic in all seasons. Takes to the wing more readily than other grebes. No wing patch. In spring utters characteristic, far-reaching, whickering trill. RW

PIED-BILLED GREBE *Podilymbus podiceps* L 35 Rare straggler from North America. The chicken-like bill and stocky appearance are characteristic. V

Great Crested Grebe

winter

summer

courtship display

Red-necked Grebe

winter

summer

Slavonian Grebe

Horned

winter

summer

Black-necked Grebe

Black-necked

winter

summer

Little Grebe

winter

summer

Pied-billed Grebe

imm. partly submerged

23

Tubenoses

(order *Procellariiformes*) have external tubular nostrils. They are birds of the ocean, coming ashore on remote islands and shores to breed. They nest in colonies; feed on squid, fish and other marine life, usually at or near the surface. All have hooked beaks. The sexes are similar. Silent away from the breeding grounds.

Families of tubenoses occurring off the European coasts

Albatrosses (family *Diomedeidae*), large birds including the largest flying species, long narrow wings, very heavy hooked beak.

Fulmars and shearwaters (family *Procellariidae*), large birds, though considerably smaller than the albatrosses. The bill is generally thinner with a pronounced tooth at the end.

Storm petrels (family *Hydrobatidae*), small birds, scarcely larger than swallows. Bills are short and the legs fairly long.

Albatrosses

are primarily birds of the southern hemisphere, only occurring off the European coasts as accidental visitors. They have tremendously long wingspreads. Though capable of powerful direct flight, they are gliders, soaring with stiffly held wings. The single egg is laid on the ground. The Black-browed Albatross is the species which has occurred the most often.

BLACK-BROWED ALBATROSS *Diomedea melanophris* L 79 W 2m Very rare, but the most likely of the albatross species to be met in Europe. Enormous size is distinctive. General coloration of adult shared with even rarer Yellow-nosed and Grey-headed Albatrosses, but combination of yellow bill and dark streak through the eye are diagnostic features of this species. Immatures have dark grey crowns and blackish bills. Most often encountered in the summer months. V

Wandering
Albatross
subadult

WANDERING ALBATROSS *Diomedea exulans* L 114 W 3m Extremely rare. Juveniles are dark brown with white face, throat, underwing and belly.

Fulmars

strongly resemble gulls in appearance and in scavenging habits, but typically range much farther out to sea. Nest usually on sea cliffs; lay one egg.

FULMAR *Fulmarus glacialis* L 46 W 107 A large gull-like tubenose. In its light colour phase (the most numerous) it can be told from gulls by the stiff flight, the habit of flapping and gliding, the heavy head and neck, the shorter tail, and, at close range, by the tubular nostrils. Dark phase birds are paler than Sooty Shearwaters, have shorter wings and a broader tail. Fulmars follow ships, often over long distances. When swimming, the bird floats high on the water. RS

tern

skua

gull

petrel

shearwater

albatross

albatross
head

shearwater
head

petrel head

shearwaters

petrels

albatross

imm.

Black-browed
Albatross

adult

Fulmar on nest

head-on silhouette

Fulmar

dark phase

light phase

light phase

25

Shearwaters (family *Procellariidae*), differ from fulmars in having longer, narrower wings, narrower tail, and longer, thinner bill. Flight pattern is similar, a few, fast, deep wingbeats and a long glide, usually close to the water. Feed on small fish and crustaceans. Nocturnal on breeding grounds. Lay a single egg. The gadfly petrels are members of this family but shown on p. 29 for identification purposes.

MANX SHEARWATER *Puffinus puffinus* L 36 W 81 Most common and numerous European shearwater. Completely dark upper side and light underside and small size distinguish it from the larger shearwaters. A sub-species with darker underside and less distinctive contrast is found in the Mediterranean. Flight rapid, tilting from side to side. Does not follow ships but gathers in large 'rafts' on sea. Nests in colonies along shores. SP

LITTLE SHEARWATER *Puffinus assimilis* L 28 Very rare visitor to European coasts north to Denmark, particularly in late spring. Closely resembles Manx Shearwater but has more white in front of eye, and some have dark under tail-coverts. Flight very rapid, with fluttering wing-beats between short spells of gliding. If direct comparison with Manx is possible, smaller size should be evident. V

GREAT SHEARWATER *Puffinus gravis* L 48 W 114 A large, fairly common Atlantic shearwater, breeding November to April in the Tristan da Cunha Islands. Black cap and white on tail are pronounced. In May and June migrates north to the western Atlantic and in October and November south through eastern Atlantic. Told from Cory's by distinctive black cap bordered with white. S

CORY'S SHEARWATER *Calonectris diomedea* L 48 W 112 Breeds in Mediterranean and north African islands, occurring from August to November in the North Atlantic. Largest of the Atlantic shearwaters. Some may have white upper tail-feathers resembling Great Shearwater, but always lacks the black-capped appearance. Flight slower, more albatross-like than that of other shearwaters. The only Atlantic shearwater to soar. Does not follow ships but trails schools of whales and dolphins.

SOOTY SHEARWATER *Puffinus griseus* L 41 W 11 Less numerous than Great Shearwater; occurs in Atlantic from July to February, but most common August to November. More confined to coastal waters than most shearwaters. Easily recognised by large size and uniform brown colour, with lighter stripe on underside of wing. Wings narrow. Wing-beats faster than those of Great Shearwater, with which it often occurs.

Assembling at dusk offshore

est Mediterranean subspecies from below

Manx swimming

baroli subspecies

boydi subspecies

Manx Shearwater

Little Shearwater

Great Shearwater

Cory's Shearwater

Sooty Shearwater

27

Storm petrels (family *Hydrobatidae*) are small birds of open

waters, feeding on tiny fish, shrimps and planktonic animals. The sturdy bill is hooked and the tubular nostrils can be seen at close range. Found singly or in flocks. Lay a single egg.

WILSON'S PETREL *Oceanites oceanicus* L 18 W 41 May be seen well out in the Atlantic, returning to its breeding grounds in the South Atlantic. Dark brown with white rump, light wing patch, long legs, and yellow webbing of feet. The tail is rounded. Dances on the surface with wings held high. Will often follow ships in loose flocks. Told from Storm Petrel by slightly larger size, light underside of feet, and slightly lighter upper side of wing; from Leach's by shape of tail.   V

LEACH'S PETREL *Oceanodroma leucorhoa* L 20 W 48 Medium-sized, dark, with prominent white rump with grey centre and pale wing patch. The tail is forked, feet are dark. Leach's is larger than Storm Petrel and is best told from this and from Wilson's Petrel by its forked tail. The flight is butterfly-like, quite different from that of Wilson's. Does not patter like Wilson's and some of the other storm petrels. The bill is noticeably heavier than that of the Storm Petrel. Does not follow ships. Sometimes blown inland after gales.   S

STORM PETREL *Hydrobates pelagicus* L 15 W 36 The most common of our petrels, also the smallest and most short-winged. The tail is square, distinguishing it from Leach's Petrel. The undersides of the feet are dark, the back and upper side of wings darker than in both Wilson's and Leach's Petrel. It has a variable but distinct white underwing-bar. The bill is very slim and weak. Flutters above the water like a bat. Follows ships. May be blown inland by storms.   S

MADEIRAN PETREL *Oceanodroma castro* L 19 W 46 A very rare visitor from Atlantic isles. Difficult to distinguish from similar petrels, but rump is pure white (Leach's Petrel), feet dark (Wilson's Petrel) and size relatively large (Storm Petrel).   V

FRIGATE PETREL *Pelagodroma marina* L 20 W 38 A very rare visitor from Atlantic isles. The colour pattern is diagnostic.   V

GADFLY PETRELS (family *Procellariidae*) are rather short-winged, strong-billed relatives of shearwaters. The tail is wedge-shaped.

SOFT-PLUMAGED PETREL *Pterodroma mollis* L 35 W 89 A very rare visitor from Atlantic isles. Grey and white pattern diagnostic.

BULWER'S PETREL *Bulweria bulwerii* L 28 W 61 A very rare visitor from breeding grounds on Atlantic isles. Dark upper rump, uniform dark colour; rather long wedge-shaped tail and short pinkish legs.   V

Wilson's Petrel

Wilson's in flight

Leach's swimming

Storm Petrel in flight

Leach's Petrel

Storm Petrel

Madeiran Petrel

Bulwer's Petrel

Frigate Petrel

Soft-plumaged Petrel

29

Pelicans and their allies (order *Pelecaniformes*)

are large, aquatic, fish-eating birds with all four toes webbed. Most species nest in large colonies and are silent outside the breeding grounds.

Families of Pelicans and their allies
Gannet (family *Sulidae*), shaped like a giant tern, fishes by diving.
Pelicans (family *Pelecanidae*), have enormous bills, they scoop up fish from the water while swimming.
Cormorants (family *Phalacrocoracidae*), often perch on poles and rocks with wings half open; they dive from the surface and swim under water; fly in V-formation.

GANNET *Sula bassana* L 92 W 172 Common in summer near breeding islands, which are rocky with steep cliffs and used year after year. Winters on the ocean, often visible from shore, especially during strong westerly winds. Note double-ended 'cigar' silhouette. Dark wingtips and white body identify adult. Immatures best told by size and shape. Feeds by diving from 50' or more into the water or by swimming under water. In migration, flies just above the water, often in lines. Wingbeats rather stiff, alternately flaps and glides. When fishing it often soars. Brown colour of immature bird gradually disappears by maturity (about three years). Sometimes follows boats, especially off Scottish coasts. Easily told from gulls by characteristic silhouette.   RS

WHITE PELICAN *Pelecanus onocrotalus* L 165 W 254 A scarce species declining in numbers. In summer found mainly in swamps and marshes, in winter also along coasts, sheltered bays and river deltas. The two European pelicans are difficult to tell apart, but in adults the wing patterns are characteristic: only a little black above, but much black below in White Pelican; much black above, hardly any below in Dalmatian. White Pelican has, in breeding plumage, a rosy tint. Feet flesh-coloured, grey in Dalmatian. Juveniles are brownish and can only be distinguished by pointed end of feathers at edge of upper mandible, as opposed to almost square ending in Dalmatian. When swimming, pelicans float very high. Flight straight, a few deliberate wing strokes interrupted by gliding. Usually fly in lines. Sometimes soar at great height.

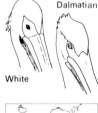

Dalmatian

White

DALMATIAN PELICAN *Pelecanus crispus* L 168 W254 Uncommon, nesting in marshes and lakes; in winter often also resorts to sheltered seashores. Distinguished from White Pelican by extent of black on upper wing, and lack of black on under wing, grey (not flesh-coloured) feet and, at very close range, yellow (not red) eyes and curly neck feathers. Immatures similar to White Pelican immatures, but distinguished by square or forked (not pointed) ending of frontal feathers at base of upper mandible. Like White Pelican, social in behaviour.

diver swan cormorant gannet pelican

Gannet

adult nesting

intermediate

juv.

adult White

adult Dalmatian

White Pelican

Dalmatian Pelican

imm. White imm. Dalmatian

CORMORANT *Phalacrocorax carbo* L92 W up to 152 Common. Usually found along seashores and in larger lakes and lagoons. Rarely very far from land. Distinguished from Shag and Pygmy Cormorant by much larger size, heavier build and white chin. The general colour is bluish black. In breeding plumage the white patch on the thighs is visible. Immatures are told from the other cormorants by the greater extent of white and yellow on underside and heavier bill. Often found in groups. Two sub-species which can be identified in the field occur. The Atlantic form *P.c. carbo*, which breeds on the Atlantic islands, Britain and in Norway, has black neck and nape, while the continental subspecies *P.c. sinensis* has almost pure white neck and nape in breeding plumage. The continental subspecies nests in colonies in trees, bushes, while the Atlantic subspecies prefers rocky cliffs. Like other cormorants it often sits on rocks or poles with half-extended wings. Fly in V-formations or lines. Usually silent, but on breeding grounds various guttural groans and moans can be heard.   RSW

imm.

SHAG *Phalacrocorax aristotelis* L 64 W 122 Common almost exclusively in salt water off rocky cliffs. Smaller than Cormorant, with more uniform blackish-green colour, lacking the white chin and thigh spot (latter only of value in breeding plumage, as is the crest). Bill and head are proportionally smaller than those of the Cormorant. In flight notice head of all cormorants is kept above the horizontal in contrast to the divers which are seen in the same habitat but fly with head held below the horizontal. The wing beats of the Shag are faster than those of the Cormorant. When swimming and sitting, all cormorants hold the bill tilted slightly upwards. Immatures have light chin and breast but darker belly than immature Cormorants (in the Mediterranean subspecies *P.a. desmarestii* lighter). Nests in colonies or rocky cliffs. Like the Cormorant, a rather silent bird.   F

imm.

PYGMY CORMORANT *Phalacrocorax pygmeus* L 38 Common. Usually prefers rivers, lagoons and freshwater lakes, often with trees and bushes on shores. Smaller than both other European cormorants, with distinctly thinner and shorter bill. In breeding plumage head and neck are rich brownish black, body black with greenish iridescence and some white spots not present in other seasons. Immatures distinguished from immature Shag by more extensive light colour on underside, from Cormorant by smaller size. Nests colonially in trees or bushes in swamps, often with different kinds of herons. Told from ducks and grebes found in the same habitat by colour, from coots by long body and tail. Wing beats are very fast like a ducks; interrupted by short glides.

imm.

Cormorant

Continental form

Atlantic form
(breeding)

flight formation

Atlantic adult
(non-breeding)

Shag

imm.

non-breeding

breeding

imm.

non-breeding

Pygmy Cormorant

imm.

breeding

33

Herons and their allies (order *Ciconiiformes*)

are wading birds with long necks, legs and bill. Most feed on aquatic animal life in shallow water. Some have long plumes ('aigrettes' or 'egrets') in breeding season. Wings broad and rounded; tail short. Clutch, 2–6 eggs.

Families of herons and their allies

Herons and bitterns (family *Ardeidae*), bill straight, flight slow with head drawn back. Most nest in colonies. Partly nocturnal. Calls are hoarse croaks.

Ibises and spoonbills (family *Threskiornithidae*), bill thin and decurved or flat and spoon-shaped. Wing-beats rather fast, neck outstretched.

Storks (family *Ciconiidae*), bill straight, flight slow with neck outstretched. They sometimes soar. Colours black and white.

Flamingos (family *Phoenicopteridae*), legs and neck extremely long; bill hooked. Flight ponderous with neck outstretched but drooped.

BITTERN *Botaurus stellaris* L 76 W 127 Rather common, but very elusive, in large reed-beds. Most active at dusk and night. Sometimes hides by freezing with head and bill pointed upward. Normal gait is crouching. Flight heron-like but low over the reed-beds. Nests singly among reeds. Distinguished from immature Night Heron by larger size, more yellowish-brown colour and lack of white spots on wing coverts and back; from much rarer American Bittern by barred upper side of wings without extensive black, lack of black 'whiskers'. The booming call, often heard at dusk in breeding season, has been compared to blowing in a bottle, or a distant foghorn and may be heard for up to three miles.   RW

AMERICAN BITTERN *Botaurus lentiginosus* L 66 W 114 Very rare visitor to westernmost parts of Europe in late autumn. Smaller than Bittern, with chestnut crown and distinctive black 'whisker' marks. On the wing blackish flight feathers diagnostic. Like European Bittern, almost exclusively found in dense reed-beds. Less crepuscular than Bittern and more often seen flying.

LITTLE BITTERN *Ixobrychus minutus* L 36 W 43 Common, but very shy and elusive, in dense vegetation of swamps and banks, with preference for larger reed beds. Once seen, easy to identify by size and coloration. In flight, large wing patch of buff contrasting with black is diagnostic. Sometimes hides by freezing. To escape danger, runs or climbs rather than flies. Flight characteristic, with fast wing-beats and long glides usually for very short distances low over the reeds. Nests singly amongst reeds and other dense vegetation, sometimes in bushes. Song is a deep croak repeated continually day and night.

crane Flamingo stork ibis heron

Bittern

Bittern fishing

juv. Night Heron
for comparison

adult in flight

**American
Bittern**

Little Bittern

adult juv.

juv. in flight

35

LITTLE EGRET *Egretta garzetta* L 61 W 97 Rather common, nesting colonially in swamps, river deltas and marshes with bushes to give support for the nest. Outside breeding season it can be met with in almost all sorts of shallow water, although it has some preference for salt and brackish marshes. Yellow feet are diagnostic. Distinguished from Cattle Egret and Squacco Heron by more 'heron-like' behaviour. Elongated scapulars (egrets) are only present in summer plumage as is the long crest. Although occasionally met with in flocks, it is less gregarious than the Cattle Egret. The Great White Egret is much larger with different bill and leg coloration and in flight the neck is held in a much more open S than is the case with the Little Egret.   V

GREAT WHITE EGRET *Egretta alba* L 89 W 140 Rather scarce. Nests in reed-beds in swamps, deltas and lagoons; outside the breeding season also met with in other types of shallow water. Much larger than any other heron with white plumage. Yellowish bill and blackish legs and feet distinguish it from the much smaller Little Egret. In flight the neck is held in a more open curve and the wing-beats are much slower than is the case with the Little Egret. Has elongated scapulars in summer.   V

SQUACCO HERON *Ardeola ralloides* L 46 W 86 Locally common in marshes, lagoons and swamps, where it nests in reeds or trees. Much more buffish in colour and stocky in appearance than other white herons, white wings and tail contrasting greatly with darkish body. In habits, closely related to the Night Heron. Often spends the day perched in the branches of a tree or bush, coming out to feed at dusk. Sociable in nesting and behaviour. Best told from Cattle Egret by bill coloration (bright yellowish green and bluish tipped black in breeding season, dark greenish outside breeding season) and much darker colours.   V

CATTLE EGRET *Bubulcus ibis* L 51 W 94 Nests mainly in bushes with other herons. Feeds on fields and dry marshes, usually in flocks and sometimes seen in association with cattle. Usually in much drier areas than other herons. Even at a long distance the Cattle Egret can be told from other herons by its white plumage, rather stocky build, characteristic flapping wing-beats and the loose flight formation of the flocks (no lines or V's). A closer range notice colour of bill and legs. Very erratic in its distribution. Can occasionally be met with all over Europe.   V

Little Egret

nesting colony

summer

winter

Great White Egret
summer

Squacco

Cattle

Squacco Heron

juv.

Cattle Egrets

juv.

Cattle Egret

adult summer

GREY HERON *Ardea cinerea* L 92 W 140 The most common and widespread of the European herons. Can be met with in lakes, seashores, lagoons, rivers, swamps and other areas of open water. Usually nests in trees near water, sometimes on ground or sea cliffs. Easily told from other European herons by large size and grey, white and black colours, and in flight, from cranes (which are also greyish) by withdrawn neck. The wing-beats are very slow and, as in other herons, the wings are held in an arch. At a distance it can be mistaken for a large bird of prey but the rounded shape of the wings and the characteristic arch with the downward pointing tips are characteristic. Call, a harsh 'kaark'. RWP

PURPLE HERON *Ardea purpurea* L 79 W 114 Common in marshes and swamps. Prefers denser vegetation than does the Grey Heron. Reddish colours are diagnostic, but at a distance the Grey Heron looks very dark. In flight the neck is held in a more open S than is the case with the Grey Heron. More active than Grey Heron. Very big feet are also characteristic. Nests in colonies, often with other species of herons. V

NIGHT HERON *Nycticorax nycticorax* L 61 W 112 Common in fresh and salt water marshes and swamps. Stockiness and black, grey and white colour pattern easily distinguish the adult bird. Immatures are told from Bittern by large white spots on wing coverts, in flight by faster wing-beats and less yellowish appearance. Night Herons often spend the day roosting in trees or bushes but can also be seen feeding in the daylight hours, particularly early in the morning and at dusk. Often seen flying in lines. The call is a characteristic 'quock'. V

GLOSSY IBIS *Plegadis falcinellus* L 56 W 94 Uncommon, usually found in marshes and on mud-flats. The curved bill and almost black appearance at a distance are diagnostic. Immatures have light undersides but do not even remotely resemble curlews. Breeds in colonies usually in reeds, sometimes in trees. The flocks fly in long, undulating lines. In flight ibises hold their necks outstretched. Wing-beats rather fast and wings stiff. Immatures may be encountered outside the breeding range in September–October. V

SACRED IBIS *Threskiornis aethiopicus* L 66 Very rare and decreasing visitor to the Caspian and eastern Black Sea regions from southern breeding grounds. White plumage with black tail and dark neck and head make this bird unmistakable.

in colony

flock

Grey Heron

imm.

Purple Heron

m.
ght Heron

adult
Night Heron

roosting

imm.
Night Heron

Glossy Ibis

Night Heron

adult

imm. Glossy Ibis

imm.

Sacred Ibis

flock in flight

39

WHITE STORK *Ciconia ciconia* L 102 W 168 Common, except in the northernmost parts of its range where it is declining in numbers. Prefers marshes, wet meadows and grassy plains. Nests near towns or farms, sometimes in colonies in trees, sometimes on specially erected constructions or on buildings. Usually rather tame and easily approached. Characteristic bird of the open farmland. Easily told from Black Stork by white upper parts. Flies with neck outstretched, sometimes soaring in loose flocks but also migrating in V-formation. Far more numerous than Black Stork. Usually silent, but bill-clattering is a characteristic feature of display. During the breeding season coughing and hissing notes may sometimes be heard. Gait is slow and deliberate.   V

BLACK STORK *Ciconia nigra* L 97 W 157 Uncommon. Prefers forests where it often frequents lakes, rivers and marshes surrounded by woods. Easily told from White Stork by glossy black plumage of upper parts. Much more shy and solitary in its behaviour than the White Stork. Nests in forest trees. During migration Black Storks usually fly singly or in small parties. Unlike the White Stork, the Black Stork has various coarse call notes and bill-clattering is less often heard.   V

SPOONBILL *Platalea leucorodia* L 86 W 137 Uncommon and scattered in its distribution. Found in shallow, open water, reedy marshes and lagoons. Nests in colonies in large reed-beds. Sometimes builds in trees and bushes. On the ground distinguished from white herons by the broad and very long bill. In flight the neck is held outstretched. The long crest is present only in summer adults. Immature birds have black-tipped wings. Flocks usually fly in lines. The flight is regular with slow gliding and soaring movements. Usually silent, but bill-clattering may occur if excited. Also utters occasional grunting sounds in summer.   SW

GREATER FLAMINGO *Phoenicopterus ruber* L 122 W 142 Common within its very restricted range. Single individuals are occasionally met with all over Europe, but may have escaped from collections. Found on mud-flats and banks with shallow water, where usually seen in large flocks. Flies in scattered groups, sometimes in lines. Neck and legs are extremely long, bill thick and hooked. Feeds by skimming surface with bill held upside down. In flight, the long outstretched neck and legs droop slightly. Nests colonially on mud-flats. Various trumpeting cries, in flight especially; also a gabble like that of a goose. Other species of flamingo occasionally occur as escapes.   V

ruber roseus

ruber chilensis

40

nest on rooftop

White Stork

Black Stork

adult

imm.

imm.

Spoonbill

Flamingo

41

Waterfowl

(order *Anseriformes*, family *Anatidae*) in Europe are divided into six groups: one each for swans and geese, and four for ducks. Waterfowl are aquatic, with webs between the three front toes. They have long necks and narrow, pointed wings, and most have short legs. They differ from divers and grebes in having flattened bills with tooth-like edges that serve as strainers. Their flattened bodies are well insulated with down feathers. Most build simple down-lined nests on the ground in thick vegetation. The young hatch down-covered and can walk and swim a few hours after hatching.

Swans, the largest of the waterfowl, are characterized by long necks — longer than their bodies. The three European species are all white. They are graceful in the air and on the water. They paddle along the surface when taking flight. The young are greyish or brownish. Swans dip for aquatic plants in shallow water. Clutch, 3–10 eggs. p. 44

Geese are intermediate between swans and ducks in size and other characteristics but form a distinctive group. Sexes are alike. Geese are heavier and longer necked than ducks. They moult once a year, as do swans. The legs of most are placed farther forward than in ducks and swans. This is an adaptation for grazing. Clutch, 3–8 eggs. p. 46

Surface-feeding ducks are the first of the four groups of ducks. Ducks are smaller than swans and geese, have flatter bills and shorter legs. Surface-feeding ducks are birds of ponds, lakes, slow rivers, where they feed on water plants. They fly strongly and take off with a sudden upward leap. Their secondary flight feathers show a bright patch — the speculum. The shelducks are larger than the rest of the surface-feeding ducks and there is much less dif-

Whooper Swan

Greylag Goose

Mallard – a surface-feeding duck

ference between the plumages of males and females. They have longer necks and look more goose-like than most surface-feeding ducks. Clutch, 5–12 eggs. p. 52

Bay ducks (the smaller, mainly freshwater, diving ducks) and the **sea ducks** fall into a single group (sub-family *Aythyinae*). All have a lobed hind-toe. Expert divers, their legs are set far back. They have flat bills. To take off they must paddle along the surface, with wings beating.

Bay ducks breed along northern lakes and many winter in huge rafts in tidal estuaries or along ice-free coasts and lakes. Feed mainly on aquatic plants and molluscs. Clutch, 4–14 eggs. p. 58

Sea ducks dive deeper than bay ducks and feed more on molluscs. Sea ducks breed along the coasts and on inland lakes. In winter they are more strictly coastal than bay ducks. Clutch, 4–8 eggs. p. 60

Mergansers have long, slender bills modified for seizing slippery fish. The bill is narrower than that of other waterfowl and the edges are heavily serrated. Mergansers take off slowly like sea ducks. Nest in hollow trees (except Red-breasted). Clutch, 6–18 eggs. p. 66

Stifftails are little, chunky ducks living in lakes and freshwater bays. Their rather long, stiff tails give them their name. Clutch, 5–11 eggs. p. 66

Pochard – a bay duck

Eider – a sea duck

White-headed Duck

Red-breasted Merganser

43

Swans

(subfamily *Cygninae*) are heavy, white, long-necked birds of lake and river shores. They dip head and neck into the water to feed on bottom vegetation, and also browse on shore grasses. No black on the wing-tips. Sexes similar. Immatures are greyish-brown above, whitish below. Swans have a rhythmical, ponderous flight with neck extended. They fly in V-formation or in lines.

MUTE SWAN *Cygnus olor* L 147 W 240 Most numerous and widespread of our swans. Nests along rivers and canals, on shores of small and larger lakes, occasionally in sheltered bays. In winter found on open water, usually in herds, and often along seashores, in sheltered bays. Mute Swans are often kept in a tame or semi-tame condition in parks. When swimming, holds its neck in a graceful S-curve, with bill pointed downwards; secondary wing feathers are often raised. Adult has orange-red bill with black knob. Dull rose bill of immature is black at base. Adult's voice is a low grunt, but cygnets are noisier. Wing-beats of flying birds produce a singing note. Sometimes mixes with other swans. Immatures told from immature Whooper and Bewick's Swans by dirty appearance of the plumage. The so-called Polish Swans are white as cygnets and in immature plumage.   R

WHOOPER SWAN *Cygnus cygnus* L 147 W 240 Rather common in winter along coasts and in larger lakes and rivers. Has a greater preference for salt water than Mute Swan. In summer, nests on islands, swamps and lakes of the north. When swimming, neck is held straight and secondary wing feathers are not raised as in Mute Swan. This makes this species and Bewick's Swan easy to distinguish from Mute Swan, even at long range. At closer range, large area of yellow on bill is noticeable. Immatures distinguished from Mute Swans by more uniform grey colour and silhouette, from Bewick's Swans by larger size. Whooper is rather noisy with characteristic deep, bugle-like whooping, which can be heard over long distances.   W

BEWICK'S SWAN *Cygnus columbianus* L 122 W 204 Least common of the swans, found in sheltered bays, lakes and larger rivers in winter; in summer nests on the Arctic tundra. Like small edition of the Whooper Swan. Yellow on bill is less extensive. Bill comparatively smaller than Whooper Swan's, giving the head a more rounded appearance. Often seen singly or in families, but some times in huge flocks probably consisting of whole populations. Immature is like a small Whooper and there is no difference in bill coloration. Call is somewhat like Whooper's but much more musical and pleasant.   W

pelican   Mallard   Eider   goose   swan

display

imm.

flock in flight

Mute Swan

imm.

Whooper Swan

feeding   imm.

Bewick's Swan

Mute Swan on nest

45

Geese

(subfamily *Anserinae*) are large, plump birds with long necks, short legs, and broad, round tipped bills. They feed on grain, grass shoots, and some marine vegetation, and fly with deep, powerful wing-beats. Geese usually migrate in noisy flocks, in V-formation or in long undulating lines. Sexes look alike.

CANADA GOOSE *Branta canadensis* L 56–76 W 127–173 Introduced in many parks. Escapes have established themselves as breeding birds in Britain as well as Sweden. In winter Swedish migrants may be met with in small numbers in most parts of western Europe, but British birds are more sedentary. Much larger than any other *Branta* species; black neck and head with white cheek patch is diagnostic. In behaviour quite similar to Bean Goose, usually feeding on the ground. Nests on islands, in lakes and in swamps. Voice is a hoarse honking, not unlike that of Whooper and Bewick's Swans. F

BRENT GOOSE *Branta bernicla* L 61 W 122 Locally common, mainly along seashores and coastal bays. Very dark and short-necked with white tail-band. Flight rapid, usually low over the water, often in flocks strung out in long lines. Sometimes mixes with grey geese. Two subspecies appear in Europe: the dark-bellied *B.b. bernicla* breeding in arctic Soviet Union, and the light-bellied *B.b. hrota* breeding in north-east Greenland and Spitzbergen. Sometimes found together but generally the dark-bellied form is found in the eastern part of Europe and the light-bellied form in the western part in winter. Often up-ends when feeding. Call is a guttural, croaking 'rronk'. W

BARNACLE GOOSE *Branta leucopsis* L 64 W 142 Very local. Breeds in mountainous areas of the Arctic and sometimes Arctic tundras. In winter rarely seen inland but prefers wet salt marshes, and tidal areas. Stragglers sometimes found in flocks of grey geese. Striking pattern of black and white is diagnostic. Wing-beats are slower than those of Brent Goose. Feeding habits are somewhat intermediate between Brent Goose and the grey geese. Call is a series of rapid, repeated short barks. W

RED-BREASTED GOOSE *Branta ruficollis* L 55 W 117 Only rare stragglers reach western Europe. In winter feeds mainly on fields and steppes, near coasts or swamps. Nests on the Arctic tundra and cliffs. In habit closely resembles the grey geese and on wintering grounds it often associates with Lesser White-fronted Geese. Vagrants are usually mixed in flocks of grey geese. Small size and striking colour pattern are diagnostic. Call is two-syllabled, staccato, rather high pitched. W

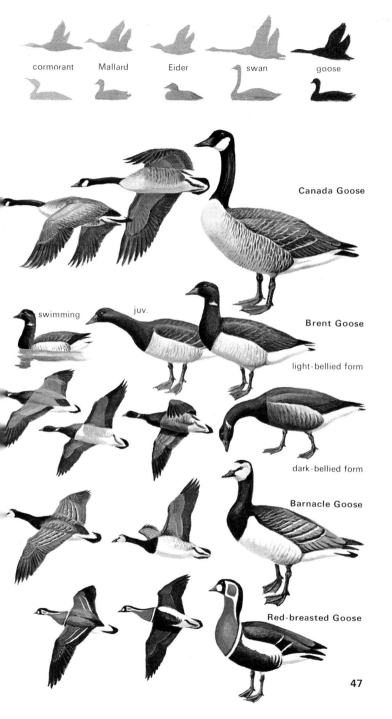

cormorant   Mallard   Eider   swan   goose

Canada Goose

swimming   juv.

Brent Goose

light-bellied form

dark-bellied form

Barnacle Goose

Red-breasted Goose

47

Seen from behind

Greylag

Bean

Greenland subspecies
flavirostris winters mostly in
Ireland and western
Scotland

White-fronted
juv.

GREYLAG GOOSE *Anser anser* L 81 W 157 The most common and widespread of the European geese. In summer found on moors, lakes and sometimes on small coastal islands. In winter it prefers salt and freshwater marshes, pastures and stubble fields. It seems considerably heavier than other geese and the bill is conspicuously large. The forewing is very light grey and contrasts sharply with the rest of the plumage. Pink-footed Goose also has a light forewing, but is smaller and darker with much shorter neck and smaller bill. Two races occur in Europe: the western European form *A.a anser* with orange bill, and the eastern *A.a. rubrirostris* with pink bill. Often breeds in loose colonies and around these colonies flocks of non-breeding birds are seen. Like other grey geese, it is gregarious in its behaviour and sometimes associates with other species. It is the wild ancestral form of the Domestic Goose and the call is similar to the familiar honking of this bird. RWF

WHITE-FRONTED GOOSE *Anser albifrons* L 7 Locally common. In winter found on open pasture and on coasts, moors and rivers, and more rarely on cultivated fields. Nests on the Arctic tundra. The adult bird is easily identified by the black belly and white front. Immature birds are best told by orange legs and unspotted bill. The much larger size distinguishes it from the Lesser White-fronted Goose, which also has a distinctly smaller bill. The subspecies nesting in Greenland *(A.a. flavirostris)* is slightly larger with a yellow bill and winters in Ireland and west Scotland. The nominate race winters in the rest of Britain. Like other geese it is gregarious in its behaviour. The call is more highly pitched than that of other large grey geese and consists of a laughing 'kow-yow'. V

LESSER WHITE-FRONTED GOOSE *Anser erythropus* L 61 W 133 Only stragglers reach western Europe. In summer found on Arctic mountain slopes, in winter on pastures and fields. Looks like a small edition of White-fronted Goose, but told from this species by the high front, the extension of the white front on to the crown, the much shorter and smaller bill and, even at a distance, a characteristic yellow rim around the eye. The immature bird also has this yellow ring and, at all stages, the wings extend beyond the tail, whereas in the White-fronted Goose they rarely do. Generally it looks rather darker than the White-fronted Goose. In western Europe it is usually seen in flocks of other grey geese. The call is higher pitched than that of the White-fronted Goose.

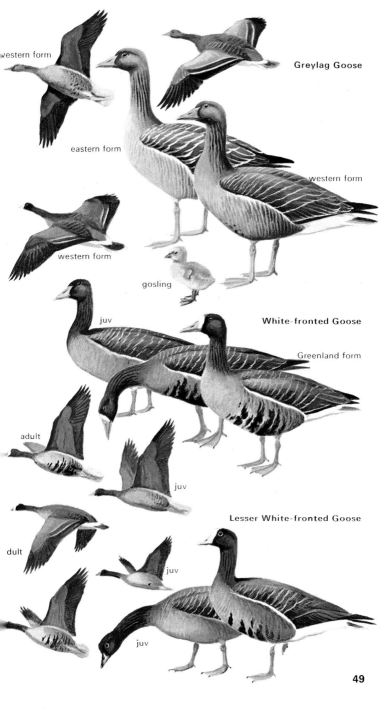

western form

Greylag Goose

eastern form

western form

western form

gosling

juv

White-fronted Goose

Greenland form

adult

juv

Lesser White-fronted Goose

dult

juv

juv

49

BEAN GOOSE *Anser fabalis* L 76 W 152 Local. In winter prefers pastures and fields close to open bodies of water, in summer tundras and the open northern woods. Distinguished from Greylag Goose by lack of pale forewing, and black and orange colour pattern on bill (varies considerably). Also told from immature White-fronted Goose by colour pattern of bill, and from the Pink-footed Goose, which by some is regarded as a subspecies of the Bean Goose, by the yellow legs, longer and lighter coloured neck, and larger bill. It is often met in large flocks, and like other grey geese it flies between the feeding grounds and lakes (where the night is spent) at dawn and dusk. Sometimes other geese are mixed with the flocks. The call is lower and more honking than that of other grey geese. W

PINK-FOOTED GOOSE *Anser brachyrhynchus* L 71 W 147 Lucally common. In winter found in pastures and fields near open water. Considered by many a subspecies of the Bean Goose, which it resembles in its habits Breeds in Greenland, in Iceland and Spitzbergen. The neck and head are very dark, contrasting sharply with the light grey forewing seen in flight. The bill is patterned pink and black and comparatively short. The feet are pink. Most difficult to tell from immature White-fronted Goose, but notice some black on smaller bill and pink feet of the Pink-footed Goose. Because of the smaller bill-size, the shape of the head is more rounded than in the other grey geese. The call is very similar to that of the Bean Goose, but slightly higher pitched. W

SNOW GOOSE *Anser caerulescens* L 71 W 150 A North American bird occurring as an accidental visitor and, more often, as an escape in western Europe usually in the company of grey geese. Unmistakable with pure white colours and black wing-tips. Immatures are so light they cannot be mistaken for any other European goose. The grey phase, the so-called Blue Goose, has white neck and head and grey body and is even rarer in Europe. Most have been observed in winter and autumn. The call is harsh and there is also a deep gabbling produced by birds together or in flocks. \

Blue Goose

BAR-HEADED GOOSE *Anser indicus* L 75 Escapes of this Asiatic goose are sometimes met with, usually in the company of other grey geese. It is easily told from other geese by the white crown with two black bars and black wing tips. Immatures lack the black colours but are very light grey.

Bean Goose

tundra form

forest form

Pink-footed Goose

Snow Goose

juv

juv

Bar-headed Goose

51

Surface-feeding ducks

(subfamily *Anatinae*) are found mostly in shallow water. Feed by up-ending and dabbling on the surface. They are agile fliers and have a nearly vertical take-off. Most are able to dive but do not do so habitually. Drake and duck have different plumages. Most have a bright, distinctive speculum. In early summer the drakes assume a drab eclipse plumage, the breeding plumage is attained again in autumn.

MALLARD *Anas platyrhynchos* L 59 W 92 Most common and widespread surface-feeding duck. Found in lakes, ponds, rivers and along sheltered coasts and in marshes. Drake easily distinguished by dark green head, chestnut breast. Both drake and duck have conspicuous blue speculum. Duck most easily confused with Gadwall and Pintail, but note heavier bill and blue speculum. Often found in flocks or pairs. Duck's voice is loud quack; drake is quieter. RWF

GADWALL *Anas strepera* L 51 W 89 Widespread but uncommon. Found in ponds, lakes, rivers and flooded meadows, rarely in salt water. Seen in pairs or very small flocks, sometimes mixed with other surface-feeding ducks. At a distance, drake looks greyish, but note characteristic red-brown, black and white speculum on both sexes. Also note white belly of duck distinguishing it from Pintail and Mallard. The orange outer edge of bill is characteristic for the duck, the grey bill for the drake. Dives readily. Call is very low and reedy. RV

PINTAIL *Anas acuta* L 71 W 89 Common, found on lakes, ponds and bays, usually in pairs or small flocks. Slim and very agile with slender, pointed wings. Female has longer neck and longer, more pointed tail than other mottled ducks. White on wing not as extensive as on Gadwall, with which it is most easily confused. Both drake and duck have grey bill. Call is short whistle. RWF

WIGEON *Anas penelope* L 46 W 81 Common in marshes, meadows and swamps where it breeds. In winter also found in lagoons, lakes and bays. In winter usually seen in large flocks. Note white forewing of male. More complactly built than other surface-feeding ducks. Flies in tight flocks or long lines, not in long open V's. Walks well and often grazes on land. Call, a high descending whistle, often reveals presence of flocks. RW

AMERICAN WIGEON *Anas americana* L 51 W 8 American counterpart to Wigeon; a rare straggler to western Europe. Drake unmistakable. Duck closely resembles Wigeon duck but has greyer appearance with more contrast between coloration of head and neck and breast, and axillaries are white, not dusky. Call is two or three soft whistles.

taking flight

up ending

landing

dabbling

♀ ♂ Mallard

Gadwall

Pintail

Wigeon

flock formation

American Wigeon

53

TEAL *Anas crecca* L 36 W 61 Very common. Smallest of the surface-feeding ducks. In summer it is found on smaller ponds, lakes, bogs and marshes, while in winter it also frequents bays, lakes and flooded marshes. Usually prefers fresh water. The female is distinguished from other small ducks by her green speculum. A very fast flier, usually in very tight flocks and only rarely in lines or V's. Most active at dusk. Call is a short whistle.

RWP

GREEN-WINGED TEAL *Anas crecca carolinensis* L 36 W 61 This North American race of the Teal is a rare straggler to western Europe. Drake has a vertical, not horizontal, white band on his side. Female is indistinguishable from the European Teal duck. Behaviour and call are the same.

V

Blue-winged Teal

BLUE-WINGED TEAL *Anas discors* L 38 W 61 Rare straggler from North America. The drake is unmistakable. The duck is much like Garganey duck but is darker, with bright blue forewing and a longer bill.

V

Garganey

BAIKAL TEAL *Anas formosa* L 38 W 61 Rare straggler from its Asiatic breeding grounds. Note the drake's distinctive facial pattern. The duck has a green speculum and a distinct white patch at base of bill.

V

adult ♂   juv ♂   ♀

FALCATED TEAL *Anas falcata* L 51 Very rare straggler to eastern Europe from its Asiatic breeding grounds. The drake is unmistakable. The duck resembles Gadwall duck, but speculum is different.

GARGANEY *Anas querquedula* L 38 W 63 Widespread but not very numerous. Found in ponds and lakes and flooded meadows with rich shoreline vegetation. Notice conspicuous white stripe over eye of drake. The duck does not have as pale forewing as male and is best told from Teal duck by facial pattern. See also Blue-winged Teal. Usually met with in pairs or very small flocks. The call of male is a strange crackling sound. SF

SHOVELER *Anas clypeata* L 51 W 79 Common, found mainly in ponds and flooded marshes where it feeds in shallow water. The drake is unmistakable. Note the flat head, long spatulate bill and large blue wing patch of both sexes. On the water it rides low in front with bill held downwards. Often met with in small flocks, sometimes consisting only of drakes. Quacks like a Mallard; also has a low clucking.

RW

Teal

Green-winged Teal

Blue-winged Teal

Baikal Teal

Falcated Teal

Garganey

Shoveler

55

MARBLED DUCK *Marmaronetta angustirostris* L 41 W 64 Uncommon and local. Prefers sheltered ponds and swamps with much vegetation. Notice very light colours, dark eye-stripe and lack of speculum. Large head and long neck visible in silhouette. Often hides and is difficult to approach. Usually met with singly or very few together. The male utters a low croak, the female a low quack which is difficult to hear.

MANDARIN DUCK *Aix galericulata* L 46 W 71 Escapes have established themselves in a feral state, particularly in some parts of England. Prefers ponds with wooded edges, nesting in tree-holes. The beautiful drake is unmistakable. The duck is less strikingly coloured, but notice the characteristic facial pattern. The flight is direct and swift. Feeds mainly on land.   R

SHELDUCK *Tadorna tadorna* L 61 Common on coastal flats and estuaries; sometimes found on inland lakes and swamps, nesting in holes and under bushes along shores. Drake and duck are similar and share the striking pattern of dark green, black, chestnut and white. Drake has large red knob on bill. The immature looks much whiter than the adults. The flight is low over the water with rather slow wing-beats. Sometimes seen in very large flocks and in huge numbers when moulting. Ducklings often appear in large flocks attended by one or few adults during moulting season. They are strikingly coloured black and white. The call is a characteristic 'ag-ag-ag', rather like the flight call of divers. Silent outside breeding season.   RS

RUDDY SHELDUCK *Tadorna ferruginea* L 61 Uncommon, but escapes may occur well outside usual range. More terrestrial than Shelduck. In winter found along river banks, sandy lakeshores and in fields and steppes. Usually seen in pairs or small flocks. The orange-brown colour is characteristic and white area on wing is striking in flight. Male has narrow black neck-band. Resembles Shelduck in shape and habits. Flight resembles that of Shelduck with rather slow wing-beats. Nests in burrows and holes. The call is nasal, Shelduck-like.   V

EGYPTIAN GOOSE *Alopochen aegyptiacus* L 71 Very rare straggler to south-easternmost Europe from breeding grounds in Africa, but escaped birds established in parts of England. The sexes are similar. Notice large white area on wing and long legs.   F

Marbled Teal ♂ ♀

Mandarin Duck ♂ ♀

Shelduck ♂ ♀ juv ♂

near nesting hole

Ruddy Shelduck ♀ ♂ ♂ ♂

Egyptian Goose ♂

57

Bay ducks

(part of subfamily *Aythyinae*) nest on lakeshores and swamps; in winter occur in flocks in protected coastal bays, larger lakes, river mouths. Dive from the surface, swim under water, and run along the surface to take off. Calls of most are short, low croaks.

RED-CRESTED POCHARD *Netta rufina* L 56 Uncommon, local, but escapes occur. Breeds by ponds and lakes with reeds; in winter also found on open lakes, sometimes along seashores. Resembles surface-feeding ducks in many aspects of behaviour. Red bill, broad white wing-band very distinctive. Facial pattern of duck resembles Common Scoter duck. Usually seen singly or in pairs, sometimes with other species.   P

SCAUP *Aythya marila* L 46 W 79 Common in winter along coasts, often on deeper water than Tufted and Pochard. Flocks usually smaller than those of Tufted, but very large aggregations can occur in favoured places. Notice grey back of male, extensive white area around bill of female. Head looks noticeably rounded.   WP

TUFTED DUCK *Aythya fuligula* L 43 W 71 Most numerous bay duck, nesting near lakes and swamps. In winter found in large flocks on lakes, bays, seashores, often with other species. Black back and long tuft of drake diagnostic. Ducks and immatures usually have a hint of a tuft and some white at base of bill. Under-tail area of female can be pale but not as white as in smaller Ferruginous. Flight fast; flocks usually fly in irregular formation with lines or V's interspersed.   RW

Ring-necked
Duck

RING-NECKED DUCK *Aythya collaris* L 43 W 71 Very rare winter straggler to western Europe from North America. Drake easily told from male Tufted by head shape and vertical white stripe on grey flank. Duck harder to identify, but head shape, facial pattern and grey (not white) wing-bar of both sexes are characteristic.   V

POCHARD *Aythya ferina* L 46 W 79 Common, nesting in reeds near open fresh water; in winter on larger lakes and sheltered bays, often with Tufteds. Triangular head shape and heavy, compact bill help identify. Drake easily told from other red-headed ducks by black breast, grey back. Female more drab, but notice dark breast, facial pattern and steel-grey ring on bill. Both sexes have grey wing-bars.   RW

FERRUGINOUS DUCK *Aythya nyroca* L 41 W 66 Common, nesting by freshwater lakes and in swamps with much vegetation. In winter found on larger lakes, sheltered bays. Rarely occurs in salt water. Smallest bay duck. Notice rich brown colour of male, white eye, distinctive white under tail-coverts. Wing-bar white. Floats higher than relatives; holds tail higher, revealing striking white of under tail-coverts. Duck more drab, lacking white eye.   W

Red-crested Pochard

Scaup

Tufted Duck

Ring-necked Duck

Pochard

Ferruginous Duck

59

Goldeneye, imm ♂
moulting

GOLDENEYE *Bucephala clangula* L 48 W 79
Common on lakes and rivers and in forested country of
the north, where it nests in cavities and even nest boxes.
Winters along the coasts and on larger lakes and rivers.
The shape of the head of both sexes is characteristic and
the large, white wing patches are striking when seen in
flight. The wings make a loud, musical whistle. The
drake has a rather small, round white facial spot. The
duck has a white collar. Usually seen in pairs or small
flocks, sometimes mixing with other species. Flight is
very fast. They are the best divers of this group and go
further out to sea than any related species. The display is
characteristic and often seen in early spring on the wintering ground, the drakes throwing their heads back with
bills pointing upward.   WF

BARROW'S GOLDENEYE *Bucephala islandica* L 53
W 79 Very rare outside its only European breeding
ground, Iceland. Nests along mountain streams and
lakes. In winter also found along coasts and in rivers. The
drake is told from Goldeneye by the crescent-shape of
the white facial spot, completely different shape of head,
purple (not green) gloss of the black head and much
more extensive black on back and wings. The duck has
less white on wings than Goldeneye and in breeding
season the bill is often all yellow, lacking the Golden
eye's black base. Like the Goldeneye, an expert diver

Sea ducks
(part of subfamily *Aythyinae*) are heavy, rather large,
short-necked diving ducks, usually seen along coasts in
winter, some species only resorting to inland waters
during the breeding season. In winter they often occur
in large flocks, frequently of mixed species. All are expert
divers, finding their food, mainly molluscs, on the bottom
of the sea.

HARLEQUIN *Histrionicus histrionicus* L 41 W 6
Like Barrow's Goldeneye, very rare outside its only
European breeding ground, Iceland. It nests on islands
in swift rivers and is found in winter in heavy surf
along rocky coasts. Drake easily recognized by dark and
light pattern (at a distance the blue and red colour
look almost black), small size, and long tail which seem
to be in constant movement. The duck is smaller and
darker than Goldeneye, lacks white wing patch in flight
and has three distinctive head spots. Usually does no
mix with other ducks and is very shy, difficult to
approach. In winter generally seen in very small parties
Usually silent. Male sometimes utters a soft whistle
female a harsh croak.

Harlequin ♀

Long-tailed Duck ♀

Goldeneye

♀

♂

♂

♀

♂

♀

nest hole

Goldeneye displaying

Goldeneye

♀ winter   ♀ summer

Barrow's Goldeneye

♀   ♂

♀ ♂ Goldeneye

♀ ♂ Barrow's Goldeneye

Harlequin

♂   ♂

♀

♂

♂

♂

♀

♀

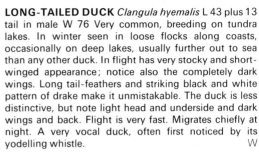

LONG-TAILED DUCK *Clangula hyemalis* L 43 plus 13 tail in male W 76 Very common, breeding on tundra lakes. In winter seen in loose flocks along coasts, occasionally on deep lakes, usually further out to sea than any other duck. In flight has very stocky and short-winged appearance; notice also the completely dark wings. Long tail-feathers and striking black and white pattern of drake make it unmistakable. The duck is less distinctive, but note light head and underside and dark wings and back. Flight is very fast. Migrates chiefly at night. A very vocal duck, often first noticed by its yodelling whistle. W

VELVET SCOTER *Melanitta fusca* L 56 W 97 Common, though not as abundant as Common Scoter. Nests along rivers and lake shores in the Arctic and along the Baltic coast. In winter usually encountered along coasts, but often also on larger inland lakes. Drake is all black with white spot by the eye and white wing-bar (often not detectable when the bird is swimming). Larger, does not appear as compact as male Common Scoter, and the protuberance at the base of the bill is less pronounced. Facial pattern of duck is same as that of female Surf Scoter but white wing-bar distinguishes the Velvet Scoter. Usually met with in medium-sized flocks, riding close together in the water. Often the whole flock submerges at the same time, leaving only one or two birds on the surface. Flies in loose flocks over short distances, in long lines when migrating. WP

SURF SCOTER *Melanitta perspicillata* L 51 W 84 Rare winter and spring visitor from North America to extreme north-west coasts. White markings on nape and forehead of drake identify it easily. Duck has facial pattern like Velvet Scoter but lacks white wing-bar of this bird. Shape of bill indistinct except at very close range. Habitats and habits like those of other scoters. V

COMMON SCOTER *Melanitta nigra* L 51 W 84 Common, nesting on the shores of lakes and rivers; in winter found along coasts and rarely in large freshwater lakes. Seems more plump and stocky than other scoters. Drake is all black with yellow protuberance on black bill. Duck has a dark cap and grey face like Red-crested Pochard duck, whose lighter colours and striking white wing-bars should make confusion impossible. Most noisy of the scoters: call of male is a bell-like whistle heard at night when migrating overland. Often encountered in large unmixed flocks, sometimes in company with eiders or other scoters. Migrate in lines or V-formation; short distances are covered in loose flocks. RWF

summer

summer

Long-tailed Duck

winter

winter

Velvet Scoter

Surf Scoter

Common Scoter

Scoters at sea, swimming, taking off, flying

EIDER *Somateria mollissima* L 61 W 104 Common and by far the most numerous European eider. Nests along seashores, rarely far from water. In winter found along seashores, only occasionally resorting to large fresh-water lakes or rivers. In winter, may form large flocks numbering 10–1000, usually outside the surf. Often mixes with scoters. Flocks of Eiders are usually more loose in formation than those of scoters. Most often flies in lines or V-formation low over the water. The head is held low, and the wing-beats are rather slow and deli-berate. White back and black belly are diagnostic of Eider drake. Immature drake has mainly dark-brown plumage, but usually some white on the back distin-guishing it from immature King Eider. Both immatures and drakes in eclipse are very variable. Duck is uniformly brown with black mottling. At close range duck and immature drake told from female King Eider by sloping profile and long slender frontal shield, which extends much farther up the forehead than in King Eider (twice as far from the nostril). Best-known note is conversational 'oo-oo' of drakes when courting.   RW

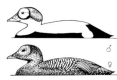

SPECTACLED EIDER *Somateria fischeri* L 54 Rare straggler to Arctic coasts mainly in winter. Faded green head and large white eye patch diagnostic in drake which otherwise resembles Eider drake. Duck told from Eider duck by faint spectacle and low feather line of upper mandible.

KING EIDER *Somateria spectabilis* L 58 W 94 Common in the Arctic where it breeds along seashores and on shores of freshwater lakes and rivers. Very rare south of Arctic Circle. King Eider behaves very much like Common Eider with which it often occurs. Black back, white neck and breast, and heavily shielded bill are good field marks for the drake. Large white wing patches are distinctive against the black back. Duck told from Common Eider by bill profile and often richer more reddish-brown plumage. Immature drakes never show white on back and differ from Common Eiders in shape of head.

STELLER'S EIDER *Polysticta stelleri* L 46 W 70 This small Asiatic eider is uncommon, usually found along rocky shores. General shape is like a Mallard, but bill is stubbier and tail longer. White upper parts and reddish-brown underside of drake are characteristic. Duck is uniform dark brown except for blue speculum widely bordered with white. Both sexes have tiny rounded crest giving the head a characteristic shape. Wings whistle in flight like Goldeneye's. In take-off Steller's Eider is not as heavy as other eiders, and flight and wing-beats are faster. Usually very tame. Both 'upends' and dives.

Eider

♂ imm.

♀

♂

♀

♂

♂

King Eider

Common Eider

♀

♀

King Eider

♂ imm.

♂

♀

♂

Steller's Eider

♂

♀

♀

♂

♀

♂

♀

Common Eiders at sea, swimming, taking off, flying

65

Mergansers

(subfamily *Merginae*) are fish-eating diving ducks with long thin bills serrated on sides. Flight is rapid with body held very straight and horizontal. All three species have white wing patch and all except drake Goosander show a more or less distinctive crest.

RED-BREASTED MERGANSER *Mergus serrator* L 56 W 84 Common, in the breeding season found along freshwater and saltwater shorelines, placing nest under bushes or hidden among rocks or dense vegetation. In winter almost exclusively found in salt water. Both sexes have shaggy crest. Drake distinguished by reddish-brown chest patch. Duck, which has more crest than female Goosander, lacks the contrast between head and throat. Smaller and more slender than Goosander. Often encountered in flocks after breeding season. Call consists of low short quacks. RW

GOOSANDER *Mergus merganser* L 64 W 94 Common, usually found on lakes and rivers with wooded shores. Nests in tree holes and other cavities (will use nest boxes). At a distance, drake looks much whiter or salmon-coloured than male Red-breasted Merganser and green head has only the hint of a crest. Duck is more crested and distinct white throat and sharp contrast between neck and breast distinguish it from duck Red-breasted Merganser. Usually seen in small flocks. Call consists of low short quacks. RW

SMEW *Mergus albellus* L 41 W 66 Locally common, found on lakes and rivers surrounded by trees. In winter also found on sheltered bays in salt water. Nests in tree cavities. Drake unmistakable with very white plumage. Female much greyer, with distinctive dark chestnut cap. Also notice very short bill. Often associates with Goldeneyes, even in breeding season, and hybrids between the two are known. Most often seen in small parties with other ducks. W

Stifftailed ducks

(sub-family *Oxyurinae*) are small and stubby, with short, thick necks. In swimming the tail is often held up at a jaunty angle. They dive and sometimes sink slowly, as grebes do.

WHITE-HEADED DUCK *Oxyura leucocephala* L 46 Uncommon in freshwater swamps and lakes with much vegetation and in brackish lagoons. Very characteristic shape with large head, short neck and long tail which is often jerked upwards, revealing whitish under tail-coverts. Outside breeding season often associates with bay ducks. Notice facial pattern of both sexes.

RUDDY DUCK *Oxyura jamaicensis* L 41 Escapes established in England. Drake chestnut. Duck best told from White-headed Duck by shape of bill. P

Ruddy Duck

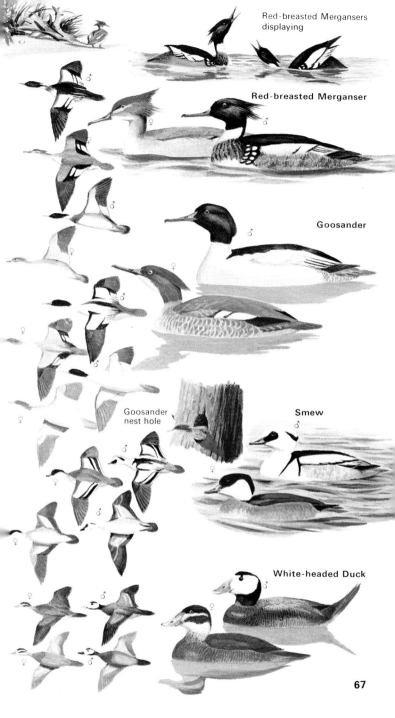

Red-breasted Mergansers displaying

Red-breasted Merganser ♂

Goosander

Goosander nest hole

Smew ♂

White-headed Duck ♂

67

Birds of prey

(order *Falconiformes*) are diurnal flesh-eaters. Most take live prey caught on the ground, in water or in the air; many of the larger species will also eat carcasses. All have heavy, sharp, hooked bills, and toes with strong, curved talons, with which they seize and hold their prey. Sexes usually alike, but females are generally larger than males. Because of this, measurements are given as a range rather than an average. Much individual variation in colour. Immatures differ from adults, and some species have light and dark forms. All are excellent fliers and the larger species are inclined to soar on widely extended wings. They ride on thermal updraughts, circling higher and higher, almost without wing-beats, then gliding to another place with strong updraught. The position of the wings when soaring is often helpful in identification at a long distance. The smaller species are more often seen in active flight, a few wing-beats interrupted by gliding on stiff wings, but many will sometimes soar. Some species notably Short-toed Eagle, Rough-legged Buzzard Osprey, Kestrel and Lesser Kestrel, often hover high above the ground watching for prey.

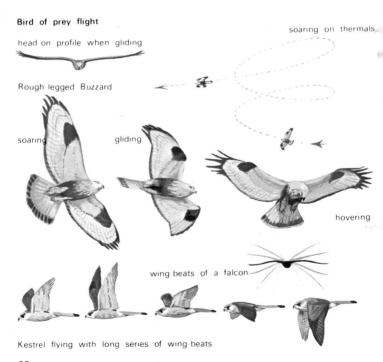

Bird of prey flight

head on profile when gliding

soaring on thermals

Rough-legged Buzzard

soaring   gliding

hovering

wing-beats of a falcon

Kestrel flying with long series of wing-beats

Vultures are very large, broad-winged scavengers. Usually seen soaring, often in flocks. Nest in trees, or on cliffs. Clutch, 1–2 eggs.   p. 70

Eagles are large, broad-winged and broad-tailed, mostly brown birds of prey. Usually seen soaring. Wings are usually proportionally larger than those of buzzards. Sea eagles have longer necks and shorter tails. Heads and bills large. Usually solitary. Nest in trees or on cliffs. Clutch 1–2 eggs.
p. 72

Buzzards are medium-sized, broad-winged and broad-tailed, mainly brown but with much individual variation in colour. Usually seen soaring. Also hunt from perches. On migration often form flocks. Nest in trees or on cliffs. Clutch 2–6 eggs.
p. 78

Accipiters are medium-sized with rounded wings and long tails. Mainly active flight, sometimes soar. Nest in trees. Clutch, 3–6 eggs.   p. 80

Kites are medium-sized, with rather broad wings held angularly and long forked tails. Soar and hunt from perch. Largely scavengers. Nest in trees. Clutch, 2–4 eggs.   p. 82

Osprey is large, broad-winged with very light underside. Soars and hovers over water. Eats fish exclusively. Nests in trees. Clutch, 3 eggs.   p. 82

Harriers are medium-sized, broad-winged and long-tailed. Often coast low over the ground with wing-tips held high. Sometimes soar. Sexes very different. Nest on ground. Clutch, 4 or more eggs.   p. 84

Falcons are medium-sized to small, and long-tailed with pointed wings. Occasionally soar. Sexes are often different. Nest on ground, cliffs, or old nests of other birds. Clutch, 3–7 eggs.
p. 86

vulture

Golden Eagle

sea eagle

buzzard

accipiter

kite

Osprey

harrier

falcon

69

Vultures

(part of family *Accipitridae*) are very large, sluggish birds of prey living mainly on carcasses and refuse. Wings are very long. Vultures are usually seen soaring, sometimes very high. They are most easily confused with eagles, but have smaller heads and different flight silhouettes.

EGYPTIAN VULTURE *Neophron percnopterus* L 59–69 W 145–150 Smallest and most numerous European vulture. Encountered in almost all habitats, but most commonly in mountainous areas. Often frequents refuse dumps. Easily told from other European vultures by smaller size and whitish plumage with black wing-tips. Immatures are brownish, but can be distinguished from all other birds of prey by their characteristic silhouette. Plumage becomes gradually whiter, reaching full adult whiteness after 6 years. Wings pointed. Notice small, pointed head and long, rather thin bill. Often seen soaring. Roosts in treetops or on rocks and buildings. Usually silent. V

GRIFFON VULTURE *Gyps fulvus* L 102–109 W 234–277 Common in some open, mountainous regions. In flight looks rectangular as tail and head only protrude slightly. Distinguished from eagles by very large size, spread out primaries and very short, square tail. Told from rarer Black Vulture by square tail and (in good light) lighter plumage contrasting with almost black wings. Whitish ruff is rarely visible. Immatures darker brown with brown ruff. When soaring the wings are held in an open V as Golden Eagle. Often seen soaring, sometimes several together. Roosts in trees or on rocky ledges, often in flocks. Various unmusical croaks and whistles are sometimes heard. V

BLACK VULTURE *Aegypius monachus* L 102–112 W 234–274 Uncommon. Usually only found in desolate mountains and plains. Told from eagles by large size, spread out primaries and very long wings; from similar Griffon Vulture by longer, more rounded tail, larger head and bill, much darker plumage. Ruff dark brown in immatures, becoming paler with age. Dark pattern on neck and head rarely visible. Immatures have head and neck covered with uniform dark brown down. Although often seen with Griffon Vultures around carcasses, it is more solitary in behaviour. Usually silent.

LAMMERGEIER *Gypaëtus barbatus* L 104–117 W 249–277 Rare. Was almost extinct in Europe but is slowly gaining in numbers. Almost exclusively found in wild, mountainous areas. Easily identified by long, narrow wings, held slightly bent, and long, wedge-shaped tail. From below, notice contrast between creamy front and belly and dark wings and tail. Immatures have dark head and breast. Although often seen soaring, it is more active than other vultures. More solitary in behaviour. Usually silent, but at breeding grounds utters loud, high-pitched whistles.

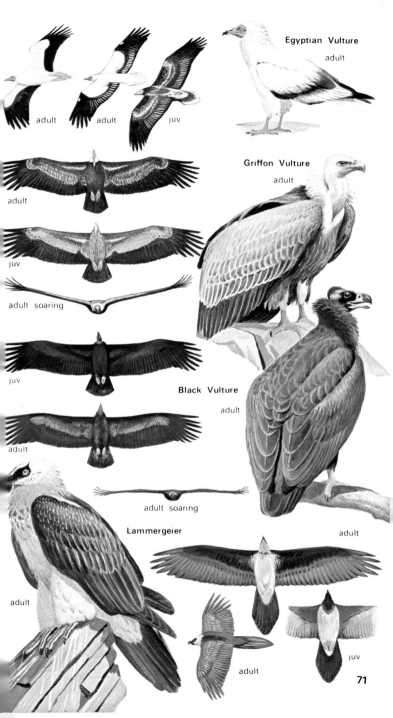

Egyptian Vulture

adult

adult

adult

juv

adult

Griffon Vulture

adult

juv

adult soaring

juv

Black Vulture

adult

adult

adult soaring

adult

Lammergeier

adult

adult

adult

juv

71

Eagles

(part of family *Accipitridae*), although they are not all very closely related, have certain features in common. They are large, broad-winged birds of prey with large heads and bills. Often soar. The plumage changes are slow and identification of immature birds can be very difficult; the subtle differences in silhouettes should be used. Sexes are very similar, females generally being slightly larger than males. Usually found singly or in pairs. Most eagles are scarce in numbers owing to persecution, the effect of poisonous chemicals and a slow reproduction rate. Nest singly, far from human habitation. Many eagles eat only carcasses and are completely harmless to man.

Reintroduced on Inner Hebrides in 1970s

WHITE-TAILED EAGLE *Haliaeetus albicilla* L 79–92 W 198–234 Uncommon. Also called Sea Eagle, it prefers coastal areas or large inland waters. Adult unmistakable with pure white, wedge-shaped tail. Immature is dark brown with varying numbers of cream-coloured spots, gradually attaining adult plumage over 5 years. The flight silhouette is characteristic with long neck and head, short wedge-shaped tail and very broad wings held horizontally or pointing slightly downwards. Wing-beats are sluggish. On favoured haunts several may be seen together. Often seen soaring. V

PALLAS'S SEA EAGLE *Haliaeetus leucoryphus* L 69–89 W 173–198 Uncommon. Only found in easternmost parts of European Russia. Prefers open steppe country close to rivers and lakes. Adult is unmistakable. Immatures very similar to White-tailed Eagle immatures but have darker, longer tails and shorter wings as well as light band on the underside of the wing. In behaviour and silhouette it resembles the White-tailed Eagle.

GOLDEN EAGLE *Aquila chrysaetos* L 79–87 W 188–299 Most common of the eagles but declining in numbers. Primarily found in mountainous areas, but sometimes, particularly in winter, in woods and fields. Easily told from Sea Eagle by more harmonious proportions (long tail, short neck), stronger, more well-controlled wing-beats and squarish (not wedge-shaped) tail White wing patches and inner tail of immatures are diagnostic. These characteristics are lost when adult plumage is attained at the age of 5 years. The tawny-golden nape is present at all ages. When soaring, this species holds its wings above horizontal and the wingtips point slightly upward and forward. Both the spotted eagles hold their wings low. Imperial Eagle has proportionally shorter tail and is smaller. Steppe Eagle has smaller head, narrower wings and shorter tail. Golden Eagles are usually seen singly or in pairs and hunt by searching mountainsides and fields from low flight. F

head-on flight

tree nest

adult

juv

White-tailed Eagle

juv

adult

adult

juv

adult

juv

Pallas's Sea Eagle

adult

iff nest

adult

juv

diving

head on flight

Golden Eagle

adult

juv

73

IMPERIAL EAGLE *Aquila heliaca* L 79–84 W 175–185 Uncommon. Prefers open fields, plains and swamps. Silhouette very similar to Golden Eagle, but tail proportionally shorter and wings held at more horizontal level. White scapulars, particularly prominent on Spanish form which also has white leading edge to wing, are diagnostic. This characteristic (attained when 3 years old) is lacking in immatures, which are light reddish-brown with streaked undersides (more prominent in eastern subspecies). Very similar Steppe Eagle has smaller head. Behaviour more sluggish than that of Golden Eagle.

STEPPE EAGLE *Aquila rapax* L 69–76 W 157–173 An uncommon eagle of dry, bushy plains or steppes. Adult has dark brown plumage. Flight silhouette is very similar to that of the Golden Eagle, but head is proportionally smaller. Difficult to distinguish from Spotted Eagle, but seldom has white upper rump. In flight, wings are held horizontal with slight bend. Immatures are very light, almost cream-coloured. They resemble immature Imperial Eagles but have wider white trailing edge of wings and tip of tail. From below the light stripe through the centre of the wing is characteristic. Very sluggish in behaviour, rarely soaring high. Often perches on the ground. Tawny Eagle, the African subspecies, is an accidental visitor to the Mediterranean and can be distinguished by the absence of a light stripe through the centre of the wing.

SPOTTED EAGLE *Aquila clanga* L 69–74 W 160–170 An uncommon eagle of extensive woods and bushy country, most often found near lakes, rivers and marshes. Adult is uniformly dark brown, sometimes with a little white on upper tail-coverts. Immatures have boldly spotted upper parts. Silhouette is rather disproportionate with short, rounded tail. Wing-tips point downward as wings are held with a downward bend from carpal joints. Wing-beats feeble. At close range seven primaries can be counted, as opposed to only six in Lesser Spotted Eagle. From below the dark wing-coverts distinguish it from the Lesser Spotted. Wings and base of tail are wider than in Lesser Spotted, and wings are held straight out from body, not slightly forward.

Spotted Eagle
light variety
(*fulvescens*)

LESSER SPOTTED EAGLE *Aquila pomarina* L 64–69 W 140–160 Uncommon, usually met with in extensive woods, often near water. Adult very similar to Spotted Eagle. The wing-coverts are lighter than on Spotted Eagle. Flight silhouette differs from Spotted Eagle by proportionally longer tail and more slender wings. Six primaries can be counted at close range. Immatures told from immature Spotted Eagle by fewer spots on back and lighter wing-coverts; at close range a diagnostic buff patch on the nape can be seen.

adult western form

Imperial Eagle

head-on silhouette

juv

adult

juv

adult western form

Steppe Eagle

juv

adult

adult

juv

Spotted Eagle

juv

adult

ead on silhouette

juv

adult

adult

juv

adult

ead on silhouette

Lesser Spotted Eagle

75

BONELLI'S EAGLE *Hieraaetus fasciatus* L 69–74 W 157–168 This rather small eagle is uncommon. I prefers open, mountainous areas; in winter also found in more open country. More Goshawk-like in silhouette than other eagles. Adult is recognised by light underside of body contrasting with almost black underside of wings and long, barred tail with broad, black terminal band Upper side is dark brown with a white area on the back Immature in first year has rusty head, red-brown underside and rather heavily barred tail. In second year it is almost uniformly brown but with black terminal band on tail. Characteristic plumage of the adult is attained after 3–4 years. Flight is swift and strong. Often seen in pairs, gliding along mountain sides. Exceptionally swift and progressive in its hunt. Call resembles that of Goshawk.

BOOTED EAGLE *Hieraaetus pennatus* L 46–5† W 109–117 Uncommon. This is the smallest European eagle, the size of a Buzzard. Found in mixed and deciduous woods with clearings, usually in low mountains but also in flatter country. Flight is swift and agile Does not soar as often as Buzzard. Told from Buzzard by much longer and narrower tail. Occurs in two colour phases, a more common pale and a rarer dark phase Pale phase is told from all other birds of prey by light wing linings and dark primaries. Scapulars are white forming a characteristic white V when seen from above Dark phase is uniformly dark brown with paler tail Both phases have small white spot on the leading edge of the wing, close to the body. Immatures resemble adults of the same phase, but in pale phase they have buffish, not white underparts. Call is a high-pitched trilling cry.

SHORT-TOED EAGLE *Circaetus gallicus* L 66–69 W 155–160 Uncommon. Prefers mountain slopes, gorges secluded marshy plains and woodlands, where it hunts snakes and lizards. A very pale and long-winged eagle with entire underside of wing white except for wing-tips Two colour phases occur, a more common with rather dark head and breast and a rarer almost pure white Juvenile is browner below with dark barring. Tail is long and head large. Wings are held at horizontal level with tips pointing slightly forward. Seen from in-front the wings are curved with primaries bent upward. Often seen soaring but will also hover like a Kestrel with dangling feet; an almost diagnostic feature for so large a bird Easily told from Osprey by larger size, broader wings and dark upper side. Does not hover over water. More vocal than most other birds of prey. Plaintive and harsh 'jee and a weaker but sharper 2–3 syllable call.

Bonelli's Eagle

adult

juv

adult

juv 2 year

juv 1 year

adult head on

light phase

dark phase

head on dark phase

adult

dark phase adult

Booted Eagle

light phase adult

stooping

Short-toed Eagle

dark phase

light phase

hovering

head-on silhouette

Buzzards

(part of family *Accipitridae*) are medium-sized, broad-winged birds of prey which are most often seen soaring. Often migrate together. Look like miniature Golden Eagles in flight silhouette.

BUZZARD *Buteo buteo* L 51–56 W 117–137 Common. In summer, in wooded areas with openings and surrounding fields; in winter also on moors, plains and extensive open areas. In Britain, on rocky coasts and hillsides in both seasons. Plumage varies from almost pure white to almost black. Told from Long-legged Buzzard adult by barred tail, from Rough-legged by dark band on upper breast, lack of white tail and black wing patches. Sometimes difficult to tell from Honey Buzzard but is generally heavier and without pellucid wings. Eastern Subspecies, Steppe Buzzard *B.b. vulpinus*, is smaller with only faint barring on the tail. Soars or migration in flocks. Perches on poles or branches Usually silent but in breeding season gives high-pitched drawn-out mewing call. Sometimes hovers.   R P

ROUGH-LEGGED BUZZARD *Buteo lagopus* L51–64 W 130–152 Common. Nests in mountainous, barren country. Winters in open habitats, marshes, fields and moors. Black carpal patches, black shield on belly and white tail and broad black terminal band diagnostic Varies in colour; immatures have less pronounced characteristics. Feathered tarsi visible at very short range In flight similar to Buzzard, but heavier. The 'arms' are held upward, the 'hands' horizontal. Soars like Buzzard often seen hovering.   W

LONG-LEGGED BUZZARD *Buteo rufinus* L 61–66 Uncommon, but probably often overlooked. Inhabits dry open plains and steppes, more rarely mountains. Occurs in two colour phases, a more common light and a rare dark phase. Light phase can be told from Buzzard by very light head and unbarred tail. Chocolate-coloured dark phase looks almost black at a distance but has light unbarred tail. Immatures of both phases are difficult to distinguish from Buzzards but longer wings and tail flight silhouette resembles Rough-legged Buzzard Habits closely resemble those of Buzzard.

A few pairs breed in southern England

HONEY-BUZZARD *Pernis apivorus* (although more closely allied to the kites it is treated here for identification purposes.) L 51–56 W 119–127 Common. Nests in open forests with clearings; on migration more varied habitats. Very variable in plumage—ranges from chestnut brown to creamy white, but more sombre brown with greyish head most common. Immatures often very light with large brown spots. Easily confused with Buzzard with which it often mixes during migration. Notice longer, broadly barred tail, outstretched neck and narrower, pellucid wings. Not as sluggish in flight Migrates in flocks. Does not hover.   S

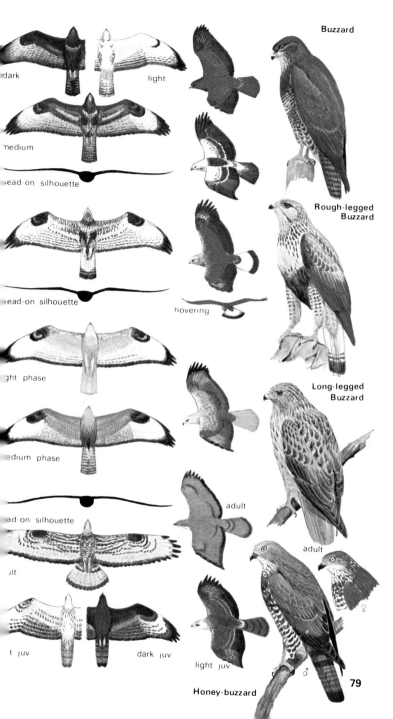

dark

light

medium

head-on silhouette

head-on silhouette

light phase

medium phase

head-on silhouette

adult

light juv

dark juv

hovering

adult

light juv

Buzzard

Rough-legged Buzzard

Long-legged Buzzard

adult

♀

♂

Honey-buzzard

79

Accipiters

(part of family *Accipitridae*) are medium-sized birds of prey with rather short, rounded wings and long tails. Fly with rapid, stiff wing-beats interrupted by glides. Sometimes seen soaring.

GOSHAWK *Accipiter gentilis* L 48–61 W 99–119 Common, but secretive in woodlands with preference for coniferous forests with many clearings. Looks like a large, heavy, short-tailed Sparrowhawk. White fluffy under tail-coverts are characteristic, as is the wide white stripe above the eye. Wing-beats are slower than Sparrowhawk's. Females much larger than males. Adult birds have barred, immatures have spotted undersides Hunts by quartering wood edges and clearings. Extremely fast. Rarely seen soaring. At nesting site a rapid call similar to Sparrowhawk's and a mewing cry similar to Buzzard's can be heard. R

SPARROWHAWK *Accipiter nisus* L 30–38 W 61–79 Common. Mainly found in forested country but also in open country with groves and scattered trees, particularly in winter. Smaller size, longer tail and short rounded wings distinguish this species from buzzards harriers and kites. Most easily confused with falcons Kestrel in particular, but has different coloration, stiffer wing-beats and more rounded wings. Male can be quite rufous on underside. Goshawk is bigger and heavier and has white fluffy feathers at base of shorter tail. Very difficult to distinguish from Levant Sparrowhawk in the field. Flies very fast, usually along hedges or wood margins, low over the ground. Sometimes seen soaring with wings and tail more fanned-out than in direct flight. Not sociable. At nesting site a rapid 'leek-keh-leek' can be heard. R

LEVANT SPARROWHAWK *Accipiter brevipes* L 33–38 W 64–79 Less common than Sparrowhawk. Prefer drier, more open country with deciduous woods. Very difficult to tell from Sparrowhawk but in flight appears more falcon-like. In all plumages it has red iris (not yellow) and adults have white underside to wing (not barred). Male has grey, not rufous cheeks and may be almost white below. Female is less brown, more grey above with brown-spotted throat, not pure white throat and there is a more striking contrast between light underwing and dark wing-tips. Immatures have large drop-shaped spots on very white underside. It has 6– rather narrow tail-bands with a wider terminal band whereas the Sparrowhawk has 4 tail-bands with wide terminal band. Migrates in flocks. Beside Sparrowhawk-like calls, it has distinct 'vee-vit'.

Goshawk

adult soaring

juv.

♂

♀

juv gliding

♀

♀

Sparrowhawk

juv.

♂

♀

♀

soaring

juv. gliding

♂

soaring

juv. gliding

♂

Levant Sparrowhawk

juv.

♂

♀

81

Kites (part of family *Accipitridae*) are medium-sized, long-winged and long-tailed birds of prey often seen soaring.

RED KITE *Milvus milvus* L 61–66 W 145–155 Quite common. Prefers wooded hills and open country with scattered groves and trees. Told from all other birds of prey by long, deeply forked tail and rufous plumage with white patches on underside of wings. Immatures have less deeply forked tail, but can be distinguished from Black Kite by lighter colour of plumage. Soaring flight is characteristic with angled wings. Flight is more buoyant than that of other birds of prey. Long tail is constantly tilted and twisted. On migration often seen with buzzards. Call is buzzard-like.   RS

BLACK KITE *Milvus migrans* L 51–56 W 112–117 Common. Usually near lakes and rivers bordered with woods or scattered trees. In southernmost Europe also in drier and more open habitats. Not infrequently in or near towns where it scavenges. Quite similar to Red Kite, but has much darker plumage and shorter, less deeply forked tail. Immatures have white patches on underside of wings but have much darker plumage than Red Kite. Adults lack white wing patches. Sociable. Sometimes fishes like Osprey but will also take refuse on the ground or on shores. Often nests in colonies.   V

BLACK-WINGED KITE *Elanus caeruleus* L 33 W 74 Extremely rare and local in dry cultivated areas with scattered trees and bushes in southern part of Iberian peninsula. Colour pattern can be difficult to distinguish at a distance. Often seen hovering like a Kestrel, but also quartering the ground like a harrier. Flight pattern can be almost gull-like.

Ospreys (family *Pandionidae*). Monospecific family.

OSPREY *Pandion haliaetus* L 53–61 W 147–163 Common. Always found near lakes, rivers or sheltered coasts, as it lives almost exclusively on fish. Dark upper parts with white crown, white underparts with poorly marked, narrow breast-band distinguish it from all other birds of prey. Flight silhouette is characteristic. Wings are held at an angle and slightly arched. Usually seen flying slowly 20–30 feet above the water. Often hovers when prey is spotted. Plunges feet-first into the water. Sometimes sociable in nesting. Sometimes soars. Call is a rapid series of descending high-pitched whistles.

SP

Red Kite

adult

juv.

adult

juv.

head-on

Black Kite

dult

juv.

juv.

adult

Black-winged Kite

ead-on adult

hovering

juv.

adult

Osprey

juv

hovering

adult

ad-on adult

Harriers

(part of family *Accipitridae*) are medium-sized, long-winged, long-tailed birds of prey found in open country. Males and females differ greatly in plumage. Glides with wing-tips pointed upwards forming an open V. Flies low over the ground when hunting. Nest on the ground or in marshes.

MARSH HARRIER *Circus aeruginosus* L 48–56 W 115–130 Common. Nests in large, dense reed-beds. Also seen over open fields and marshes. Colour pattern characteristic. Notice lack of white rump. Heavier and broader winged than the other harriers and wings are held in a more open V. Wing-beats slower. On breeding grounds the nasal, high-pitched whistling call can be heard. RS

HEN HARRIER *Circus cyaneus* L 45–52 W 105–120 Common. Nests in open country and moorlands. Also seen hunting over marshes and swamps. Although not as large as Marsh Harrier, it is larger, heavier and less buoyant in flight than Montagu's and Pallid Harriers. More white on rump. Male told from male Montagu's by lack of black stripes on wing and unstreaked underside, from Pallid Harrier by more extensive black on wing-tips and grey breast. Females and immatures are similar and very difficult to distinguish from female Montagu's and Pallid Harriers. They are more brownish in general colouring and appear heavier with shorter and stubbier wings. Usually seen singly flying low over the ground; at favourable hunting grounds sometimes a few together. RWF

Pallid   Montagu's

MONTAGU'S HARRIER *Circus pygargus* L 43–47 W 105–120 Uncommon. Found in marshes, moors, heath and cultivated land. Slim, long-winged harrier with narrow, pointed wings and buoyant flight. Male told from male Hen by lack of white rump and by narrow black wing-bars, from male Pallid by dark grey breast wing-bars and much more extensive black on wing-tips. Immatures have unstreaked rich rufous underside but are almost indistinguishable from immature Pallid Harriers. Females told from female and immature Hen Harrier by longer and narrower wings and more elegant appearance. They are almost indistinguishable from female Pallid Harrier in the field but dark bars on secondaries below are more widely spaced. Black phase is very rare. Sometimes nest sociably.

Montagu's
adult ♀

Pallid adult ♀

PALLID HARRIER *Circus macrourus* L 40–48 W 95–120 Uncommon. Although frequenting marshes and moorlands, it prefers dry steppes and plains. Male told from Montagu's and Hen Harriers by paler grey upper parts, white cheeks and breast, and very limited amount of black on wing-tips. Female and immature very similar to female and immature Montagu's but have narrow light neck-band and more prominent dark stripe through the eye.

head-on silhouette

Marsh Harrier

juv

♂

♂

♀

Hen Harrier

♂

♂

♂

imm
♂

Montagu's
♀

Hen

♀

Montagu's Harrier

juv.

♂

adult

♂

sub-adult
moulting

♂

Pallid Harrier

imm

juv. Montagu's juv. Pallid

♀

♂

Montagu's

♂

dult

adult

♂

♂

sub-adult

Falcons (family *Falconidae*) are small to medium-sized birds of prey

with long, pointed wings and long tails. Head is large. Perfect flyers. Moustachial stripe present on most species. Females often larger than the males.

GYRFALCON *Falco rusticolus* L 56–61 W 124– 132 Uncommon. Found in mountainous open country. Outside breeding grounds most often found on sea coasts and other open areas. Largest of the falcons. Told from Peregrine by larger size, proportionally longer tail, slower wing-beats and much broader base of wing. Lacks the contrast between dark upper side and light underside so characteristic of Peregrine. Easternmost birds are dark, while the Icelandic are intermediate in colour. The almost white Greenland birds are very rare. Flies low over the ground but sometimes soars. Often perches on rocks or poles.   V

Very rare throughout the whole of its European range.

PEREGRINE FALCON *Falco peregrinus* L 41–51 W 81–112 Formerly common, now much reduced in number, apparently due to the effects of poisonous chemicals on its prey. Usually found in open or semi-open country with trees or cliffs, where the nest is built. Also open woods. Coastal in Britain. Outside breeding season often found on marshes and moors. Told from Gyrfalcon by smaller size and greater contrast between dark upper side and light underside; from Lanner and Saker by darker back and head. Female larger than male. Immatures have brown, not black upper side, but head is always dark. Moustachial streak is broad and well-pronounced. Flight swift and strong with fast wing-beats interrupted occasionally by gliding. Sometimes soars. Usually solitary. Often perches on stones and poles in the open.   RP

LANNER *Falco biarmicus* L 43 W 99 Uncommon. Found on mountain slopes and plains, rocky shores and brushland. Very similar to Peregrine, but has light brown crown and lighter back. Breast in adult has only few spots; immature more heavily spotted. Moustachial streak narrow but well-defined. Upperside of tail clearly barred. Behaviour and habits much like Peregrine but less bold.

SAKER *Falco cherrug* L 46 W 104 Uncommon. A bird of the open plain, semi-desert and desert. Often nests in heronries. Looks like very pale Peregrine (paler than Lanner). Light underside, crown and nape finely streaked. Moustachial streak pale and narrow. Slightly larger than Peregrine with proportionally longer wings and tail. Immatures have darker and bolder streaks on crown and underside. Upperside of tail less distinctly barred than in Lanner. Behaviour and habits as Peregrine but more confined to open country.

adult intermediate phase

Gyrfalcon

adult light phase

adult intermediate phase

juv. dark phase

Peregrine Falcon

juv

adult

dult

adult diving

juv

Lanner

adult

lult

Saker

adult

ult

juv

87

ELEONORA'S FALCON *Falco eleonorae* L 36 W 89
Local and uncommon. Found on rocky Mediterranean islands and sea cliffs. Nests colonially. Breeding season delayed to feed on autumn migrants. Occurs in two colour phases: a dark slate grey (25%) and a more common light phase with dark upper side and rusty, heavily streaked underside. Dark phase can be confused with the smaller Red-footed Falcon male, but it lacks the red under tail-coverts. Light phase can be confused with larger immature Peregrine, but has yellow cere, narrower moustachial streak, more heavily streaked underside and longer tail. Immatures of light and dark phases are correspondingly coloured. Larger than Hobby, which it closely resembles in flight but wings are exceptionally long. Hunts birds and insects in dashing elegant flight. Hawks for insects at dusk like Hobby. Will also stoop on small birds in similar manner to Peregrine and sometimes hover like kestrel. Call is harsh 'keya', sometimes repeated.

HOBBY *Falco subbuteo* L 28–31 W 69–76 Quite common in some parts of its range. Found in open woodlands and heaths with many groves. Nests in abandoned crows nests. Looks like small Peregrine but is more heavily streaked on underside, and adults have chestnut thighs and under tail-coverts. Immatures are more heavily streaked and lack chestnut areas. Moustachial streak is well defined. Immatures told from immature Red-footed Falcon by dark forehead and more heavily streaked underside. Does not hover like Red-footed Falcon. Manoeuvres with extreme elegance when hunting insects and small birds. Flight silhouette is characterized by long sickle-shaped wings and comparatively short tail distinguishing it from much larger Peregrine Falcon. Does not look as compact as the slightly smaller Merlin. Call is a repeated 'kick'.   S

MERLIN *Falco columbarius* L 28–31 W 61–66 Common. A bird of prey of the open, nesting on moors and tree-less hills; outside breeding season also found on marshes, cultivated fields and along seashores. A very small, very fast falcon. Male has bluish back and tail. Larger female has dark brown back and tail. Told from Hobby by longer tail with broad black band near tip, smaller size and less sickle-shaped wings. From Kestrel by colours, shorter tail and more compact appearance. Moustachial streak ill-defined. Immatures resemble female closely. Easily told from Sparrowhawk by pointed narrow wings. Flies fast low over the ground. Often seen perched low on stones and fence posts. Nests on the ground. Call is a Kestrel-like chattering 'ki-ki-ki'. Female has similar but lower pitched chatter and also a much slower, rather plaintive call, 'eep-eep'.
RWF

Eleonora's Falcon

adult dark phase

adult light phase

juv light phase

adult light phase

adult dark phase

Hobby

adult

juv

juv.

adult

eating dragonfly

adult

♂

♀

Merlin

♂

Merlin charging

RED-FOOTED FALCON *Falco vespertinus* L 25–30
W 69–76 Common, often seen in flocks. Found on open
and semi-open plains, wood edges and open agricultural areas with scattered trees. Male is slate-black with
red feet and rusty under tail-coverts, the latter distinguishing it from dark phase Eleonora's Falcon. Female
very light rufous, resembling female Kestrel, but with
lighter head and unstreaked breast. Immatures resemble
immature Hobby but are paler with pale forehead and
less bold streaking of underside. Very long wings and
tail. Behaviour resembles Kestrel's but it is often seen in
flocks hunting insects, particularly at dusk. Often hovers.
Will also take insects and small rodents from the ground.
Nests colonially in old nests of other birds, especially
Rooks. Call is Kestrel-like, but higher pitched.   V

LESSER KESTREL *Falco naumanni* L 28–31 W 61–66
Very common. Often seen in surroundings of villages and
towns, hunting in open agricultural country and marshes. Roosts in flocks in trees. Very similar to Kestrel but
slightly smaller with smaller bill and white claws (black
in Kestrel); wing beats faster. Male has unspotted back
and wings with clearer blue and red markings. Seen from
below, wings and tail look much paler than Kestrel's.
Female indistinguishable in field except for gregarious
noisy habits and light claws seen at close range. Hunts
insects in the air and on the ground. Does not hover as
frequently as Kestrel. Call is more chattering, not as shrill
as Kestrel's. Nests colonially in ruins, cliffs or quarries. V

KESTREL *Falco tinnunculus* L 30–33 W 69–74 Most
common and widespread of the falcons. Breeds in old
nests on cliffs and buildings, sometimes in the centre of
cities. Found in almost all types of open and semi-open
habitats. Male has blue head and nape, reddish back and
wings with dark spots and blue tail with broad sub-
terminal black band. Can only be confused with Lesser
Kestrel which has unspotted back and wings. Female
and immatures have barred reddish-brown upper side
and apart from black, not light claws and more solitary
habits, are almost indistinguishable from female and
immature Lesser Kestrels. Told from female and immature
Red-footed Falcons by spotted breast, dark forehead
and broad, dark sub-terminal band on tail. Flight
silhouette is characteristic with long, pointed wings and
very long tail. Often hovers at 20–30 feet with tail fanned
out on the lookout for prey, insects and small mammals
on the ground. Occasional short glides between hovering. Usually solitary in habits. Call is a series of shrill
'keh-leek' notes and also a repeated 'kee-kee-kee'. RV

Red-footed Falcon

adult ♂
imm ♂
adult ♀
juv

juv
♀
♂

Lesser Kestrel

♂
♀

♂
♂

hovering

♂
♀

♂
♂

Kestrel

♂

♀

91

Birds of prey in flight

are often difficult to tell apart and colours are usually obscure. Special notice should therefore be made of shape and length of wings and tail, position of wings when the bird is soaring, and pattern of wing-beats and flight. As birds of prey are reluctant to cross open water, they concentrate on promontories and along coastlines during migration. Well-known gathering places are Falsterbo (south

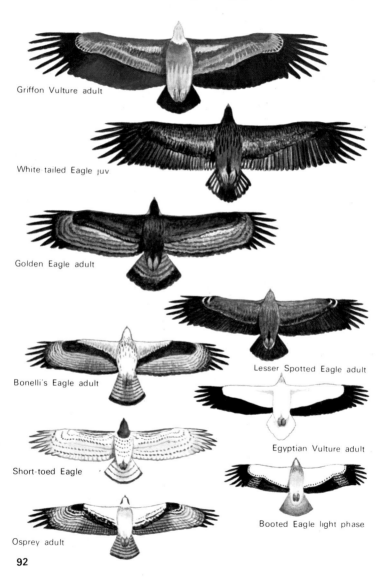

Griffon Vulture adult

White tailed Eagle juv

Golden Eagle adult

Lesser Spotted Eagle adult

Bonelli's Eagle adult

Egyptian Vulture adult

Short-toed Eagle

Booted Eagle light phase

Osprey adult

Sweden), the Bosporus, and Gibraltar, where more than 1000 birds of prey can be seen in a single day. Falsterbo is best in the autumn, whereas the Bosporus and Gibraltar are passed by large numbers of birds of prey in both autumn and spring. Migrating birds of prey also concentrate along mountain ridges. In winter, areas with concentrations of other birds are usually also good places for watching birds of prey.

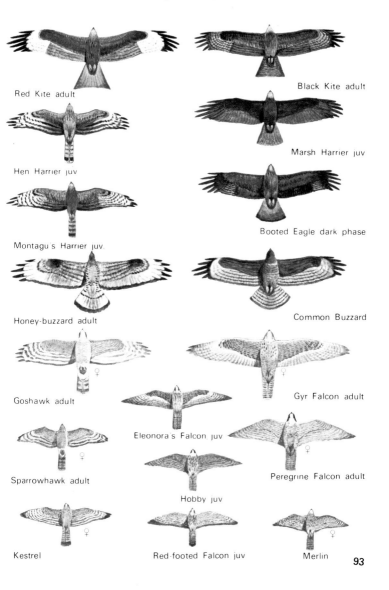

Red Kite adult

Black Kite adult

Hen Harrier juv.

Marsh Harrier juv.

Montagu's Harrier juv.

Booted Eagle dark phase

Honey-buzzard adult

Common Buzzard

Goshawk adult

Gyr Falcon adult

Eleonora's Falcon juv.

Sparrowhawk adult

Peregrine Falcon adult

Hobby juv.

Kestrel

Red-footed Falcon juv.

Merlin

93

Gallinaceous birds (order *Galliformes*) are heavy-bodied, chicken-like land birds. All have a short, heavy bill. Wings short and rounded. Legs rather long. Flight with rapid wing-beats interrupted by short glides seldom lasts more than a few hundred yards. Capable runners, they forage on the ground for seeds and insects. Cocks of most species more colourful. Many species have an elaborate courtship display.

Grouse (family *Tetraonidae*) are stocky, medium-sized, with moderate to long tails. Nostrils and feet covered with feathers. Clutch, 5–12 eggs.

WILLOW GROUSE *Lagopus lagopus* L 41 Common, but abundance varies. Found in moors with low scrub, often near rivers. Usually at lower altitudes than Ptarmigan but not uncommon a little above tree limit. Difficult to tell from Ptarmigan but is larger with proportionally larger bill, more rufous colours in summer, and in winter neither cock nor hen has dark stripe between eye and bill characteristic of cock Ptarmigan. In autumn, Willow Grouse is patchy dark brown and white, and not grey above like Ptarmigan. Winters in small flocks. When flushed, gives rapid laughing call.

RED GROUSE *Lagopus lagopus scoticus* L 38 The Red Grouse of Britain and Ireland are now regarded as races of the Willow Grouse. Common on upland moors and heaths. Dependant on heather at different stages for food, nesting and cover. In cold spells may go down to fields. Wings dark in all plumages. Colour predominantly dark rufous, distinguishing them from Greyhen (female Black Grouse), Hazelhen and partridges. Hens paler than cocks and Irish race yellower than British. Voice like Willow Grouse's. F

PTARMIGAN *Lagopus mutus* L 36 Common in mountain areas, normally above the tree line. Usually found at higher elevations than Willow Grouse. In summer, cock lighter and more yellow than larger Willow Grouse, but hens are virtually identical except for size and bill. In winter both sexes are white with black tail, and cock has black line through eye. Found in pairs in summer, in flocks in winter. When flushed, utters peculiar, dry croaking, very different from Willow and Red Grouse. F

Caucasian
Snowcock

CAUCASIAN SNOWCOCK *Tetraogallus caucasicus* L 55 Resident in Caucasus above tree limit. Greyish brown with white throat. Cannot be confused with any other gallinaceous bird. Very large (bigger than Black Grouse).

CASPIAN SNOWCOCK *Tetraogallus caspius* L 65 Resident eastern Turkey, Caucasus eastward. Similar to Caucasian Snowcock but darker and less rufous.

sandgrouse

dove

Ptarmigan

partridge

Black Grouse

foot of grouse

chick

Capercaillie display

partridge

foot of partridge

covey of partridge

Willow Grouse

summer ♂

♂ winter

♂ autumn

♂ summer

♀ summer

♂ winter

Red Grouse

♂ summer

♀ summer

♂ summer

♀ summer

♀ winter

♂ autumn

Ptarmigan

♂ summer

♂ winter

♂ winter

CAPERCAILLIE *Tetrao urogallus* L male 87, fem. 61 Common in large coniferous woods, sometimes seen at edges and in clearings. Retiring in habits. Enormous size, black plumage and rather long, fan-shaped tail make cock unmistakable. Hen is less characteristic but told from Greyhen (female Black Grouse) by more closely barred plumage, much longer, rounded tail, rufous in colour. In flight, cock easily recognized even at a distance by size, long neck, very short wings with rapid wing-beats and light underside of wings. When flushed, bursts out of cover very noisily. Display of cock is magnificent; he stands on a rock with tail cocked and fanned and bill pointing upwards, calling. Feeds on buds, shoots, berries and some insects. Often polygamous; cock takes no part in domestic duties. F

BLACK GROUSE *Tetrao tetrix* L male 53, fem. 41 Common on heath and moors, wide open woods, fields and in winter also in open birch woods. Blackcock (male) can hardly be confused with any other European species except perhaps Capercaillie, which is found in coniferous woods, is much larger, not as black and has rounded, not lyre-shaped, tail. Greyhen (female) has slightly forked tail, is larger and more brownish-grey than hen Red Grouse, and smaller and not as barred as hen Capercaillie. At short range, very narrow white wing bar can be seen. Flies high for a game bird and takes rather long glides. Sometimes hybridizes with Capercaillie, Red Grouse and Pheasant. Most often seen at dawn and dusk. Displays are picturesque, the cocks performing beautifully with fanned-out tails and puffed-up plumage, on special areas called 'leks'. Feeds on shoots and buds. Cocks are often polygamous and do not help rear the young.

Caucasian
Black Grouse

CAUCASIAN BLACK GROUSE *Tetrao mlokosiewiczi* L 51 Resident in Caucasus in scrubland. Resembles Black Grouse but tail-feathers of male less lyre-shaped. Female has rounded tail. In habits resembles Black Grouse.

HAZEL GROUSE *Bonasa bonasia* L 36 Common but retiring, in woods near rivers and on mountainsides with thick undergrowth. Cock has black throat; hen's throat is whitish. Black band on grey tail of both sexes is very distinctive in flight. General colour of plumage varies from rufous to greyish-brown. Unlike most other grouse it does not crouch when danger approaches, but immediately takes to wing with characteristic burring sound. Often perches in trees. Usually seen in pairs or families. Call is repeated whistling.

Capercaillie

chick

courtship display

Black Grouse

chick

males displaying

Hazel Grouse

chick

97

Quails, partridges and pheasants

(family *Phasianidae*) are small to large birds of fields and open country. Quails, the smallest, lay 6–16 eggs; partridges are larger laying 8–16; the Pheasant, introduced from Asia, is the largest and may lay 18 or more.

CHUKAR *Alectoris chukar* L 33 Common, preferring open, rocky and barren lands. Closely resembles Rock Partridge but barring on flank more strongly marked and black ring around mottled greyish-white throat, does not surround the bill. Call is chicken-like.

ROCK PARTRIDGE *Alectoris graeca* L 33 Common in rocky evergreen forests and scrub, also found above tree limit. Closely resembles Red-legged Partridge but has larger snow-white throat patch with very distinct, clean-cut black border including bill. Upper parts greyish-brown rather than red-brown. Call is characteristic three-note whistle.

BARBARY PARTRIDGE *Alectoris barbara* L 33 Common in arid scrub. Barbary, Red-legged and Rock Partridges and Chukar are almost indistinguishable at long range. At shorter range, Barbary Partridge told from all others by chestnut-coloured, rather than black border of the grey, not white, throat-patch. Call consists of fast and slow cackling notes.

RED-LEGGED PARTRIDGE *Alectoris rufa* L 34 Common on farmland and heaths with preference for more arid regions. At a distance difficult to tell from Partridge, as both have reddish tail and brownish back. At closer range notice red bill and legs, heavily barred sides and lack of chestnut-brown patch on belly. Immatures spotted rather than streaked. Much more reluctant than Partridge to take wing or run long distances. Coveys spread out when flushed. Has characteristic call with repeated first note: 'chuck, chuck-or'.

PARTRIDGE *Perdix perdix* L 30 Most widespread and numerous European partridge, found in almost any kind of open land, cultivated or uncultivated. The numbers in Britain have recently declined. Notice small size, rust tail, orange-brown unbordered throat and face, and chestnut patch on belly. Like other partridges, often encountered in pairs or family groups. When flushed bursts into flight with noisy wing-beats. Coveys usually do not spread out widely. Rather silent, except during spring courtship, when cocks call 'chirrick, chirrick'. Also calls when flushed.

Black Francolin

BLACK FRANCOLIN *Francolinus francolinus* L 33 Found in densely vegetated areas in Turkey and southern shores of the Caspian Sea eastward. Very dark with chestnut nape, also present in female.

Chukar

Rock Partridge

Red-legged in flight

juv. Red-legged

Barbary Partridge

Red-legged

♂

Red-legged Partridge

juv.

♀

♂ Partridge

covey exploding

99

PHEASANT *Phasianus colchicus* L male 84, fem. 59
Common in open woods and on farmland in scrub,
hedgerows and fields. Both sexes have long pointed
tails and short, rounded narrow wings. Cock very
colourful with distinctive red eye patch on black head
and neck. Plumage is variable, depending on the origin
of the released stock. Some have distinct white ring on
neck. Hen is mottled brown but long, pointed tail is
diagnostic. Bursts upward into flight noisily if flushed,
and flies strongly but only for short distances. Roosts in
trees, often in small flocks. Feeds mostly on waste grains,
seeds and berries. Often seen in the open. The cock's
loud, two-syllabled call is followed by the muffled
sound of rapidly beating wings.   P

Lady Amherst's
Pheasant

LADY AMHERST'S PHEASANT *Chrysolaphus am-
herstiae* L male 89, fem. 63 Established in the wild in
some forests in England. Cock unmistakable. Hen
resembles Pheasant hen but is paler with longer more
strongly barred tail. Other pheasants are introduced in
various parts of Europe but are less well established.

QUAIL *Coturnix coturnix* L 18 Formerly abundant but
has declined in numbers. Found in grassland and fields.
Usually keeps out of sight, hidden in vegetation. Smaller
than any other game bird. Sandy coloured, with striped
back and sides. Cock is striped on throat, hen unmarked.
Best told from Andalusian Hemipode of similar size and
build by striped, not spotted, side and sandy, not orange
breast. Very hard to flush. Once on the wing, flight is low
and slow with very fast wing-beats and the very short
tail looks sandy coloured, not red like that of Partridge
which it resembles somewhat in build and colours. Our
only migrating gallinaceous bird. On migration, seen in
small bevies (flocks) but otherwise usually solitary. Call
can be heard day and night but most often at dusk. Consists of repetition of liquid, three-syllabled notes: 'wet-
my-lips' or 'quip-ip-ip'.

Hemipodes
(order *Gruiformes,* family *Turnicidae*) are small quail-
like birds related to cranes and rails (but treated here for
identification purposes). Males take care of the nest and
females are more boldly coloured.

ANDALUSIAN HEMIPODE *Turnix sylvatica* L15 Very
local in Spain and Portugal. Nests in dense vegetation.
Very secretive, usually found in well-covered brush and
grassland. Very similar to Quail but has bright orange
patch on breast and black spotting on sides. More
closely related to the cranes and rails than to the
gallinaceous birds. Usually seen singly or in pairs and
family groups. Very hard to flush. Call is a characteristic
resonant 'hoo-hoo-hoo', heard particularly often on
clear nights at dawn and dusk.

Pheasant

Quail

Quail in flight

Andalusian Hemipode

101

Cranes and their allies (order *Gruiformes*) are a diversified group. All are wading birds with long legs, but other features are very variable.

Cranes (family *Gruidae*) are tall, stately birds with long legs. The long neck is held extended in flight. Sociable outside breeding season. Perform picturesque dancing display. Clutch, 2 eggs. p. 102

Bustards (family *Otididae*) are medium-sized, rather long-legged and long-necked birds. Terrestrial, with a preference for large open fields and steppes. Gait slow and deliberate. Very shy. Clutch, 2–5 eggs. p. 104

Rails, gallinules and coots (family *Rallidae*) can be divided into two subfamilies:
Rails and gallinules are medium-sized to small, compact birds, with short necks, long legs and long toes which dangle in flight. Rather secretive in behaviour, not sociable. Clutch, 5–15 eggs. p. 106–8
Coots are duck-sized birds with lobed feet. The bill is short and thick. Sociable outside breeding season. Clutch, 5–12 eggs. p. 108

CRANE *Grus grus* L 113 W 203 Locally common, nesting in bogs and wooded swamps. Outside breeding season found in marshes and on sandbanks, along rivers, in grasslands and fields. Larger size and outstretched neck in flight distinguish it from herons, grey colour from storks, spoonbills and ibises. Much larger than Demoiselle Crane but in flight can be difficult to tell from this species. Flies in V-formations or long lines, often very high, sometimes soaring. On the ground the tail looks very bushy. In spring both sexes perform the fantastic courtship dance consisting of jumps and bows. Call is trumpet-like. Voice deeper than Demoiselle Crane's. V

SIBERIAN WHITE CRANE *Grus leucogeranus* L 11S Rare, but regular in autumn along coast of Caspian Sea. Extremely rare in rest of Europe. Pure white colour with black primaries diagnostic. Behaviour is like that o Crane.

DEMOISELLE CRANE *Anthropoides virgo* L 9 W 178 Less common than Crane. Breeds on dry ground on open plains and high plateaux. In winter found o grasslands, in marshes and fields. Distinguished from Crane by much smaller size, long white ear tufts, elon gated black breast feathers and elongated but not fluff inner secondaries. In flight very difficult to tell from Crane, but is smaller and has higher pitched call. Ofte mixes with Cranes. Like Crane, it flies in V-formation o long lines, often at great height. Performs courtshi dance more often than Crane. Escapes are common.

duck   coot   rail

heron   stork   crane

Crane dancing

Water Rail in reeds

Coot taking off

juv.   Crane

Crane in flight

Siberian White Crane

Demoiselle Crane
in flight

Demoiselle
Crane

103

GREAT BUSTARD *Otis tarda* male L 102 W 229 fem. L 81 W 178 Rare and local, found on open plains and cultivated fields, where it feeds on cereals and other vegetable matter, also on insects, frogs and other small animals. Extremely shy and difficult to approach. Easily told from other bustards by its enormous size. In its strong flight the large white area on the wing is striking. Has been compared with a goose with eagle wings. Wing-beats are rather slow. Usually met with in flocks where the size difference between males and females is striking. Females outnumber males. In winter, vagrants can occasionally be found far away from regular range. Communal or single displays, usually performed in the early morning hours, are spectacular, the males bending their legs and suddenly displaying white under tail-feathers, underside of wings and moustachial feathers. The head is thrown backwards and the throat inflated. Cannot be confused with any other European bird. Usually silent but has a gruff bark in breeding season. V

LITTLE BUSTARD *Tetrax tetrax* L 43 W 89 Fairly common on open plains and farmland. Shy, although not as unapproachable as Great Bustard. Notice black and white neck markings of male in breeding plumage. In winter plumage he resembles the female. Told from larger Houbara Bustard by lack of dark stripes along neck, more extensive white on wing and much smaller size. Flies higher than Great Bustard, with much faster wing-beats, resembling flight of game birds. Appears very light-coloured in flight. Males produce whistling sounds in flight. Seen in small flocks, outside the nesting season often far from the breeding grounds. In the courtship display the male puffs up, raises his tail and occasionally leaps into the air and emits a sharp 'irr' note. V

HOUBARA BUSTARD *Chlamydotis undulata* L 64 W 152 A very rare straggler from its African and Asiatic breeding grounds. Prefers very dry steppes but can occur in farmland. In western Europe most often seen in autumn, usually singly although it is quite sociable where more numerous. Told from other bustards by having less white on wing, longer wing and tail, and long, black lines on sides and neck. It has a short crest, more pronounced in the male than the female. Flight resembles that of Great Bustard but longer neck is characteristic. V

Great Bustard

Great Bustard display

Little Bustard

Houbara Bustard

WATER RAIL *Rallus aquaticus* L 28 Common in swamps and ponds with dense vegetation. The largest of the rails, with a very long reddish bill, and pure white under tail-coverts. Although secretive in behaviour, less so than the crakes. Most often seen at dusk and dawn. More often heard than seen. Has a large vocabulary of calls which are more penetrating than musical and are most often heard at night, or when birds are disturbed. These include various squeals, grunts, groans and wails, which often are heard bursting from a dense reed bed at night. Also a sharp 'kik-kik-kik', very similar to calls emitted by Little and Baillon's Crakes.   RSW

SPOTTED CRAKE *Porzana porzana* L 23 Common in swamps and ponds with dense vegetation. Very shy and difficult to observe. Best identification is call. Resembles Water Rail but has short orange bill, greenish legs and buff under tail-coverts. Can also be confused with Corncrake, but notice dark brown, not reddish, wings. When suspicious jerks tail upwards. Usually solitary and most often seen or heard at night. Call is repetition of high-pitched, explosive short 'wheet' notes, rather like the cracking of a whip.   SWP

BAILLON'S CRAKE *Porzana pusilla* L 18 Fairly common in swamps and ponds with dense vegetation. Adult birds are told from male Little Crakes by having boldly barred sides, flesh-coloured legs and no red spot at base of greenish bill. Immatures resemble immature Little Crakes, but are more strongly barred. Call is an unmusical trill somewhat like that of the Garganey drake or Edible Frog. Secretive in behaviour.   V

LITTLE CRAKE *Porzana parva* L 18 Fairly common in swamps and ponds with rich vegetation. Very secretive in behaviour. Male is distinguished from Baillon's Crake by having less strongly marked barring on sides, green legs and red spot at base of bill. Female is buffish, rather than grey, with green legs and red base of bill. Immatures resemble immature Baillon's Crake but have less distinctive barring on the side. Usual call is a series of barking notes ending in a trill. Secretive in behaviour.   V

CORNCRAKE *Crex crex* L 26 Locally common in meadows and fields with dense vegetation. Much larger than other crakes. Told from other crakes by buffish plumage and distinctive reddish colour of wings, very obvious in flight. Secretive, but call, which is a repeated 'crex-crex', may be kept up for hours in the breeding season, most persistently at night.   S

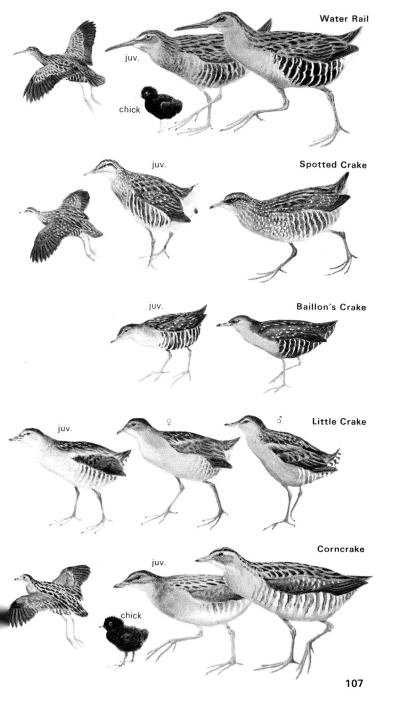

Water Rail

juv.

chick

Spotted Crake

juv.

Baillon's Crake

juv.

Little Crake

juv. ♀ ♂

Corncrake

juv.

chick

107

PURPLE GALLINULE *Porphyrio porphyrio* L 48 Uncommon, preferring swamps with dense vegetation especially extensive reed-beds. Unmistakable, with large, red bill and long, red legs. Immatures best told by large size and shape of bill. Secretive in behaviour. Call is trumpet-like.

ALLEN'S GALLINULE *Porphyula alleni* L 26 A very rare visitor to the Mediterranean countries and occasionally further north from its African breeding grounds. Found in swamps with dense vegetation. Small size, red bill and legs easily distinguish this species from other gallinules.

MOORHEN *Gallinula chloropus* L 33 Very common in swamps, ponds and lakes with shore vegetation. Often in parks. Nests in bushes beside water, reeds and aquatic vegetation, sometimes builds floating nest attached to vegetation on open water of river, and occasionally uses old nest. Swims well. Adult easily distinguished by black colour of body, red base of bill, white line on side and white under tail-coverts with a black line through them. The last two characteristics also distinguish immature Moorhens from immature Coots. Tail is held high and often jerked both when swimming and walking. Flight is weak and fluttering. Calls include a number of harsh, unmusical notes, the most common rendered 'creck' and 'whittuck'. RW

COOT *Fulica atra* L 38 Very common in lakes and ponds and in winter also in sheltered bays. Nests among reeds or aquatic vegetation. Adult easily recognized by black plumage with white frontal shield and bill. Immatures are distinguished from immature Moorhens by having black under tail-coverts and the characteristic Coot silhouette. Dives after an upward jump. Swims with nodding movement of head. Takes to the wing only after a long run along the water. In winter it congregates in flocks at suitable feeding areas, often in large numbers. Usual calls are a loud 'kowk' and a double 'ke-kowk'. RW

CRESTED COOT *Fulica cristata* L 41 Resembles Coot closely and the two red knobs above the frontal shield distinguishing this species are hard to see at a distance. Wing is pure black without the whitish areas found in Coot. Common, and like Coot in habits although more secretive. Call is of two syllables, distinctly different and deeper than call of Coot.

winter

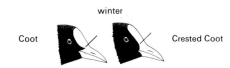

Coot   Crested Coot

Purple Gallinule

juv.

Allen's Gallinule

juv.

Moorhen

juv.

adult

chick

Coot

juv.

chick

display

Crested Coot

juv.

Shorebirds, gulls and auks (order *Chara-driiformes*) form a very large and diverse group of birds all of which, in habitat, are associated with water, in which they either swim (phalaropes, gulls and auks) or wade (the remainder).

Oystercatchers (family *Haematopodidae*) are large, chunky shorebirds with bright red bills and black heads. The long bill, which is compressed laterally, is used to open bivalves obtained along the shores.   p. 112

Shorebirds (waders) (family *Charadriidae*) are small to medium-sized, long-legged birds with long bills and legs. Wings are long and pointed and flight is swift and elegant. Sexes are in most cases similar although striking examples of sexual dimorphism occur like that of the Ruff. Most are highly migratory, often occurring in large flocks on passage. Related species frequently mix outside the breeding season. Breeding habitat often very different from preferred habitat in other seasons. Courtship behaviour is often elaborate and characteristic. Most nest on the ground. Eggs, 2–4, are spotted and well camouflaged. At the nest many species readily feign injury to lead an intruder away. Young are covered with down at hatching and leave the nest immediately. They are usually spotted for camouflage, and crouch when approached. Calls of shorebirds are usually far-reaching and characteristic, and are important in identification.
p. 112

Thick-knees (family *Burhinidae*) are closely related to shorebirds. The Stone-curlew is the only European representative.   p. 136

Pratincoles and coursers (family *Glareolidae*) are more aberrant in looks and behaviour.   p. 136

Gulls and terns (family *Laridae*) are closely related to **skuas** (family *Stercorariidae*). They are short-legged web-footed birds of the open sea, seashores or large stretches of open inland water. Sexes are similar. Juvenile plumages differ and full adult plumage is attained gradually. Winter plumage differs from summer plumage.   p. 140

Auks (family *Alcidae*) are chubby, short-winged, web footed birds of the open sea, only coming ashore to breed. Sexes are similar. Winter plumage differs from summer plumage   p. 160

The **habitats** preferred by our native shorebirds at breeding time and at other seasons are listed on the opposite page. Although they are most often met with in the habitats indicated, they can occur in other places

In breeding season

Sandy beaches
  Kentish Plover
Stony beaches
  Lapwing
  Oystercatcher
  Ringed Plover
  Turnstone
  Grey Phalarope
Marshes with mud-flats
  Lapwing
  Dunlin
  Redshank
  Marsh Sandpiper
  Terek Sandpiper
  Black-tailed Godwit
  Curlew
  Snipe
  Great Snipe
  Jack Snipe
  Black-winged Stilt
  Avocet
  Pratincole
Inland fields and ponds
  Little Ringed Plover
  Lapwing
  Stone-curlew
    (not ponds)
Along lakes and rivers
  Common Sandpiper
Upland moors and tundra
  Oystercatcher (locally)
  Dotterel
  Golden Plover
  Grey Plover
  Lapwing
  Dunlin
  Temminck's Stint
  Little Stint
  Purple Sandpiper
  Knot
  Sanderling
  Broad-billed Sandpiper
  Greenshank
  Wood Sandpiper
  Bar-tailed Godwit
  Curlew
  Whimbrel
  Grey Phalarope
  Red-necked Phalarope
Marshes and bogs in forests
  Common Sandpiper
  Spotted Redshank
  Greenshank
  Wood Sandpiper
  Terek Sandpiper
Woods
  Woodcock

Outside breeding season

Open sea
  Grey Phalarope
  Red-necked Phalarope
Sandy beaches
  Oystercatcher
  Ringed Plover
  Kentish Plover
  Grey Plover
  Knot
  Sanderling
  Common Sandpiper
Rocky beaches
  Turnstone
  Purple Sandpiper
  Common Sandpiper
  Redshank (locally)
Coastal mud-flats
  Oystercatcher
  Ringed Plover
  Little Ringed Plover
  Kentish Plover
  Golden Plover
  Grey Plover
  Lapwing
  Little Stint
  Dunlin
  Curlew Sandpiper
  Knot
  Broad-billed Sandpiper
  Redshank
  Spotted Redshank
  Greenshank
  Common Sandpiper
  Terek Sandpiper
  Bar-tailed Godwit
  Curlew
  Whimbrel
  Avocet
Marshes with some mud-flats
  Golden Plover
  Lapwing
  Temminck's Stint
  Little Stint
  Dunlin
  Curlew Sandpiper
  Broad-billed Sandpiper
  Redshank
  Marsh Sandpiper
  Greenshank
  Green Sandpiper
  Wood Sandpiper
  Common Sandpiper
  Black-tailed Godwit
  Snipe
  Jack Snipe
  Black-winged Stilt
Inland fields
  Dotterel
  Golden Plover
  Lapwing
  Curlew
  Whimbrel
  Great Snipe
  Stone-curlew
Woods
  Woodcock

OYSTERCATCHER *Haematopus ostralegus* L 43
Very common along coasts, locally also breeding on inland moors, plains and river valleys. Unmistakable black and white with long coral-red bill. In flight the broad wing-bar is striking. Immature birds have incomplete white band on the throat. Outside breeding season usually occurs in large flocks frequenting mud-flats and beaches. Flight is strong and direct. Flight formation lines or V's. Probes deep into mud when feeding but also takes shellfish from rocks. Very noisy. Call is a shrill, loud 'bleep'. Song, heard on breeding ground only, is a high-pitched trill ascending in frequency and volume.
RWP

SPUR-WINGED PLOVER *Hoplopterus spinosus* L 28
Uncommon and local, in marshes and irrigated fields. Black and white pattern makes this species unmistakable. It has a slight crest but distribution of black and white and the brownish upper parts easily distinguish it from Lapwing. In behaviour it resembles Lapwing, but lacks the characteristically rounded wings of this species and usually flies lower over the ground. The call is a noisy 'zeet-zeet-zeet'.

LAPWING *Vanellus vanellus* L 30 Abundant, in marshes, meadows, moors and fields. Easily identified by long, thin crest, black and white colour pattern and, in flight, the broad, rounded wings, unique among waders. Immatures have shorter crest and less distinct black and white pattern. Outside breeding season usually recorded in flocks of varying sizes, sometimes mixed with Golden Plovers. Flock pattern is either that of a 'cloud' or an irregular line with a larger group at the head. Wing-beats are rather slow and in breeding season the erratic display flight is conspicuous. In cold weather between October and March, huge flocks may be involved in 'cold-weather movements' from one locality to another. The call is a nasal 'vee-veet'.
RSW

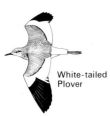

White-tailed
Plover

WHITE-TAILED PLOVER *Chettusia leucura* L 28
Very rare visitor from western Asia, mainly in spring. It resembles the Sociable Plover, but has very pale facial pattern, white belly and tail, and yellow legs. Call resembles Lapwings, but is lower pitched.
V

SOCIABLE PLOVER *Chettusia gregaria* L 30 Nests on steppes. A very rare visitor to western Europe, mainly in autumn, when it occurs on shores, meadows and fields. Black crown bordered with white and black and white pattern of wings and tail are diagnostic. Very characteristic chestnut colour of belly is almost lost in winter. On the ground at a distance the bird looks greyish brown. The legs are dark grey. The call is unlike that of Lapwing, consisting of a short whistle and a harsh chatter.
V

Oystercatcher

flight formation

Spur-winged Plover

Lapwing

juv.

Sociable Plover

imm.

113

RINGED PLOVER *Charadrius hiaticula* L 18 Common along shorelines, on tundra and sometimes marshes. Notice prominent wing-bar and orange legs and bill (tipped with black). Flight is fast and low, with fast wing-beats. Outside breeding season often encountered in small flocks, sometimes mixed with other small shore-birds. Call is a mellow 'choo-ee'. Best told from Little Ringed Plover by wing-bar and voice. Immatures do not always have complete breast-band but are told from Kentish Plover by tail pattern and yellow legs.   RSWP

LITTLE RINGED PLOVER *Charadrius dubius* L 15 In summer locally common on inland localities: shores of lakes, river shingle beds, gravel pits and sandy ground. Often difficult to distinguish from Ringed Plover, but in all plumages notice lack of white wing-bar and pale pink legs. Also notice facial pattern and bill colour of adult, and prominent yellow eye-rim. Call is a character-istic high-pitched, two-note whistle: 'pee-oo'. In winter found along coasts.   S

KENTISH PLOVER *Charadrius alexandrinus* L 19 Fairly common on sandy and stony beaches. Upper parts paler than in the ringed plovers, neck-band interrupted and in flight shows white wing-bars. Legs are always black, distinguishing it with certainty from immature Ringed Plover. Also notice tail pattern. Usually encoun-tered singly or in pairs. Call is a low-pitched 'chu-uu-ee'.   P

CASPIAN PLOVER *Charadrius asiaticus* L 19 Breeds on steppes. Very rare in western Europe, mainly during summer when found on open land. Reddish-brown breast-band of summer male indistinct in winter and in female. Notice whitish head and Golden Plover's upright stance.   V

GREATER SANDPLOVER *Charadrius leschenaultii* L 22 Rare vagrant to parts of Europe from west and central Asia. Found on sandy coasts and mud-flats. Somewhat similar to Caspian Plover but has dark facial pattern and Ringed Plover's more horizontal stance. The legs are grey with a greenish tint, the long bill is black.

KILLDEER *Charadrius vociferus* L 25 A rare visitor to western Europe from North America. Usually met with on marshes and farmland. Notice large size, long rufous tail and two black breast-bands. Call is a loud and characteristic 'kill-deer'.   V

Greater
Sandplover
♂ summer

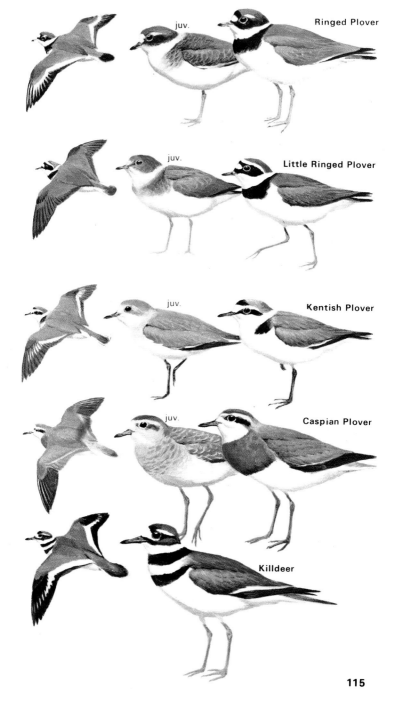

Ringed Plover

juv.

Little Ringed Plover

juv.

Kentish Plover

juv.

Caspian Plover

juv.

Killdeer

115

GREY PLOVER *Pluvialis squatarola* L 28 Common. Breeds on tundra. In winter found on shorelines with mud-flats and sandy beaches. Resembles Golden Plover, but can be distinguished by white rump and striking black axillaries under the wing. It is greyer above than Golden Plover and bill is larger. Does not migrate in large flocks like Golden Plover, but is usually encountered singly or in small groups. Call is plaintive, slurred whistle: 'whee-oo-ee'. WP

GOLDEN PLOVER *Pluvialis apricaria* L 28 Common except in southernmost part of its range where it is becoming increasingly scarce. Nests on moors; in winter found in fields, on mud-flats and meadows. Distinguished from Grey Plover by golden-brown upper parts, faint wing-bar but lacks white rump. Outside breeding season often encountered in very large flocks, sometimes mixed with Lapwings. Call is a sad-sounding, melodious, single-note whistle: 'whoo-ee'. Also note white axillaries distinguishing it from Grey Plover (black axillaries) and Lesser Golden Plover (grey axillaries); habit of raising wings when standing helps in using this as a field mark. RWP

LESSER GOLDEN PLOVER *Pluvialis dominica* L 25 Very rare visitor from Arctic Asia and North America. Mainly seen in autumn. Resembles Golden Plover closely but not as heavy and has grey, not white axillaries. It has no wing-bars and in summer plumage black on belly reaches under the wing. Wings and legs are proportionally longer than those of Golden Plover. Habitat similar. Call is a clear, short, whistled 'oodle-oo' V

DOTTEREL *Charadrius morinellus* L 23 Rare, nesting usually on tundra and mountains. Outside breeding season found on fields and marshes. Adult with its cinnamon underparts is unmistakable. Female is slightly larger than male, who incubates and rears brood. In autumn could be mistaken for Golden Plover, but broad white stripes over eyes meet on nape, and at close range pale breast-line is visible and diagnostic. Usually seen singly or in small groups. Call is a soft trill. S

TURNSTONE *Arenaria interpres* L 23 Common along rocky and stony shores, rare inland. Also frequent sandy beaches. Prefers rocky types of shores, feeding among seaweed. Note head and breast pattern an short orange, red or yellow legs, and in flight the striking black, brown and white pattern of wings, rump and tai Usually seen singly or in small groups. Sometimes foun with other small waders. Call, one to eight fast, low slurred, whickering notes. W

Grey Plover

winter

winter

summer

southern form
summer

Golden Plover

northern form
summer

winter

**Lesser
Golden Plover**

winter
Golden Plover

winter

winter
Lesser
Golden Plover

winter

Dotterel

summer

winter

Turnstone

winter   summer   winter

summer

117

Snipes and woodcock

(family *Charadriidae*, part of subfamily *Scolopacinae*) are primarily inland birds of moist woodlands, marshes and river banks. Rather secretive in behaviour. Necks and legs are relatively short and bills are extremely long. Probe deep into soft ground to find burrowing invertebrates.

SNIPE *Gallinago gallinago* L 25 Very common in marshes, meadows and swamps. The most numerous of the snipes. Told from Great Snipe by white belly, only little white on tail and when flushed, by characteristic zig-zag flight; from Jack Snipe by pattern on crown, larger size, longer bill and tail pattern. Outside breeding season it can be encountered in rather large, loose flocks. Call is a low, rasping note. In display flight, produces strong vibrating sound with outer tail-feathers, called 'drumming', as it dives repeatedly at great height.

RWF

Pin-tailed Snipe

PIN-TAILED SNIPE *Gallinago stenura* L 25 Rare visitor from Asia. More common in drier habitats than very similar snipe. Told by lack of white trailing edge of wing and in the hand by extremely narrow outer tail feathers.

GREAT SNIPE *Gallinago media* L 28 Uncommon, declining in numbers. Breeds in marshes and swamps or on drier land with small streams. Outside nesting season found on fields and marshes. Told from very similar Snipe by slightly larger size, more rounded appearance, barred breast and belly, white outer tail-feathers and straight, heavy flight (immature Snipes sometimes have similar flight pattern). The facial markings are less distinct, the wing pattern more distinct than in Snipe. Usually silent when flushed. Communal display is seen at dusk. During display a twittering sound is produced, but also characteristic accelerating clicking sound.

JACK SNIPE *Lymnocryptes minimus* L 20 Common in marshes and swamps. Distinguished from the larger Snipe by shorter bill, crown pattern and brown unmarked tail. Very difficult to flush. Generally silent when flushed and the flight is then usually short without the characteristic zigzag of the Snipe. During spectacular display flight, a call resembling the sound of a galloping horse is produced.

W

WOODCOCK *Scolopax rusticola* L 36 Common in woods with bogs and wet ground. Easily told from Snipe by larger size and more rounded wings. Flight fast and agile among the trees. When flushed, a clattering of wings is heard. Usually nocturnal. Ideal camouflage makes it difficult to observe during the day. Solitary in behaviour although it can occur in very scattered groups on migration. In the breeding season the soft, croaking call, 'roding', of the displaying male is heard at dusk and early in the morning as the bird flies just above the trees.

RSV

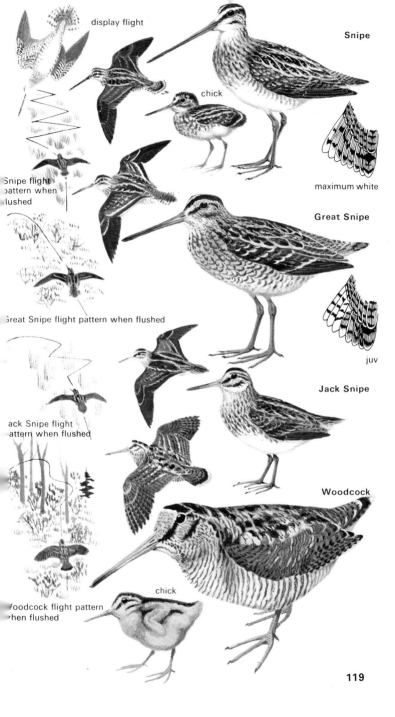

display flight

Snipe

chick

maximum white

Snipe flight pattern when flushed

Great Snipe

Great Snipe flight pattern when flushed

juv

Jack Snipe flight pattern when flushed

Jack Snipe

Woodcock

chick

Woodcock flight pattern when flushed

Curlews and godwits (family *Charadriidae,* part of subfamily *Scolopacinae*) form two rather distinct groups: the genera *Numenius* and *Limosa.* They are large, long-legged, long-billed brownish or greyish shorebirds. Curlews have down-turned bills and are brownish with dark stripes and spots, whereas godwits have straight or slightly upturned bills and are reddish in breeding plumage, greyish in winter. The sexes are similar. Outside breeding season usually gregarious.

CURLEW *Numenius arquata* L 56 Common, nesting on moors, marshes and fields. Outside breeding season also on mud-flats. Very large, with very long down-curved bill and long legs. Lacks distinctive crown pattern of Whimbrel and underparts are striped rather than spotted (compare with Slender-billed Curlew). In flight the neck is withdrawn and the wing beats are relatively slow. Usual call is a mellow whistle: 'curlee'.   RWF

WHIMBREL *Numenius phaeopus* L 41 Common, nesting on moors and upland meadows. In winter found in fields, marshes and on mud-flats. Told from Curlew by smaller size, faster wing beats and much shorter bill and characteristically striped crown. Often mixes with Curlew. Call is a short, mellow whistle, repeated rapidly 6–7 times resembling the call of female Cuckoo.   SF

SLENDER-BILLED CURLEW *Numenius tenuirostris* L 41 Uncommon, breeding on wet steppes. In winter found in marshes and mud-flats. Told from Whimbrel by lack of crown pattern, from Curlew by smaller size and shorter bill. From both by rounded spots on underside which, however, are absent in immatures. Call resembles Curlew's but is higher pitched and shorter.

BLACK-TAILED GODWIT *Limosa limosa* L 41 Fairly common, nesting in meadows and marshes, wintering on mud-flats and marshes. The flight is strong and powerful. In all plumages easily distinguished by long bill, distinctive white wing-bars and solid black band on tail. In summer, chestnut breast, neck and head. Call is loud 'wicka' repeated three times.   RW

BAR-TAILED GODWIT *Limosa lapponica* L 3? Common, nesting in Arctic marshes. In winter found along shores and on mud-flats. In all plumages told from Black-tailed Godwit by barring of tail, lack of wing-bar and comparatively shorter legs and bill. In summer chestnut colours cover entire underside. Flocks are usually very closely packed. Call is a harsh, nasal two-note 'irrick'.   W

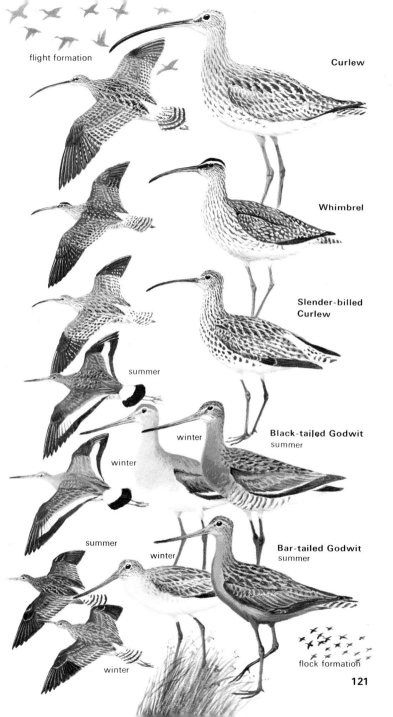

flight formation

Curlew

Whimbrel

Slender-billed Curlew

summer

winter

Black-tailed Godwit
summer

winter

summer

winter

Bar-tailed Godwit
summer

winter

flock formation

121

Larger sandpipers

(family *Charadriidae*, part of sub-family *Scolopacinae*) are a group of medium-sized, slender and elegant shorebirds with rather long, slender bills and legs. In identification, pattern of upper rump plays an important role, as do the calls.

COMMON SANDPIPER *Actitis hypoleucos* L 20 A very common sandpiper breeding along freshwater shores, wintering along freshwater as well as saltwater shores. Characteristic stance is with body tilted forward, head lowered. It bobs the tail up and down almost continuously. In flight the wings are held stiffly downward, with very shallow wing-beats. Usually seen singly or in small flocks, nearly always along water edges or flying low above the water. Sometimes associates with Dunlins or Ringed Plovers. The American counterpart, Spotted Sandpiper (see. p. 126) is a rare vagrant. Call is a shrill piping, often rendered 'kitty-wiper'.　　　　SP

GREEN SANDPIPER *Tringa ochropus* L 23 Common, breeding in woodland swamps and marshes using old nests of songbirds. Outside breeding season usually found in freshwater marshes and shores. Notice dark upper parts, strikingly white rump and dark underside of wings. The dark breast ends abruptly in front of the white belly. Usually seen singly or in small parties. When flushed it often throws itself from side to side a few times. Call is a musical, penetrating three-note whistle: 'tit-looet'.
　　　　WP

WOOD SANDPIPER *Tringa glareola* L 20 Fairly common, nesting in marshes and on the tundra. Outside breeding season found in marshes and swamps and along shores. Notice yellowish legs, spotted upper parts, white rump and light underwing. The striped breast and sides merge into the white belly. More elegantly built than Green Sandpiper. Overall appearance lighter than Green Sandpiper and less contrast between dark and light parts is noticeable, particularly in flight. Usually seen singly but can occur in small flocks. Noisier and more vocal than Green Sandpiper. Call is a high-pitched, three-note whistle: 'chip-ip-ip'.　　　　SP

TEREK SANDPIPER *Xenus cinereus* L 23 Uncommon, nesting on inland marshes. Outside breeding season also encountered along seashores and on marshes. Notice relatively short yellow legs and long upturned bill. On the wing, note pale grey rump and white trailing edge of wing. Flight resembles that of Common Sandpiper but is not as close to the surface of the water. In habits it resembles the smaller Common Sandpiper. Gait is characteristic with breast and bill held low and forward giving the impression it is about to topple forward. Bobs like Common Sandpiper. Call is a fast repetition of flute-like notes.　　　　V

bobbing tail

Common Sandpiper

Green Sandpiper

Wood Sandpiper

winter

Terek Sandpiper

winter

obbing tail like
ommon Sandpiper

summer

123

REDSHANK *Tringa totanus* L 28 Very common in marshes, meadows and swamps, in winter also along shores. Notice conspicuous white rump and wide trailing edge of wing in flight. On ground, bright orange-red legs and partly red bill. Spotted Redshank has dark red legs and bill and is more uniformly greyish in winter plumage. Like many of the larger sandpipers, Redshank occasionally bobs its tail in the same way as Common Sandpiper. Outside breeding season often seen in flocks. Call is a musical, three-note whistle: 'tew-hee-hee'. Alarm call is a loud rapid 'chip-chip-chip'. RSWP

SPOTTED REDSHANK *Tringa erythropus* L 30 Rather common, nesting in marshes and meadows of the forested regions of the north, wintering along shores and in marshes and swamps. In summer unmistakable with black plumage and white upper rump extending very far up back. In winter lighter than Redshank and more uniformly grey, lacking the white trailing edge on wing. Larger and more elegant-looking than Redshank. Usually seen singly or a few together. Call is a musical, somewhat drawn-out whistle: 'tew-it'. WP

GREENSHANK *Tringa nebularia* L 30 Locally common, nesting on moors and marshes in northern forested regions, wintering along coasts and in marshes and meadows. Notice dark grey upper parts with lighter underside, lack of white trailing edge on wing, white upper rump reaching far up back, green legs and slightly upturned bill. Usually seen singly or in small groups. Call is a three-note whistle: 'tu-tu-tu', more melodious than that of Redshank. SWP

MARSH SANDPIPER *Tringa stagnatilis* L 23 Uncommon on marshes and lakeshores. Greenshank-like, but much smaller and more delicate with very slender, straight bill and paler head. In flight the relatively longer legs extend further back than those of Greenshank. Outside breeding season often seen with other larger sandpipers. Usual calls consist of a variety of rather mellow whistles and a twittering trill. V

RUFF *Philomachus pugnax* L male 30, fem. 23 Fairly common in marshes, meadows and lakeshores, only very occasionally seashores. Male in breeding plumage unmistakable. In all plumages notice scaly appearance of back due to pale margins of dark brown feathers, and white areas on edge of dark tail, forming a characteristic pattern. Very variable in details of colours of plumage and soft parts. Males have communal display ground where the picturesque 'fights' take place. Often found in small, close flocks. Call is a rather low, two-note whistle seldom heard. WF

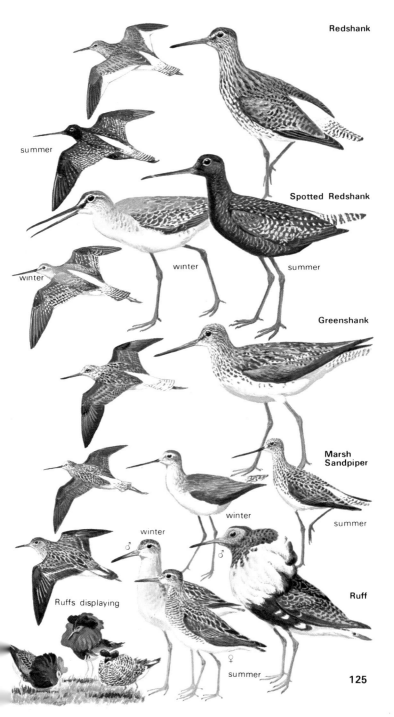

Redshank

summer

Spotted Redshank

winter

winter

summer

Greenshank

Marsh Sandpiper

winter

summer

Ruffs displaying

♂

winter

♂

Ruff

♀

summer

125

Accidental larger sandpipers

are visitors from North America. Most occur in autumn along the westernmost parts of western Europe.

SPOTTED SANDPIPER *Actitis macularia* L 20 Very rare. In winter plumage almost indistinguishable from Common Sandpiper, of which some authorities consider it to be the American race. However, it has more distinct barring on wing-coverts, the legs are brighter yellowish or flesh coloured and it has more white on wing and tail. Call is 'weet-loo-eet'. In summer distinguished by spotted underparts and yellow base of bill.

SOLITARY SANDPIPER *Tringa solitaria* L 20 Very rare autumn visitor. Told from rather similar Green Sandpiper by lack of white upper rump (dark centre) and prominent eye ring. Call is a shrill, high-pitched 2–3 note piping.

STILT SANDPIPER *Micropalama himantopus* L 20 Very rare autumn visitor. Unmistakable in breeding plumage with barring and rusty facial pattern. In winter plumage notice white upper rump, very long greenish legs and 'drooping' bill. Behaviour is snipe-like. Call is a low, rather hoarse, single-note whistle.

GREATER YELLOWLEGS *Tringa melanoleuca* L 36 Very rare autumn visitor (occasionally spring). Resembles Greenshank but with dark back. Notice white upper rump and rather long, slightly upturned bill, yellow legs and characteristic sharp, 3–4 note whistle.

LESSER YELLOWLEGS *Tringa flavipes* L 25 Rare autumn visitor (occasionally spring), but more numerous than Greater Yellowlegs. Notice yellow legs and white upper rump. Bill is shorter and more slender than that of Greater Yellowlegs and general outline more like Redshank's. Call is a soft, 1–3 note whistle.

LONG-BILLED DOWITCHER *Limnodromus scolopaceus* L 30 Very rare autumn visitor. Notice very long bill, plump build, rather short legs and white upper rump reaching far up on the back. Told from Short-billed Dowitcher by barred flanks (summer) and more finely barred tail (winter). Call is a single, thin, piping note, or series of notes.

SHORT-BILLED DOWITCHER *Limnodromus griseus* L 30 Very rare autumn visitor (occasionally spring). Only told from Long-billed Dowitcher with difficulty. Usually has less barring on the flanks and spotted (not barred) under tail-coverts. Best distinguishing feature is the call, a low, mellow three-note whistle.

UPLAND SANDPIPER *Bartramia longicauda* L 2 Very rare autumn visitor. Notice brown colour, long tail, small head and short bill. Often ends rapid flight on post holding the wings high. Airports are favoured haunts. Call is a mellow Whimbrel-like whistle.

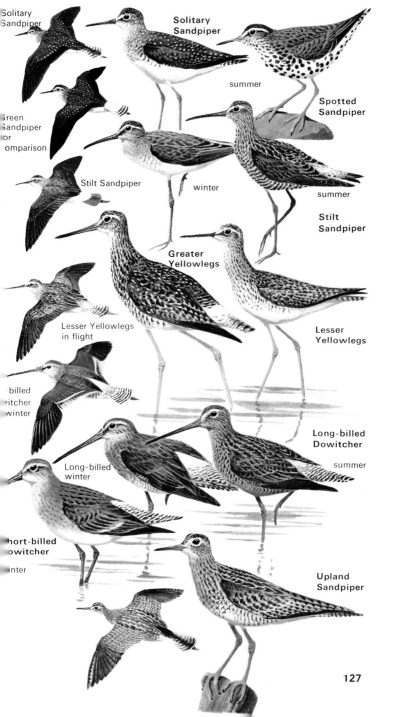

Solitary
Sandpiper

Solitary
Sandpiper

summer

Spotted
Sandpiper

Green
Sandpiper
for
comparison

Stilt Sandpiper

winter

summer

Stilt
Sandpiper

Greater
Yellowlegs

Lesser Yellowlegs
in flight

Lesser
Yellowlegs

billed
itcher
winter

Long-billed
Dowitcher

summer

Long-billed
winter

Short-billed
Dowitcher

winter

Upland
Sandpiper

Small sandpipers

(family *Charadriidae*, part of sub-family *Scolopacinae*) are a group of small, rather chunky, short-legged and rather long-billed shorebirds. Outside breeding season they occur in flocks, often many species mixed together, feeding on mud-flats and along shores. Flocks fly in tight, cloud formation. In America the species belonging to this group are called Peeps.

KNOT *Calidris canutus* L 25 Common. Breeds in the high Arctic, wintering along seashores with mud-flats. In red summer plumage unmistakable. In winter greyish, but notice rather large size, light rump and tail, and faint wing-bars. Usually seen in flocks sometimes with other small sandpipers, when larger size of this species becomes obvious. Bill is comparatively short. Usual calls are a single, rather quiet 'wut' or a whistling 'thu-thu'.
WP

PURPLE SANDPIPER *Calidris maritima* L 20 Fairly common on rocky coasts and in harbours. Nests on Arctic tundra. The darkest and plumpest of the small sandpipers. Often tame. Orange-yellow base of bill and yellow legs are noticeable at a long distance. Usually seen in small flocks, often with Turnstones or Sanderlings. Call is a short 'wit', sometimes repeated.
WF

DUNLIN *Calidris alpina* L 18 Most numerous of the small sandpipers. Nests on moors and marshes; outside breeding season found in flocks along seashores and on mud-flats of fresh as well as salt water. In summer plumage notice bright rusty back and black belly. Winter plumage is grey-brown above, white below. Distinguished from Curlew Sandpiper and larger Knot by dark upper rump. Call is a rapid, low, grating reel.
SW

CURLEW SANDPIPER *Calidris ferruginea* L 1? Common, more numerous in autumn than spring. Nests in the Arctic. Outside breeding season found on mud-flats and marshes, fresh as well as saltwater. In red summer plumage unmistakable. In winter plumage resembles Dunlin, but has white upper rump, longer legs and longer neck and more pronounced down-curved bill. It is generally paler with less streaked underparts. Stance is more upright than that of Dunlin. In Britain and western Europe immatures outnumber adults on autumn passage and are easily told from adults and Dunlins by pinky buff breast and sides of neck. Call is soft whistle 'chirrup'.

winter

summer

Knot

winter

Purple Sandpiper

winter

summer

Purple Sandpipers
and Turnstones
in winter

winter

Dunlin

winter

summer

flock formation

Curlew Sandpiper

summer

winter

winter

129

LITTLE STINT *Calidris minuta* L 13 Fairly common breeding in the Arctic tundra. In winter found in marshes and mud-flats. On migration and in winter often seen with other small waders. Little Stint and Temminck's Stint are easily picked out in these mixed flocks by their smaller size, shorter and straighter bills and more active behaviour. This greater activity is most characteristic of Little Stint. Told from Temminck's Stint, which is the same size, by more distinct light V-pattern on back and grey, not white outer tail-feathers. It is lighter on breast and face and has noticeably longer legs. Call is a sharp short, high-pitched note, quite distinct from the trill of Temminck's Stint.

TEMMINCK'S STINT *Calidris temminckii* L 13 Fairly common, nesting on mountain moors, tundra and along lake and seashores. Outside breeding season found on mud-flats and marshes, primarily of fresh water. Differs from the similar Little Stint in having more uniform dark back, white outer tail-feathers and usually pale legs (black in Little Stint). The pectoral patches give appearance resembling that of Common Sandpiper (p 122). Breast and face darker. Often mixes with Dunlin although it has a greater tendency to occur in small unmixed flocks than the more active Little Stint. Call is a short, high-pitched trill, very different from the sharp high-pitched note of the Little Stint.

BROAD-BILLED SANDPIPER *Limicola falcinellus* L 15 Uncommon, nesting on mountain moors and tundra. In winter found on mud-flats and marshes. Notice very dark colours with Snipe-like pattern with forked eye-stripe, kinked bill and extremely short legs. White belly distinguishes it from Dunlin in summer. Rather sluggish in behaviour. Only at very short range is the drooping flattened tip of the bill noticeable. In winter plumage prominent white eye-stripe and dark spot on the front of wing are the best field marks. Only rarely mixes with other small sandpipers, usually occurring singly or in small flocks. Call is a rather deep trill, 'crrrooit'.

SANDERLING *Calidris alba* L 20 Common, breeding in the Arctic. Outside breeding season found along sand beaches at the water's edge. In winter plumage notice very white appearance with prominent black spot on front of wing, in summer replaced on the upper parts by rich brown. In flight the white wing-bar is striking. The bill is short and dark. Very active, keeping close to the retreating waves. Often allows a close approach before flying off. Usually occurs in unmixed flocks. Flight call a sharp, distinctive 'plick'.

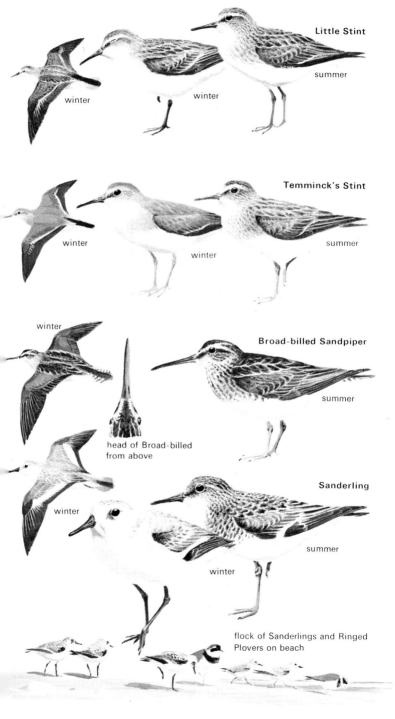

Little Stint

winter

winter

summer

Temminck's Stint

winter

winter

summer

winter

Broad-billed Sandpiper

summer

head of Broad-billed
from above

winter

Sanderling

summer

winter

flock of Sanderlings and Ringed
Plovers on beach

Accidental small sandpipers are visitors

from North America and Asia, most often met with in western Europe in autumn, although there are occasional spring records. Often seen in company with our own small sandpipers.

LEAST SANDPIPER *Calidris minutilla* L 15 Very rare visitor from North America. Resembles Temminck's Stint, but has brownish outer tail-feathers and is slightly darker above especially with darker crown. Bill is thin and short. Legs are yellow. Call is a distinctive high 'breep'.

SEMIPALMATED SANDPIPER *Calidris pusilla* L 18 Very rare visitor from North America. Resembles Little Stint, but back pattern less well-defined and bill thicker and heavier. Call, a short 'kripe', is lower pitched than Least Sandpiper's.

WHITE-RUMPED SANDPIPER *Calidris fuscicollis* L 18 Rare visitor from North America. Has distinctive white upper rump but differs from Curlew Sandpiper in having short, straight bill and more horizontal stance. The wings are long, projecting beyond tail. Call is a thin 'jeet'.

PECTORAL SANDPIPER *Calidris melanotos* L 15 Rare visitor from North America, often found in drier locations than other small sandpipers. It is larger than Dunlin with scaly back like Ruff. Note the abrupt border between streaked breast and white underparts. When flushed, zig-zags like Snipe. Call is a low 'prrrp'. Occurs annually on west coast of Britain in very small numbers.

SHARP-TAILED SANDPIPER *Calidris acuminata* L 18 Very rare visitor from Asia. Resembles Pectoral Sandpiper, but in autumn its breast is buffish, narrowly streaked at sides, and there is no abrupt border between breast and underparts. The supercilium is creamy and prominent, the crown rufous. Legs are darker than those of Pectoral Sandpiper. Call is a high-pitched 2-note whistle.

BAIRD'S SANDPIPER *Calidris bairdii* L 18 Very rare visitor from North America, often found on drier ground than other sandpipers. Notice scaly back, horizontal stance and relatively long wings. Call is a rather liquid 'keep'.

BUFF-BREASTED SANDPIPER *Tryngites subruficollis* L 20 Rare visitor from North America. Prefers short grass habitats (airports). Notice buffish colour with distinctive white underwing and upright stance. When flushed, zigzags rather like Snipe. Call is a low trill.

winter

Least Sandpiper

Least

Semipalmated

winter

summer

Semipalmated Sandpiper

winter

winter

summer

White-rumped Sandpiper

winter

winter

Sharp-tailed Sandpiper

Pectoral Sandpiper

Pectoral

Baird's Sandpiper

Baird's

Buff-breasted Sandpiper

Buff-breasted

Avocets and stilts

(family *Charadriidae*, subfamily *Recurvirostrinae*) are very elegant, black and white shorebirds with extremely long legs and long, thin bills.

AVOCET *Recurvirostra avosetta* L 43 Locally common. Prefers sheltered bays and lagoons. Elegant white and black with extremely long, lead-coloured legs and thin, black, upturned bill. Flight graceful with rather slow wing-beats. Often in large flocks. Sometimes flies in V-formation but more often in loose cloud formation. Nests in colonies of varying size. Call is soft, melodious 'klui-it', hence Dutch name Kluut. SWP

BLACK-WINGED STILT *Himantopus himantopus* L 38 Locally common. Prefers marshes and lagoons with open water. Extremely long pink legs and thin, straight bill are unmistakable. Easily told from Avocet by these, and by solid black back and upper side of wing. Nests in small, loose colonies. Can be seen in small groups but not as sociable as Avocet. Call is a sharp, repeated 'kik'. V

Phalaropes

(family *Charadriidae*, subfamily *Phalaropodinae*) look like small sandpipers, but have lobed toes and swim readily. Outside breeding season the two European species are highly pelagic. Females slightly larger, more colourful than males. Phalaropes often spin in circles in shallow water to stir up food.

Wilson's
Phalarope
winter

WILSON'S PHALAROPE *Phalaropus tricolor* L 23 Rare visitor from N. America in late spring, summer and autumn. More likely seen inland than other two phalaropes. Bill very thin and rather long. With white rump and dark wing, it resembles some of the larger sandpipers, but notice chestnut pattern in summer plumage. Very active. Call is low and grunting. V

GREY PHALAROPE *Phalaropus fulicarius* L 18 Uncommon pelagic species most often seen during storms along the coast. Breeds on Icelandic coastal lagoons. Yellow-based bill is short and much stouter than Red-necked Phalarope's. Notice also less bold pattern on back and much paler appearance in winter. Usually seen singly or in small flocks flying low, far out to sea. Call suggests Turnstone's. P

RED-NECKED PHALAROPE *Phalaropus lobatus* L 17 Uncommon, though more numerous than Grey Phalarope. Nests by tundra lakes. Bill longer and thinner than Grey Phalarope's. Flying birds in winter plumage resemble Sanderling, but have darker back, more slender bill and black line through eye. Usually seen singly or in small flocks. Call consists of low, short, scratchy notes. SP

Avocet

juv.

chick

Black-winged Stilt

winter

♂

♀

♂ summer

juv.

Wilson's Phalarope

summer

adult winter

♂

summer

Grey Phalarope

adult winter

summer
♂

adult winter

♀
summer

Red-necked
Phalarope

adult winter

♂ summer

adult winter

♀
summer

Thick-knees

(order *Charadriiformes*, family *Burhinidae*) are rather large, sand-coloured, large-headed and large-eyed terrestrial birds of dry habitats. Only one species is found in Europe, the Stone-curlew.

STONE-CURLEW *Burhinus oedicnemus* L 41 Scarce or locally common on dry, open localities. Notice large head and eyes and streaked plumage. Often escapes danger by running in a crouched position. Sometimes stands very erect, when characteristic head shape and large eye are prominent features. Flight is usually low over the ground with deliberate wing-beats and the wing pattern is distinctive. Outside breeding season often seen in small flocks. Largely nocturnal in habits. Call is Curlew-like but higher pitched. S

Pratincoles and coursers

(order *Charadriiformes,* family *Glareolidae*) are aberrant southern shore-birds, only rarely encountered in northern Europe.

COLLARED PRATINCOLE *Glareola pratincola* L 25 Locally common on mud-flats, marshes and open plains. Notice tern- or swallow-like silhouette in flight and dark brown underwing. Stance horizontal but runs very well on rather short legs. Can be told from the more eastern Black-winged Pratincole by the reddish-brown, not pitch-black, underwing and narrow white trailing edge of wing. Nests colonially and is usually encountered in flocks, which are often very noisy. Call is tern-like V

BLACK-WINGED PRATINCOLE *Glareola nordmanni* L 25 Locally common on open steppes and dried-out mud-flats. Has pitch-black underwing with no white or brown but this can only be seen properly when the bird takes off or is seen flying in good light. It lacks the white trailing edge of wing present in Collared Pratincole. Also, intermediate forms occur. Otherwise almost identical with Collared Pratincole, of which some authorities consider it a race. V

CREAM-COLOURED COURSER *Cursorius cursor* L 23 Rare straggler to most of Europe from its African and Asian breeding grounds. Usually encountered in localities resembling its desert home, such as sandy beaches and dried-out fields. Notice very light brown colour with black eye-stripes and black tips to wings. Runs very fast, interrupted by sudden stops. Often tries to escape danger by crouching. Call is unmusical and harsh. V

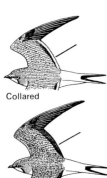

Collared

Black-winged

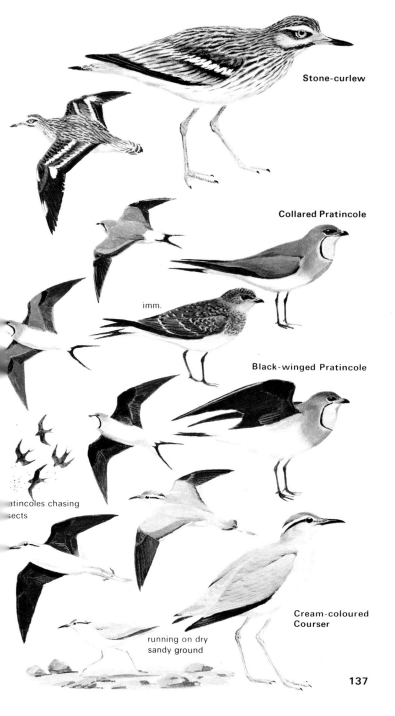

Stone-curlew

Collared Pratincole

imm.

Black-winged Pratincole

atincoles chasing
sects

running on dry
sandy ground

Cream-coloured
Courser

137

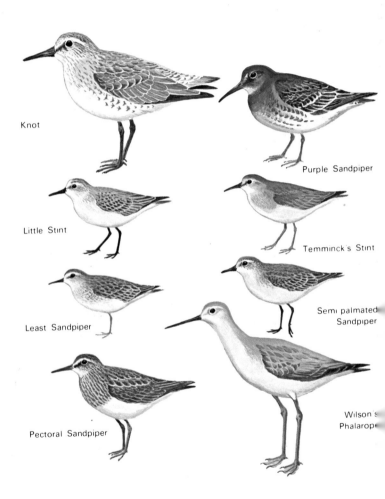

Knot

Purple Sandpiper

Little Stint

Temminck's Stint

Least Sandpiper

Semi palmated
Sandpiper

Pectoral Sandpiper

Wilson's
Phalarope

Winter plumage of smaller shorebirds

The smaller shorebirds usually occur in flocks outside the breeding season, frequenting mud-flats. These flocks are often mixed, offering good possibilities for comparison between species. Identification is often difficult and requires much patience and close observation. Features of special importance are: overall size; length and shape of bill; colours and pattern of back, wings and rump; pattern of breast; and colour of legs. Also notice calls when flushed.

Dunlin

Curlew Sandpiper

Broad-billed Sandpiper

Sanderling

White-rumped Sandpiper

Baird's Sandpiper

Red-necked Phalarope

Grey Phalarope

Skuas

(order *Charadriiformes*, family *Stercorariidae*) look like dark gulls with elongated central tail-feathers, but their silhouette, flight, and feeding habits are very different. The slender wings are sharply bent at the 'wrist' and the tails are frequently fanned as they suddenly change course. Wing-beats are powerful and rapid. The three smaller species show light and dark plumage phases with intermediate grades. Skuas are most often seen robbing other sea birds of fish. They seldom come ashore except to nest and are generally silent. Immatures lack the long tail-feathers and are hard to tell apart. Clutch, 2–3 eggs.

GREAT SKUA *Stercorarius skua* L 59 Very local. At a distance it looks like a dark short-tailed Herring Gull, but it can be distinguished by the large white patches at the base of the primaries. More of a scavenger than other skuas and often seen soaring with gulls. Like the other skuas, it nests colonially on moors and tundra.   SF

POMARINE SKUA *Stercorarius pomarinus* L 51 Uncommon. Larger than Arctic Skua. Bill is proportionally larger than those of Arctic and Long-tailed. Flight is heavier and more steady. The long central feathers are broad and twisted. In the light phase, sides are barred and breast-band is more distinct than in other skuas. Immatures only told from Arctic Skua by larger size and broader wings. It has less white in wing than Great Skua. Immatures more barred than Great Skua. Dark phase is rare.   P

ARCTIC SKUA *Stercorarius parasiticus* L 46 Most common skua, frequently seen pursuing terns. Adults are told from larger, heavier Pomarine Skua by short, flat, pointed central tail-feathers; from Long-tailed by tail length alone. Proportion of dark to light phase birds is greatest in the south of the breeding range. Immatures are browner than Long-tailed and have more white on wing. Immatures very hard to tell from Pomarine Skua immatures, but notice smaller size and narrower wings.   S

LONG-TAILED SKUA *Stercorarius longicaudus* L 5 Uncommon except on breeding grounds. The smallest bodied and slimmest of the skuas and the one least inclined to rob other sea birds. Central tail-feathers of adult extend 5–8" behind the others. On nesting grounds it often hovers over its prey, the Lemming. Dark phase unknown. Immature is also grey rather than brown and has less white on wing. Flight is more graceful and tern-like than that of other skuas.

shearwater

falcon

gull

tern

Arctic Skua

Great Skua
chasing
Herring Gull

Great Skua

Pomarine imm.

Arctic imm.

dark phase

Pomarine Skua

light phase

imm.

light phase

dark phase

Arctic Skua

light
phase
Arctic

Long-tailed
hovering

juv.

**Long-tailed
Skua**

141

Gulls

(order *Charadriiformes*, family *Laridae*, subfamily *Larinae*) are sturdy, robust birds with webbed feet, long pointed wings, stout hooked bill, and usually a square tail. Colours are generally white, grey and black. They are primarily scavengers. Some species gather by thousands at garbage dumps and fish docks. They rarely dive from the air, but alight on the water to seize food. The flight is deliberate and powerful; some species soar frequently. Sexes are similar; immatures are usually brownish, and those of the largest species take several years to acquire adult plumage. They nest in colonies. Clutch, usually 2 or 3 eggs.

IVORY GULL *Pagophila eburnea* L 46 Rarely encountered outside the Arctic. During breeding season found along the coast, otherwise over open water and along pack ice in the Arctic Ocean. Ivory is much smaller than other all-white gulls; it is easily distinguished by the short black legs and black bill (yellow-tipped in adult). Standing it resembles a pigeon. Immatures are speckled with black on the upper side. Flight is elegant and light. Call is tern-like. V

GLAUCOUS GULL *Larus hyperboreus* L 69 Uncommon, usually seen along the coast in the company of other large gulls. Distinguished from Iceland Gull by size (larger than Herring Gull), heavier bill and by flatter forehead and somewhat shorter wings (not constant). Immatures of both Glaucous and Iceland Gull easily told from other immature gulls by their very light colouring, particularly of the wings. In first winter they are generally ochre, easily distinguishing them from other gulls. In second winter lighter, and by third winter adult plumage is almost attained. More albinistic Herring Gulls are completely white. Immatures told from immature Iceland Gulls by heavier bill and more extensive flesh colour at its base. In all plumages of Glaucous and Iceland, note in flight the translucent 'windows' at base of primaries. Yellow eye-ring of adult very hard to see. Fiercely predatory in its behaviour. Call resembles that of Herring Gull. W

1st winter

ICELAND GULL *Larus glaucoides* L 56 Rare, usually seen along the coasts, often in company with other large gulls. Slightly smaller than Herring Gull but has no black on wings. When sitting, folded wings protrude beyond the tail in most individuals. Head looks small for the body and bill seems still smaller. The shape is more rounded than in Glaucous Gull. Like Glaucous Gull, immatures are very light in plumage. Immatures are best told from immature Glaucous Gulls by smaller size, longer wings and much smaller and darker bill. Reddish eye-ring of adult is very hard to see. The feet are always flesh-coloured in both species. Call resembles that of Herring Gull. W

1st winter

2nd winter

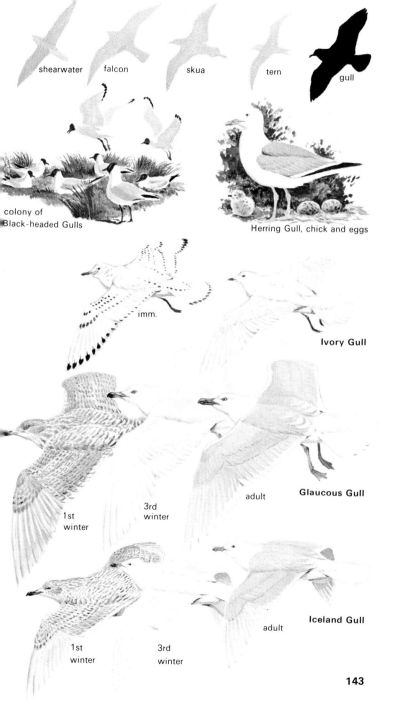

shearwater falcon skua tern gull

colony of Black-headed Gulls

Herring Gull, chick and eggs

imm.

Ivory Gull

1st winter

3rd winter

adult

Glaucous Gull

1st winter

3rd winter

adult

Iceland Gull

143

GREAT BLACK-BACKED GULL *Larus marinus* L 69

Common along coasts, rarely found inland. Nests singly or colonially, often with other gulls. Distinguished from similar Lesser Black-backed by larger size, noticeably larger and heavier bill, more solid black of wing and back, pinkish legs and, from below, by lesser extension of black on wing-tips. Wing-beats measurably slower than Lesser Black-backed's. Immatures difficult to tell from immature Lesser Black-backed and Herring Gulls, but note shape and extent of black band on tail, contrast between light head and dark back, and heavy bill. Characteristics helpful in distinguishing it from Lesser Black-backed Gull are also lighter inner primaries and light tips to primary coverts. Sometimes follows ships but not as much Herring Gull. Predatory, especially on nesting colonies of other sea birds. Call is low pitched 'kow-kow-kow'.   RSW

1st winter

LESSER BLACK-BACKED GULL *Larus fuscus* L 53

Very common, usually along coasts and in harbours but also inland. Scandinavian subspecies migrates along European rivers towards the south, and is also becoming more common in southern areas. Nests colonially on islands, beaches and moorland. Adults of both British and Scandinavian subspecies told from Great Black-backed by smaller size, lighter bill, yellow legs and more extensive black on underside of wing. British subspecies *L.f. graellsii* has much lighter (slatey-grey) mantle and wings than Great Black-backed, whereas Scandinavian subspecies *L.f. fuscus* is much darker. Immatures very hard to tell from immature Herring Gulls but wings have all dark primaries and primary coverts. In the second winter, legs become yellow and contrast between dark and light areas becomes more pronounced. Call is loud, clear and bugle-like, only slightly deeper than that of Herring Gull. Often follows boats.   RSWF

1st winter

HERRING GULL *Larus argentatus* L 56 Abundant

along coasts, particularly in harbours and on rubbish dumps, but also common inland by lakes and rivers. Breeds colonially on cliffs, islands and beaches. Adult is best told from Common Gull by larger size and yellow bill. Leg colour is usually flesh, but legs of subspecies in Mediterranean and eastern Europe are yellow. Immatures very hard to tell from immature Lesser Black-backed but note pale inner primaries and light tips to primary coverts. Told from immature Great Black-backed by less contrast in colours and distribution of dark and light on tail. Primarily a scavenger, Herring Gull will also break molluscs by dropping them on a hard surface. Sometimes seen diving clumsily in tern-like fashion in shallow water. Commonly seen high overhead, soaring like a hawk. Usual call is loud, clear and bugle-like. RV

1st winter

1st winter

1st winter

Great Black-backed Gull

adult

Lesser Black-backed Gull

L.f.graellsii

L.f.fuscus

2nd winter

adult **Herring Gull**

2nd winter

1st winter

Herring Gulls at refuse dump

COMMON GULL *Larus canus* L 41 Common inland and along shores, in harbours, parks and sometimes on refuse dumps. Nesting colonies are found on islands, beaches, marshes and moors. Adult resembles Herring Gull but is much smaller, and greenish colour of bill should be noticed. Distinguished from rare Audouin's Gull by green bill, more defined black and white wing-tips and greenish yellow legs; from Kittiwake by white on otherwise black wing-tips. Immatures have distinctive black band on tail. Call is higher pitched than that of Herring Gulls. Often follows boats.   RSWP

AUDOUIN'S GULL *Larus audouinii* L 48 Very rare and local. Breeds in small colonies on rocky islands. Less coastal in behaviour, staying further out to sea, than most other gulls. Distinguished from all other gulls by characteristic bill pattern and very indistinct border between black tips and grey upper side of wing, without contrast between black and grey so obvious in other gulls. Notice also wing and head pattern of immature birds, which have greyish crown and neck and brownish upper parts. Call is harsh and weak.

SLENDER-BILLED GULL *Larus genei* L 43 Fairly common except in westernmost part of its range. Nests colonially in marshes and swamps. Outside breeding season usually found along coasts. Resembles Black-headed Gull but notice white wing-tips of adults, lack of hood, and long thin bill, which in flight is usually held pointing downwards. Also has longer, more wedge-shaped tail than Black-headed Gull. Iris is light coloured. Immatures told from immature Black-headed Gulls by much fainter markings and shape of bill. Even at a distance, bill and head shape differ markedly from those of other gulls. Call is very nasal.   W

Ring-billed Gull

imm.

RING-BILLED GULL *Larus delawarensis* L 48 Very rare winter and spring visitor from North America. Plumage resembles small Herring Gull but pattern of black or yellow (adult) or flesh (juv.) bill is diagnostic. Black tail band very distinct.   W

KITTIWAKE *Rissa tridactyla* L 41 Very common, but usually stays far from shores as it is one of the few truly pelagic gulls. Breeds in large colonies on ledges of cliffs on coasts, sometimes on buildings and beaches. Notice square-cut tail and solid black wing-tips of adult bird. When standing, very short black legs are characteristic. Immature resembles several of the dark-headed gulls but is distinguished by combination of dark neck-band, white crown, short black legs, black wing-tips and very slightly forked tail. Flight is elegant, almost tern-like, often in lines low over water. Call is a characteristic 'kittiwake'.   R

Common Gull

imm.

bill of adult

bill of imm.

ack-headed
m.

Audouin's Gull

Slender-billed Gull

head of
Slender-billed

Slender-billed
imm.

adult

imm.

Kittiwake

flock of Kittiwakes over sea

147

MEDITERRANEAN GULL *Larus melanocephalus*
L 38 Fairly common, nesting colonially in shallow water in lakes, swamps, and marshes. Outside breeding season found on coasts, in harbours and occasionally inland. Slightly larger and heavier than Black-headed Gull. Adult is told from similar Black-headed Gull by having more extensive, solid black (not brown) hood in summer, no black at all on wing, and heavier, dark, banded bill. Immatures have much darker wing-tips than Black-headed (only a few white spots) without white fore-edges of wing. Has more distinct black mark behind the eye. Call is lower pitched than that of Black-headed Gull. Annual visitor to Britain in very small numbers.   V

BLACK-HEADED GULL *Larus ridibundus* L 36 Abundant, nesting colonially in swamps, marshes and lagoons. Occasionally found nesting on cliffs in the far north where the species is spreading. Outside breeding season found along coasts, in harbours, along rivers and lakes and on farmland, often far from large bodies of water. Adult told from other hooded gulls by brown hood which does not extend down the neck. Also note white leading edge of wing, black rear edge of tip. Underside of wing is dark, distinguishing it from rare Bonaparte's Gull. Immatures are told from immature Common Gulls by much narrower black band on tail and characteristic pattern on upper side of wing and on head. From immature Mediterranean Gulls by lighter wing-tips with a white fore-edge of the wing. Smaller than Mediterranean Gull, larger than Bonaparte's and Little Gull. Call is a very harsh cackling 'kwuririp'.   RSWF

BONAPARTE'S GULL *Larus philadelphia* L 33 Rare visitor from its North American breeding grounds to western European countries, where it often associates with very similar Black-headed Gull. Mostly seen in winter months. In summer, adult easily told from Black-headed Gull by solid black (not brown) hood and black bill. In all plumages, undersides of primaries are white not dark. Smaller and more elegant, particularly in flight than Black-headed Gull. Bill is black, shorter and thinner in appearance than Black-headed Gull's. Immatures resemble immature Black-headed Gulls, but dark wing pattern is more pronounced. Flight buoyant and tern-like, with bill held down. Call is a low quacking.   V

LAUGHING GULL *Larus atricilla* L 41 Very rare visitor from North America to Western Europe. Adult has black hood and slaty back and upper wings. Immatures are sooty brown above with very dark primaries and white trailing edge to wing. The breast is sooty brown. Tail feathers are grey with black tips. Legs black.

juv.

adult winter

Mediterranean Gull

imm.

adult summer

Black-headed
Gull

imm.

summer

Black headed
winter

summer

summer

summer

Bonaparte's Gull

Bonaparte's winter

imm

Great Black-headed Gull juv.

Little Gull juv.

Sabine's Gull

GREAT BLACK-HEADED GULL *Larus ichthyaetus* L 64 Fairly common, nesting along lagoons, in marshes and lakes. Rare visitor to western Europe, with occurrences at all times of the year, usually along sea coasts. In summer, adult unmistakable by enormous size and black hood. In winter, yellow bill with black band and dark feathers on head are characteristic. Immatures told from other large immature gulls by striking wide black band on white tail and characteristic long, dark-tipped bill. In habits it resembles the other other large species, but is even more ferocious, often parasitising other gulls. Call is harsh and crow-like.   V

LITTLE GULL *Larus minutus* L 28 Fairly common, nesting in marshes and swamps, often in association with other *Laridae*. Outside breeding season found on inland lakes and rivers as well as along coasts and quite far out to sea. Smallest of the European gulls, in summer plumage easily distinguished by black hood extending far down on neck, uniformly grey upper side of wing and black underwing. Immatures have light underwings, but characteristic Kittiwake-like wing pattern. In spite of the very rounded wings, flight is buoyant and elegant, almost tern-like. Also swims buoyantly, like a paper boat. Usually encountered singly or in small flocks. Often associates with Black-headed Gull. The call: 'kek-kek-kek'.   WP

SABINE'S GULL *Larus sabini* L 33 Common on breeding grounds, elsewhere seen singly or in small flocks, wintering far out to sea. Only rarely encountered inland or along canals. Adult in summer plumage unmistakable with slate-coloured hood and black bill tipped with yellow. In all plumages notice characteristic upper side of wing with triangles of black, white and brown or grey. Tail is forked. Immatures have more dark on head than other hooded gulls. In behaviour it resembles Little Gull but may parasitise Arctic Terns. Flight is very buoyant and tern-like. Call is harsh and tern like.   W

ROSS'S GULL *Rhodostethia rosea* L 30 Very rare visitor to the northernmost coasts from its Arctic Asiatic breeding grounds. A very light-coloured gull with wedge-shaped tail (the only European gull to have this). Adult birds are tinged rosy and in summer have narrow black neck-band. Immatures have wing pattern similar to that of Kittiwake immatures, but notice wedge-shaped tail. Flight is pigeon-like. Call is more melodious and higher pitched than most gulls. Also variable. Typical is 'klaw' or a repeated 'a-wo'.   V

adult winter

Great Black-headed Gull

summer

imm.

Little Gull

summer

summer

imm.

imm.

adult winter

Sabine's Gull

summer

adult winter

imm.

Ross's Gull

imm.

adult

Immature gulls

are very difficult to identify. Only typical plumages are shown here. The time it takes to acquire adult plumage differs from species to species. In general, small gulls take two years, larger ones four. For example, the Black-headed Gull acquires adult plumage

Ivory
imm.

Glaucous
1st winter

Glaucous
3rd winter

Herring
1st winter

Herring
3rd winter

Herring
2nd winter

Great
Black-headed

1st winter

Lesser Black-backed
2nd winter

Common
1st winter

Ross'
imm.

Sabine's
imm.

Kittiwake
imm.

the second winter after partial moults in the autumn and spring. The larger Herring Gull acquires adult plumage in the fourth autumn after two partial moults the first year, and one complete and one partial moult each following year. This sequence of moults is important in understanding the intermediate plumages not shown here. Also note colours of soft parts.

Iceland
1st winter

Iceland
3rd winter

Great
Black-backed
1st winter

Great
Black-
backed
2nd winter

Great Black-backed
3rd winter

Slender-billed
imm.

Little
imm.

Mediterranean
imm.

Black-headed
imm.

Bonaparte's
imm.

Terns

(order *Charadriiformes,* family *Laridae,* subfamily *Sterninae*) are slender birds with long, narrow wings, forked tails, and pointed bills. They are mainly black and white, and winter plumage is different from summer plumage. Their flight is buoyant, with bill pointed downwards as they search for small fish or insects. They dive from the air. Nest colonially. Clutch, 1–4 eggs.

BLACK TERN *Chlidonias niger* L 24 Common, nesting in colonies by inland waters, swamps, marshes and lakes. Outside breeding season also found along seashores. Summer plumage unmistakable, with all dark upper parts but white underside of wing and tail. In winter told from White-winged Black Tern by longer bill, darker upper side and a dark mark on side of lower neck. The white leading edge of wing is narrow. Black Terns dive little, but take insects from the surface and in the air. Flight is erratic. Call is nasal. P

WHITE-WINGED BLACK TERN *Chlidonias leucoptera* L 24 Common, nesting in inland marshes, swamps and lakes; in winter also frequents seashores. In summer plumage, told from Black Tern by shorter, red bill, white upper side of wings, white tail, black underside of wings and red legs. In winter very similar to Black Tern, but is lighter above, particularly rump, and lacks dark mark on side of neck. The white leading edge of wing is wider than in Black Tern. Wing lining is white at this season. Behaviour like that of Black Tern with which it often associates. P

WHISKERED TERN *Chlidonias hybridus* L 24 Fairly common, breeding in marshes, lakes and swamps; in winter also found along seashores. In summer plumage, easily told from other dark terns by white cheeks and heavier bill. Underside more dusky than that of other dark terns. In winter plumage, lighter than other dark terns and has considerably more white on crown. Notice distribution of dark on crown of the three species in winter plumage. Bill slightly heavier on Whiskered Tern than on the other two dark species. Associates freely with Black and White-winged Black. Call is harsher and consists of two syllables. V

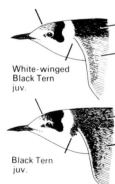

White-winged
Black Tern
juv.

Black Tern
juv.

SOOTY TERN *Sterna fuscata* L 41 Very rare visitor to Atlantic and Mediterranean coasts from subtropical and tropical oceanic islands. Pelagic in behaviour. Adult is black above with white front and white below (the only European tern to have this distribution of colours) Immature is dark brown with white under tail-coverts. Does not dive; catches surface fish in flight. Call is a nasal 'wide-a-wake'. V

shearwater   skua   gull   tern

imm.

moulting

Black Tern

summer

Black Tern
over marsh

winter

summer

White-
winged
Black Tern

imm

moulting

Whiskered
Tern

winter

summer

imm.

winter

Sooty Tern

155

GULL-BILLED TERN *Gelochelidon nilotica* L 38
Uncommon, nesting colonially on coastal marshes and sandy beaches. Also seen over land and along shores. Recognized in all plumages by short, thick, black, gull-like bill and broad, very white wings. Tail is less forked than in most terns and legs are black and long. The rump is pale grey, not white. Flight is more gull-like than that of other terns. Looks considerably heavier and more stocky than Sandwich Tern. Juvenile has buffish brown on back of head and dark patch around eye. When standing, the long legs are characteristic. Rarely dives but hawks for insects and small vertebrates over marshes. In winter plumage has only very little black on head, easily distinguishing it from somewhat similar Sandwich Tern. Nasal 2–3 syllable call is characteristic, 'za-za-sa', quite different from Sandwich Tern's call. ⁣ P

SANDWICH TERN *Sterna sandvicensis* L 41 Common, nesting in dense colonies on shores and small islands. Takes its food almost exclusively at sea. No other European tern has a black bill tipped with yellow. Note also the long, slender bill, black legs and slight crest. Forehead of juvenile is mostly black; adult has white on forehead and crown in winter, although it still has much more black than somewhat similar Gull-billed Tern. Immature has less forked tail than adult and sometimes lacks the yellow tip to bill, making it difficult to tell from Gull-billed Tern, but notice colours on head and much more 'tern-like' silhouette and behaviour. Fishes far off shore, often out of sight of land. Call is a loud

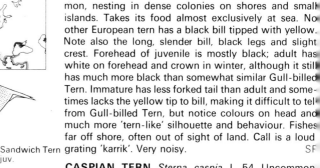

Sandwich Tern juv.

grating 'karrik'. Very noisy. ⁣ SF

CASPIAN TERN *Sterna caspia* L 54 Uncommon nesting singly or in small colonies on islands and sandy beaches. Outside breeding season usually along sea-shores but occasionally on larger inland waters. Enormous size (almost as big as Herring Gull) makes it easy to identify. Large, bright red bill is a very prominent characteristic. Wider wings give it a more gull-like appearance than most terns, and its behaviour is also more gull-like. Alights on the water, occasionally soars, robs other sea birds, and eats eggs, but fish is its chief diet. The huge coral-red bill is noticeable even at a distance. Call is a very deep and characteristic 'caw caw-cah'. ⁣ V

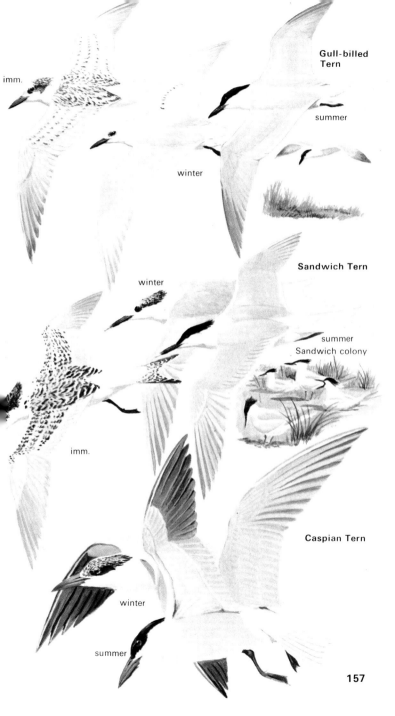

imm.

Gull-billed Tern

summer

winter

Sandwich Tern

winter

summer
Sandwich colony

imm.

Caspian Tern

winter

summer

157

juv.

wing above

juv.

wing above

COMMON TERN *Sterna hirundo* L 36 Very common, nesting colonially on islands, sandy and marshy sea coasts and on inland lakes. Most common along sea-shores. Flocks with Arctic and Roseate Terns. Wing-tips are noticeably darker than in Roseate, tail is shorter and bill in summer brighter coral-red (black tip varies in extent). Best told from Arctic Tern by black tip of bill, lighter underside, shorter tail, longer legs and more extensive black under and upperside of wing. Retains red legs in winter whereas they become black in Arctic Tern. Immatures have grey secondaries with white tips and prominent dark grey leading edge of upperside of wing. Often seen in large groups. Call is a harsh 'kee-urr'.   S

ARCTIC TERN *Sterna paradisaea* L 38 Very common, nesting colonially in marshes and on sandy and rocky beaches and islands. Less often seen inland than Common Tern. Often seen far out to sea. At close range adults can be told from Common Terns by white streak below black cap, longer tail (extending to wing-tips), short legs, blood-red bill (no black tip), and transluscent spot near wing-tip, which has less extensive black and has a more uniformly grey upperside. Bill and legs of adult are black in winter. Occasionally breeds in winter plumage. Immature has white upper wing-coverts (grey on immature Common) and the secondaries are pure white. Calls are like those of Common Tern, but more nasal and rasping.   SP

ROSEATE TERN *Sterna dougallii* L 38 Uncommon and local, often nesting with Arctic and Common Terns along the coast. Rarely occurs inland. Paler above than Common and Arctic Terns. Tail is whiter, longer, more deeply forked, wing-tips paler, and bill black (red only at base). Breast shows roseate flash at close range, otherwise looks white. Note also deep, fast, wing-beats and buoyant flight. In flight it appears more top heavy and Sandwich Tern-like than Common Tern. In winter very like Common Tern but breast whiter and bill darker. Immatures are more strongly marked on upper side than immature Arctic and Common. Calls are distinctive: a soft 'chivy' and a less frequent rasping 'z-a-a-p'.   S

LITTLE TERN *Sterna albifrons* L 23 Common, nesting colonially on sandy beaches, usually along the coasts occasionally inland. Smallest of the European terns, with a comparatively short tail. Notice the rapid wing-beats, white forehead, yellow bill (spring), and legs, yellow or yellowish at all seasons. Immature has contrasting wing pattern, similar to that of other white terns, but small size distinguishes it at a glance. Very active and noisy. Call is a rapid series of paired notes. Although once a common species, it has rapidly diminished in numbers, especially in Britain where it is now the rarest tern, fewer numbers breeding than the very uncommon Roseate Tern.   S

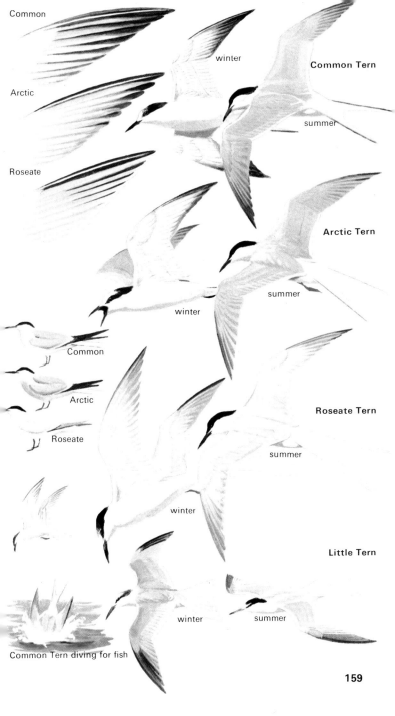

Common

Arctic

Roseate

winter

Common Tern

summer

Arctic Tern

summer

winter

Common

Arctic

Roseate

Roseate Tern

summer

winter

Little Tern

winter

summer

Common Tern diving for fish

159

Auks

(order *Charadriiformes,* family *Alcidae*) are black and white pelagic birds with short tails, narrow wings and rapid wingbeats. Except on nesting cliffs they are silent. They come ashore only to breed. Swim under water using wings. Winter plumage different from summer plumage. Immatures are usually like adults. Clutch, 1–2 eggs.

RAZORBILL *Alca torda* L 41 Common, nesting in colonies on sea cliffs, sometimes associated with Guillemots but usually not on as steep cliffs. Outside breeding season usually stays far off shore. Notice thick bill which, when the bird is swimming, is uptilted, as is the short tail. In flight, back is more arched than in Guillemot. Razorbill also looks more thick-necked and has different head shape which makes it possible to distinguish it from Guillemot even at some distance. It is also more black, rather than brownish. At sea usually seen in small flocks which fly in lines low above the water. Sometimes seen singly off rocky coasts.   RS

GUILLEMOT *Uria aalge* L 41 Common. Nests in colonies on ledges of steep cliffs along seashores. Winters at sea; rare within sight of land. Best told from Razorbill by long, narrow bill. In winter plumage, has a narrow black streak back from the eye which, when seen, is diagnostic. In a proportion of birds, Bridled Guillemots, there is a furrow along this streak which shows white in summer. In flight, back is held less arched than Razorbill Other useful field characteristics distinguishing this species from Razorbill are long, narrow bill, thinner neck more pointed head shape, and colour: dark brownish rather than black. Told from Brünnich's Guillemot by longer and more slender bill, and in winter plumage by characteristic facial pattern. Like other auks it is often seen in small flocks, flying in lines low above the water
RS

BRÜNNICH'S GUILLEMOT *Uria lomvia* L 41 Common, but more northern in distribution than Guillemot and Razorbill. Like Guillemot, it nests colonially on sea cliffs. In all plumages note shorter, thicker bill and narrow white streak at base of mouth. In winter plumage there is no white above the black eye-line. Immature Razorbills resemble Brünnich's Guillemot superficially but have more rounded, stubbier and shorter bill and cannot be confused at close quarters. In habits it resembles the Guillemot, but often roams further out to sea.

diver cormorant scoter Little Auk Guillemot

winter

breeding colony of Guillemots

Razorbill

summer

imm.

Guillemot

summer

summer
Bridled
Guillemot

winter

winter

winter summer

Brünnich's Guillemot

161

LITTLE AUK *Alle alle* L 20 Abundant in the Arctic, nesting in enormous colonies in holes in sloping cliffs. Outside breeding season truly pelagic, only rarely coming within sight of shore. After severe westerly storms, 'falls' or 'wrecks' occur far inland. Much smaller than any of the other auks. Note very short body, neck and bill, whirring wing-beats and distribution of black and white. White areas much more extensive in winter plumage. At sea usually seen in small flocks, flying in lines very low above the water, following the waves up and down. Silhouette markedly different from that of other auks, much more chubby and short-billed. Above nesting colonies they gather like a swarm of mosquitos. Call, which is only heard on the breeding grounds, is a high-pitched chattering. W

BLACK GUILLEMOT *Cepphus grylle* L 33 Common, nesting singly or in small groups among rocks along sea-shores, sometimes in holes dug out in cliffs. Less maritime in behaviour than other auks, staying closer inshore winter and summer. In summer notice black plumage with large white area on wing. In winter much whiter but white wing area is still delineated in black. Red legs seldom visible, but red gape of mouth may show up. In immatures, wing patch is usually mottled. Wing-beats are extremely fast. Always fly very low over the water. Usually seen singly or in very small flocks, often in openings in the ice. In spring quite often heard giving its characteristic, high-pitched twittering 'vee-bee' calls when red gape shows quite conspicuously. R

juv.

PUFFIN *Fratercula arctica* L 30 Common, nesting in colonies in burrows on mountain slopes along seashores. In winter far off shore, reaching further out to sea than most auks except for the Little Auk. Notice chunky body and large head and bill. On breeding grounds the small fish held in the bill give it a characteristic 'bearded' appearance. The outer layers of the bill are shed in late summer, so winter adults and especially immatures have smaller bills (rectangular at base). Although face is largely dark in winter, characteristic facial pattern is still present. When swimming, holds its fore-parts higher above water than other auks, giving it a characteristic silhouette. Usually seen in small or large flocks. Flies low above the water in short lines. In flight the very large head is characteristic. Call, heard on the breeding grounds only, consists of unmusical guttural notes.

Little Auk

flock on water and flying

winter

summer

Black Guillemot

winter

summer

esting among boulders

Puffin

imm.

summer

winter

at nest hole

Sandgrouse (order *Columbiformes,* family *Pteroclidae*) are
medium-sized birds, closely related and somewhat
similar to pigeons and doves. They have very short bills
and feet and long, pointed wings and tail. Male and
female differ slightly in plumage. Flight is swift and
direct; gait similar to that of pigeons. Nest on the ground.
Clutch, 2 eggs, sometimes 3. They are birds of the open
steppe and are usually found in flocks, sometimes of
immense size.

BLACK-BELLIED SANDGROUSE *Pterocles orientalis* L 36 Fairly common, found on steppes and outlying
fields. Very rare outside breeding grounds. Tail is shorter
than that of other sandgrouse. Much darker below and
on underside of wing than any other European sandgrouse, easily distinguishing it in flight. On the ground,
neck and breast pattern distinguish it from other sandgrouse. Female is more spotted than male but still retains
the black belly and a blackish patch on the throat. Call is
a deep 'djur-djur-djur'.

PIN-TAILED SANDGROUSE *Pterocles alchata* L 33
Fairly common on dry steppes and other dry, flat areas.
Very rare outside its normal range. Lighter in colour than
the other sandgrouse, with a brown breast-band bordered with black. Central tail-feathers elongated. It is
the smallest of our sandgrouse. In flight, easily told from
Black-bellied Sandgrouse and Pallas' Sandgrouse by
its distinct white wing-band. Female lacks the black
throat of male. Usually seen in flocks, larger than those of
Black-bellied Sandgrouse. In flight, which is fast, the
characteristic far-reaching call 'catar, catar' is often
given.

PALLAS'S SANDGROUSE *Syrrhaptes paradoxus* L
38 Common. In some years makes far-reaching eruptions
into western Europe in varying numbers. During such
invasions it has reached as far west as England and has
occasionally settled down to nest. Smaller invasions and
sporadic occurrences sometimes take place and it is the
sandgrouse most likely to be found outside its normal
range. Found on dry steppes; during invasion in sandy
and other dry areas. Elongated central tail-feathers and
black spot on belly are diagnostic. Notice also the very
light underside of wing. Female has narrow black line
around throat and lacks the orange on the neck.
Usually encountered in flocks, which are noisy. Call
consists of two or three notes.   V

partridge   Golden Plover   Rock Dove   sandgrouse

flock of Pin-tailed at water hole

Black-bellied Sandgrouse

♂

♀

flock

♂

Pin-tailed Sandgrouse

♀

♀

♂

Pallas's Sandgrouse

Pigeons and doves

(order *Columbiformes,* family *Columbidae*) are medium-sized, rather heavy birds with pointed wings and rather long tails, usually with characteristic patterns. Social in behaviour outside nesting season. The domestic forms of the Rock Dove, which have a wide variety of plumages, and escaped Collared Doves (favoured pets) can cause some confusion in ascertaining the true wild state of these two species. Clutch, 2 white eggs.

ROCK DOVE *Columba livia* L 33 Locally common; but huge populations of feral domestic pigeons which are descendants of this species are found in cities and resemble it closely. Found in mountains of moderate elevation, mainly along the coasts, also on sea cliffs where it nests in caves or on sheltered shelves. Light above, with pronounced white upper rump, and two black stripes on wings. Underside of wing is white. Resembles Stock Dove most but white rump and wider wing stripes are usually present even on domestic pigeons. Smaller, more compact and has more rapid wing-beats than Wood Pigeon. Flight is very fast. Usually encountered in small flocks. Call is similar to that of the domestic pigeon.   R

STOCK DOVE *Columba oenas* L 33 Fairly common, nesting in tree-holes in open woodland. Can also place the nest in rabbit holes and in holes in rocks. In winter also found on fields and open farmland. Rather uniformly grey, lacking white upper rump of Rock Dove, and white wing-bars and neck-patch of Wood Pigeon. Black wing-bands less prominent than on Rock Dove. Often encountered in small flocks, but also mixes freely with Wood Pigeons, in which case the much smaller size, darker colours and faster wing-beats are evident. Flight usually a little faster and more straight than Wood Pigeon's. Cooing is a monotonous, coughing 'oo-hoo-hoo', more similar to that of Rock Dove than Wood Pigeon.   RP

WOODPIGEON *Columba palumbus* L 41 Called by many the Ring Dove, it is the most common and widespread European pigeon. Found in farmland, parks, gardens, all types of woods. Has invaded many large cities in recent years. Easily distinguished by large size, white patch on side of neck, and broad white bar on wing. Outside breeding season usually found in flocks, sometimes of enormous size. In flight, dark underwing helps in identification. Wings clatter when it takes flight. Stock Doves sometimes mix in the flocks. In towns and villages often very tame, mixing with domestic pigeons. Cooing consists of five syllables, emphasis on the first.   F

Jackdaw

falcon

Golden Plover

sandgrouse

Rock Dove

Wood Pigeons on ground

Domestic Pigeons feeding

Rock Dove

Stock Dove

imm.

adult

Wood Pigeon

167

TURTLE DOVE *Streptopelia turtur* L 28 Common in parks and farmland with hedges and groves and in open woodland with plenty of undergrowth. Much smaller than Wood Pigeon. White patches with black stripes on neck are diagnostic. This characteristic is lacking in the immature bird. Tail is conspicuously dark, showing narrow white edging from above and below. Looks much darker than Collared Dove of similar size and shape. Smaller and lighter in colour than the very rare Rufous Turtle Dove. Lacks the bright blue areas found on the wing of the slightly smaller Laughing Dove. Usually seen in small flocks or pairs. Builds an open nest in trees or bushes. Song is a soft purring coo. SP

RUFOUS TURTLE DOVE *Streptopelia orientalis* L 33 Accidental visitor west to England from Asiatic breeding grounds, mainly occurring in late autumn and winter. Resembles Turtle Dove but is considerably larger and darker and more the shape of Stock Dove. The white on neck and tail of Turtle Dove is replaced with light blue and grey in Rufous Turtle Dove. Back more finely speckled. Behaviour and habitat similar to Turtle Dove. V

COLLARED DOVE *Streptopelia decaocto* L 28 Common in parks and gardens of villages and cities. Sandy coloured with wide terminal white band on tail. Black neck-band bordered with white is diagnostic. Much lighter in colours than similar-sized and shaped Turtle Dove. Usually seen in pairs or small flocks. Often very tame, feeding with domestic fowl. In flight very dark primaries contrast with the otherwise light plumage. Immatures lack black neck-band. The cooing is characteristic: three syllables with emphasis on the second syllable. From the original breeding area in the Balkans this species is still extending its range towards the north-west. This spectacular spread started in the 1930s. R

LAUGHING DOVE *Streptopelia senegalensis* L 26 Common but local in cities and villages. Very recent invader. Smallest of the European doves. Speckled band on front part of neck is hard to distinguish. Seems quite dark with white-tipped tail-feathers and brilliant blue areas on wings particularly noticeable in flight. Sexes are similar. Immatures have the same colour pattern but are much duller. Usually seen in pairs or few together. In behaviour and habitat very similar to Collared Dove. Cooing is rapid and distinctive, almost resembling call of Cuckoo.

Turtle Dove

Rufous Turtle Dove

Collared Dove

Laughing Dove

169

Cuckoos

(order *Cuculiformes,* family *Cuculidae*) are medium-sized, long-tailed birds with pointed wings. Some are brood parasitic, others not. The three species breeding in Europe lay their eggs in nests of different passerines. The family characteristic, hardly ever observed in the field, is the toes, of which two are pointed forward and two backwards.

CUCKOO *Cuculus canorus* L 33 Common in open woods, groves and areas with bushes and hedges, also on moorland. Occurs in two colour phases: the more numerous grey, and a brown form (only juveniles and females). In flight can be confused with smaller birds of prey, but notice very pointed wings, rounded tail, small head, often held slightly upward, and thin bill. Flight is fast, usually low above ground. Often chased by small passerines. Repeated 'cuckoo' song of male is diagnostic; female has babbling call. S

ORIENTAL CUCKOO *Cuculus saturatus* L 30 Fairly common in woods. Two colour phases, grey and brown, also occur in this species, but brown phase is more numerous than is the case with the Cuckoo. Very similar to Cuckoo, but is darker above and bars on underside are usually broader. Underside of wing is not whitish but yellowish. Call is distinctly different from that of Cuckoo, consisting of four syllables rather than two.

GREAT SPOTTED CUCKOO *Clamator glandarius* L 41 Common near groves and woods and on open land with scattered trees and bushes. Somewhat resembles Magpie which it parasitises, but the black and white pattern is quite differently arranged. Often seen in small flocks. Call is rasping, almost tern-like. V

YELLOW-BILLED CUCKOO *Coccyzus americanus* L 30 Rare autumn visitor to western Europe from North American breeding grounds. Secretive in behaviour. Can only be confused with rarer Black-billed Cuckoo, from which it is told by large white spots contrasting with black on undersurface of tail, by bright rufous flash in the open wing, and by yellow lower mandible. Call is guttural and toneless. V

BLACK-BILLED CUCKOO *Coccyzus erythrophthalmus* L 30 Very rare autumn visitor to western Europe from North American breeding grounds. Habits and habitat similar to Yellow-billed Cuckoo. Separated from this species by indistinct tail spots, by all-black bill and by showing hardly any rufous in spread wing. Call consists of three or four coos. V

170

Nightjar   Kestrel   Sparrow hawk   dove   Cuckoo

imm.
red phase

red phase
♀

♂

Cuckoo

display

Oriental Cuckoo

♂

♀

Whitethroat
feeding
Cuckoo nestling

adult

Great Spotted Cuckoo

imm.

Yellow-billed
Cuckoo

Black-billed Cuckoo

171

Owls

(order *Strigiformes,* family *Tytonidae* — the Barn Owl — and family *Strigidae* — all other owls) are small to large, large-headed, short-necked birds of prey, mostly nocturnal, best seen and more frequently heard at dusk. The large eyes are fixed in their sockets, so the entire head moves as the owl shifts its gaze. The flat, round or heart-shaped facial disc conceals the large external ear flaps. Some owls have erect ear tufts. All fly silently, hunting for rodents, other small mammals, birds and insects. Females are like males but larger. Immatures resemble adults. The call is a distinctive hoot, wail or whistle. Most small owls and some larger ones are cavity nesters. Eggs are round, white, 2–8 or more in a clutch.

SCOPS OWL *Otus scops* L 20 Common in gardens, groves and in ruins, usually nesting in cavities. Very small, rather uniformly brown and the only small owl with ear tufts. Slimmer, sitting more upright and not as squat in appearance as Little Owl. When ear tufts are not obvious, less flat shape of head should be noticed. Wings rather long. Call is a monotonously repeated 'piuww', usually heard at night, occasionally during the day. V

PYGMY OWL *Glaucidium passerinum* L 18 Fairly common in dense coniferous forests, where it nests in tree cavities. Occasionally occurs outside usual range in winter. Very small with rather small rounded head and short, wide tail. The flight is undulating, woodpecker-like. Partially diurnal in habits. The short tail is often jerked upwards. Call is a monotonous repetition of soft whistles. In autumn a series of shrill, rising call notes may be heard.

LITTLE OWL *Athena noctua* L 23 Common in open land with hedges and trees, often near human habitation; introduced to Britain in last quarter of nineteenth century. Nests in holes in trees and buildings, also in burrows. Notice squat appearance and large head. The white spots on neck form a characteristic V. Partially diurnal. Flight is characteristically undulating, and can hover. Bobs when nervous. Calls are shrill and sharp. F

TENGMALM'S OWL *Aegolius funereus* L 26 Fairly common in mature coniferous forests. Nests in tree cavities. Populations fluctuate and in some years invasions of areas outside the normal range take place. Distinguished from rather similar Little Owl by more rounded appearance of head (not flat on top), spotted rather than striped head, and more erect posture. Only during the Arctic summer does it feed by daylight. Call is a fast series of 7–8 whistles rising slightly at the end, 12–15 groups per minute. V

Short-eared Owl

Tawny Owl

Hawk Owl

Pygmy Owl

grey form

brown form

Scops Owl

Pygmy Owl

Little Owl

Little Owl in flight undulating with closed wings

Tengmalm's Owl

juv

173

Very rare over much
of its range

EAGLE OWL *Bubo bubo* L 69 Uncommon, found in large tracts of undisturbed land, woods, mountains and even open country. Usually nests on the ground or on rock ledges, but also in hollow trees. Huge, with large ear tufts which are not visible in flight. It is the largest European owl. Female is larger than male. Colour pattern is similar to the smaller and slimmer Long-eared Owl, but Eagle Owl's ear tufts are larger and farther apart. Hunts medium-sized mammals and birds at night, spending the day perched upright in trees. Like all owls, it is often harassed by smaller birds. Call is a far-ranging, deep 'boo-hu'. V

SNOWY OWL *Nyctea scandiaca* L 61 A rather uncommon diurnal Arctic owl. Nests on the ground. Populations fluctuate and in some winters it occurs south of its normal range in considerable numbers reaching the southern part of middle Europe. Adult males are almost pure white, females with some dark brown bars. Immatures, which are darker, go farther south than adults in winter. Large size, pale plumage, and lack of ear tufts are diagnostic. Female is larger, and generally more spotted and barred than male. Perches near the ground in open country and often allows itself to be approached. Feeds on lemmings and other rodents and rabbits. Usually hunts during the day. On breeding grounds a 2-note crow is occasionally heard; otherwise silent. V

GREAT GREY OWL *Strix nebulosa* L 69 Rather uncommon, in mature coniferous forests. Uses old nests of other large birds. In some years winter range extends south of normal range. Very large with enormous head. Looks greyish. Easily told from other large owls by enormous rounded head, bold, concentrically-barred facial disc, striking facial pattern and lack of ear tufts. The eyes are rather small. In flight notice long tail which has a dark terminal bar and wide and rounded wings with pale wing-bars. Call is deep, booming series of 'whoos', each lower in pitch than preceeding one.

URAL OWL *Strix uralensis* L 61 Uncommon, in coniferous as well as mixed woods, primarily in mountain regions. Nests in hollow trees. Large, without ear tufts, but with very long tail. Underside strongly streaked. Facial disc unmarked. Resembles Tawny Owl, but is larger with longer tail and rather small dark eyes. Also diurnal in habits. In flight told from Eagle Owl by longer tail and more streaked underside, from Great Grey Owl by shorter, narrower wings and more brownish colour. Call is divided into two parts (like Tawny Owl): a deep bisyllabic 'huh-ow', then a four second pause followed by five deep, stammering notes, 'hoh-hu ho-hoo-hu'. Alternative call is a rapid series of 6–8 deep 'hooings'.

Eagle Owl

Snowy Owl

...at Grey Owl in flight

Ural Owl

Great Grey
Owl

175

LONG-EARED OWL *Asio otus* L 36 Common in coniferous forests, occasionally in deciduous. Notice very long ear tufts held erect when nervous. Told from Eagle Owl by smaller size; from Short-eared by longer ears, shorter wings, warmer buff colours, orange eyes, whole underside streaked (only breast on Short-eared), habitat and erect posture. Wing-beats deep but slow. Outside breeding season occasionally found in small parties. Generally silent except near nest, where it makes various low hoots, whistles and shrieks.   RWP

SHORT-EARED OWL *Asio flammeus* L 38 Fairly common in open country, over plains, moors and marshes. Ears very short and hard to see. Note amount of black on facial disc, yellow eyes, black patch near bend of underwing and large, buffish area on upper wing surface. Active before dark, quartering low over fields in irregular flight. Wings are tilted upward like harriers'. In winter occasionally found in small groups. Usually silent. Territory call is a fast series of deep 'po' sounds; also wings are clapped in the air.   RW

Marsh Owl

MARSH OWL *Asio capensis* L 30 Very rare autumn visitor to southern Iberian peninsula. Like Short-eared Owl but darker above with more contrasting facial pattern.

TAWNY OWL *Strix aluco* L 38 Most common and widespread European owl. Found in woods, parks, gardens, often near human habitation. Black eyes and lack of ear tufts distinguish this species. Occurs in two colour phases, grey and more rufous. Song consists of a deep hooting. Another common call is a rather shrill 'kuvvitt'.   P

BARN OWL *Tyto alba* L 36 Common, but local, usually near buildings or ruins. Only owl with a heart shaped facial pattern. The west and southern European subspecies is dark-breasted but still lighter than most other owls except for Snowy. Usually nocturnal, hunts rats and mice in farmyards, marshes and fields. Has a peculiar habit of lowering its head and moving it back and forth. Does not hoot, but has a soft, ascending wheezy cry and a shriek. At the nest it gives a toneless hiss, compared to human snoring.   R

HAWK OWL *Surnia ulula* L 38 Fairly common in northern birch and coniferous forests. Sometimes invades areas south of its range. No other owl has the long slender tail that gives this bird a falcon-like appearance. Perches in the open on treetops, where it raises and slowly lowers its tail. Sometimes sits with tail cocked up at an angle. Flight is straight and swift, usually very low, with alternate flapping and gliding. Also hovers somewhat as the Kestrel does. Territory call is a hurried, vibrating, deep bubbling sound; also hawk-like, 'ki-ki-ki . . .'.

hiding

relaxed and in flight

Long-eared Owl

Short-eared Owl

hiding

grey phase

Tawny Owl

rufous phase

Hawk Owl

dark-breasted form

Barn Owl

177

light-breasted form

Nightjars

(order *Caprimulgiformes,* family *Caprimulgidae*) are nocturnal insect-eaters with large, flat heads, small bills and distinctive white patches on wings and tails. Eyes are mere slits by day, huge and round by night. The plumage is brown and well camouflaged. White spots on wings and tail characteristic. The daytime is spent resting on the ground or on branches, the bird being very difficult to detect in this position. Hibernation occurs in an American species but this is not true of any of the European nightjars. The two eggs are laid on the ground. No nest is built.

NIGHTJAR *Caprimulgus europaeus* L 28 Fairly common, found in open woods and clearings, or open land with scattered trees and bushes and even in sand dunes. Usually seen at dusk when hawking insects. Flight is silent, but during display wings are clapped together; twists and turns with great ease and elegance and sometimes hovers like a Kestrel. Notice white spots on wings and tail of male only. Told from slightly larger Red-necked Nightjar by dark throat and lack of reddish neck-band, from smaller Egyptian Nightjar by darker colours. Solitary in behaviour, except on migration when flocks occur. Migrates at night. Song, which is given at dusk and at night in spring and summer, is an unmistakable churring trill which often leads to the detection of this bird. It is very different from the 'cutek' note of the Red-necked Nightjar.   S

RED-NECKED NIGHTJAR *Caprimulgus ruficollis* L 30 Fairly common, found in evergreen woods and on dry, bushy wasteland. Nocturnal in habits like the Nightjar. Resembles Nightjar closely, but is larger with longer tail, has lighter colours, reddish neck-band and pure white throat. Spots on wing and tail are more distinctive than on Nightjar and are present in both sexes (only the male Nightjar having white spots). Much larger and darker in plumage than rare Egyptian Nightjar. Song, distinctly different from that of Nightjar, is fast repetition of 'cutek' notes.   V

EGYPTIAN NIGHTJAR *Caprimulgus aegyptius* L 26 Very rare visitor to Mediterranean regions in summer from African and Asiatic breeding grounds. Found in deserts but usually near water. Smaller and much paler and more uniformly coloured than Nightjar and Red-necked Nightjar, which it resembles in habits and silhouette. White spots are ill-defined and white throat band often indistinct. Churring song resembles that of Nightjar.   V

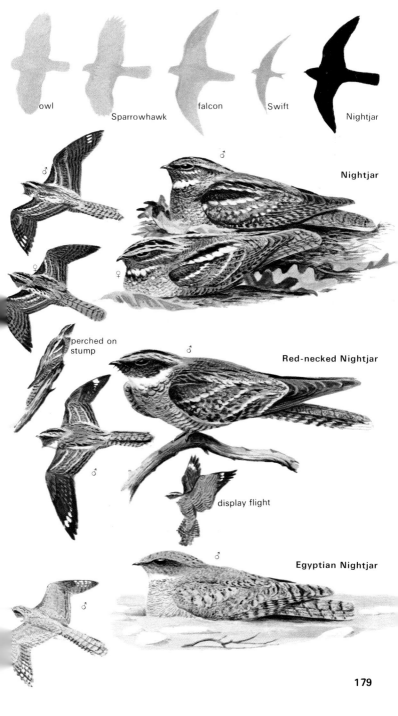

owl   Sparrowhawk   falcon   Swift   Nightjar

♂

Nightjar

♂

♀

perched on
stump

Red-necked Nightjar

♂

♂

display flight

Egyptian Nightjar

♂

Swifts

(order *Apodiformes,* family *Apodidae*) look somewhat like swallows and feed almost exclusively on insects caught on the wing with their wide mouths. Unlike swallows, with which they are often found, swifts appear to beat their wings alternately. Swifts fly continuously all day, except in heavy rain, and can roost on the wing. Their wings, built for speed, are long, stiff, slender and slightly decurved. If grounded, they can only take off with difficulty. The sexes are alike. Swifts nest in cracks and holes in cliffs, trees and buildings. Clutch, 2–3 white eggs.

SWIFT *Apus apus* L 17 Very common. Can be seen in the air almost anywhere, but most often near towns and villages which offer nesting sites. Nest is placed in hollow trees, chimneys and other protected cavities. Colonial in breeding. Larger than any of the swallows, with narrower and stiffer wings. Very dark, with black underside (Pallid Swift has brownish underside). Often flies very high, usually in small flocks. Flight is extremely fast. Call is a shrill screaming. S

WHITE-RUMPED SWIFT *Apus caffer* L 13 Very rare summer visitor to southern Iberian peninsula where it has recently begun to breed. Small and generally black with white upper rump and marked forked tail. Its behaviour is typically swift-like.

LITTLE SWIFT *Apus affinis* L 11 Very rare visitor from North Africa and Asia. It resembles White-rumped Swift but is smaller and more compact with square tail and more prominent white rump. V

PALLID SWIFT *Apus pallidus* L 15 Rather common, with a preference for rocky shores and mountains. Often mixes with Swift and Alpine Swift. Resembles Swift closely but is paler with brown on underside (not black like Swift). Also has more white on throat than Swift. Silhouette differs slightly from that of Swift, as head is broader. When seen with Swift, the slower wing-beats of this species can be noticed. Call is like that of Swift.

ALPINE SWIFT *Apus melba* L 20 Common, found in mountains and towns. Much larger than the three other swifts, with white underside and brown breast-band. Flight even faster than that of Swift, wing-beats slower. Like Swift, often encountered in flocks. Nests colonially in rocky mountainous areas; also in old buildings and along sea cliffs. Nest is cup-shaped, placed in crevice. Call is distinctly different from Swift's, consisting of a loud, descending and ascending trill. V

falcon

Nightjar

Swallow

Swift

flock of Swifts

Little Swift

Swift

Pallid Swift

Alpine Swift

White-rumped Swift

181

Kingfishers and their allies (order *Coracii-tormes*) form a highly diversified group of very colourful birds.

Kingfishers (family *Alcedinidae*) are large-headed, short-tailed birds that dive for fish, which they catch with their long, sharp beaks. Colours are bright. Seen near open water. They perch motionlessly or hover in the open over water. Their legs are very short. Solitary nesters. Usually lay 3–8 white eggs in a deep burrow in a steep bank.

Bee-eaters (family *Meropidae*) are medium-sized, slim birds with long, pointed, slightly down-curved bills, pointed wings and projecting middle tail-feathers. They live on insects which they catch in the air. Sit horizontally when perched on wires or branches. Nest colonially. Lay 4–7 white eggs in deep burrows in steep banks.

Rollers (family *Coraciidae*) are medium-sized, jay-like birds, which get their name from their rolling display flight. They live mainly on insects which are taken on the ground. Solitary nesters. The 4–5 white eggs are laid in holes in trees or in the ground.

Hoopoes (family *Upupidae*) are medium-sized, largely pink-brown birds, with long, decurved bills, rounded wings and large, erectile crests. Solitary nesters. Nest in holes, laying 6–10 greenish-white eggs.

KINGFISHER *Alcedo atthis* L 18 Fairly common along slow-running rivers and streams and by ponds rich in fish. Blue and green upper parts and orange-red underside distinguish this species. Notice the relatively enormous head, short wings, legs and tail. Perches on poles and branches by the water, often sitting motionless for long periods of time, but also has characteristic jerking of head and tail. Flight fast and direct, low over the water. Occasionally seen hovering for brief moments. Plunges headlong into the water from perch to catch fish. Call is a high, ringing repetition of 'cheet' notes.

F

PIED KINGFISHER *Ceryle rudis* L 25 Very rare, usually spring visitor from African and Asiatic breeding grounds to eastern and south-eastern Europe. Black and white plumage, large size and kingfisher silhouette easily distinguish this species from any other European bird. Male has two, female one, more or less complete breast-bands. Soars and hovers above the surface of the water before plunging head-first to catch fish. Fishes in salt and fresh water. Call is short and penetrating.

Hoopoe

Roller

Bee-eater

Kingfisher

Hoopoe nest
hole in tree

Roller nest
hole in tree

Bee-eater nest
hole in sandbank

Kingfisher nest
hole in bank

foot of Kingfisher

hovering

Kingfisher

Pied Kingfisher

183

BEE-EATER *Merops apiaster* L 28 Common in open country with scattered trees and bushes. Nests colonially in dried-out river-banks and sand-pits, but may nest solitarily. Very colourful plumage with yellow-brown upper parts and blue underside distinguish this species. Immatures have less striking colours and lack the elongated central tail-feathers. Often seen perching on horizontal wires. May be encountered in flocks. Flight is extremely elegant on long, pointed wings. Sometimes hovers. Hunts insects in the air. Call is a characteristic far-reaching 'pruik', often repeated and mostly given in flight. V

BLUE-CHEEKED BEE-EATER *Merops superciliosus* L 31 Fairly common in open steppes. Local in very restricted European range. Very rare summer visitor to western Europe. Nests colonially in holes in river-banks or sand-pits. Green colour without any brown on upper parts and reddish underside of wing distinguish it from the Bee-eater. Habits are similar to Bee-eater. Often encountered in flocks on breeding grounds but in western Europe singly. Call resembles that of Bee-eater but is shriller and not as far-reaching. V

ROLLER *Coracias garrulus* L 31 Fairly common in open country with scattered trees and bushes, and in open woodland. Nests in hollow trees or other cavities. Blue colour with chestnut back make this species unmistakable. Sexes similar. Often sits in the open on a perch from which it catches insects on the ground or even in flight in shrike-like fashion. Flight resembles that of Jackdaw, but is faster and more erratic. On the ground it is rather clumsy. Has characteristic 'rolling' display flight. Call is a loud, crow-like 'kraack'. V

HOOPOE *Upupa epops* L 28 Fairly common in open land with many trees and groves, parks and open woods, nesting in tree cavities. Erectile crest, long decurved bill, light pinky brown plumage and striking black and white wing pattern identify this species at a glance. Crest is often raised and lowered. Sexes are similar. Immatures have shorter crest. Wings are very rounded and flight is undulating. Runs well on the ground. Often seen perching on bushes, trees, rocks and buildings. Call is a characteristic deep 'hoo-poo-poo'. F

Bee-eater

Blue-cheeked Bee-eater

Roller

imm.

Hoopoe

crest up

crest flattened

Woodpeckers

(order *Piciformes,* family *Picidae*) are medium-sized to small birds with strong bills, sharply pointed for chipping and digging into tree trunks and branches for wood-boring insects, and for excavating nest holes. The stiff tail is used as a prop when climbing tree trunks. Tongue is extremely long and sticky and is used for extracting insects from holes. Most species 'drum' on resonant limbs, poles or drainpipes, especially in early spring when territories are claimed. Besides drumming, woodpeckers have several characteristic far-reaching calls. Most are brightly coloured and most males have red on crown. Flight is markedly undulating, with wings folded against body between each series of flaps. Most are residents. Although they are primarily woodland birds, some species (Green and Grey-headed Woodpeckers and Wryneck) search open ground for ants and dig them out of nests. All woodpeckers except Wryneck nest in cavities which they chisel out in a trunk or large branch. Wryneck uses a natural cavity. Clutch, 4–8 white eggs.

GREEN WOODPECKER *Picus viridis* L 30 Common in deciduous woodlands with a preference for areas with large clearings and rides. Also found in more open land with scattered trees and groves. Where range overlaps that of Grey-headed Woodpecker, Green is usually found at lower elevations. Notice green upper parts with conspicuously yellow upper rump. Only other greenish Woodpecker in Europe is the Grey-headed, but Green is told from this species by larger size and more red on crown (both male and female) and more black on face. Juveniles are spotted and are greener than juvenile Grey-headed Woodpeckers and have more red on crown. Often seen on the ground in the open, feeding on ants. Carriage on the ground is upright. Hops clumsily. Perches across branches more often than other woodpeckers. Call is a far-reaching laughing cry. Seldom drums. R

GREY-HEADED WOODPECKER *Picus canus* L 26 Fairly common in open deciduous and mixed woods, open areas with scattered trees and open mountain forests (less numerous than Green Woodpecker). Where range overlaps that of Green Woodpecker, usually found at higher elevations. Resembles Green Woodpecker, but is smaller and has less red on head in male and none in female, and less black on face (limited to narrow lines). Juvenile male has some red on forehead, female none. Juveniles are browner in colour and not spotted. Like Green Woodpecker, often seen on ground, where it finds ants. Call resembles that of Green Woodpecker, but is not as harsh and dies away slowly. Unlike Green Woodpecker, it drums frequently.

Treecreeper

Nuthatch

woodpecker

Great Spotted Woodpecker at nest

woodpecker head showing arrangement of tongue

undulating flight of woodpeckers

Green Woodpecker

♀

♂

imm.

Grey-headed Woodpecker

imm.

♂

♂

GREAT SPOTTED WOODPECKER *Dendrocopos major* L 23 The most common and widespread of the woodpeckers, found in both deciduous and coniferous woods, in gardens and parks with many trees. The black and white plumage distinguishes the spotted wood-peckers as a group at a glance. To tell the species apart it is important to note the head, neck and back pattern. Great Spotted Woodpecker has two large white areas on back, as does the Syrian Woodpecker from which it is told by bold black line across side of neck, and Middle Spotted Woodpecker from which it is told by black line reaching bill, by only a little red on neck of adult male (female has none), and by unstriped flanks. Juveniles have red crown, but black on side of head and neck extends further than on any other spotted woodpecker. Call is a loud, short 'kik'. Often drums; drumming is very fast and short (0.5 sec.). RW

SYRIAN WOODPECKER *Dendrocopos syriacus* L 23 Common in open woodland and parks, preferring less dense woods than the Great Spotted Woodpecker. Very similar to Great Spotted Woodpecker, but told from this species by lack of black stripe across side of neck. Imma-tures are told from Great Spotted Woodpecker imma-tures in the same way, from Middle Spotted Wood-pecker by moustachial stripe extending forward to the bill. In call, drumming and behaviour like Great Spotted Woodpecker.

MIDDLE SPOTTED WOODPECKER *Dendrocopos medius* L 20 Fairly common in mature deciduous forests, staying rather high in the canopy. Has white patches on shoulders, like Great Spotted Woodpecker, but has red crown in all plumages and less black on sides of head and neck. Sides of flanks striped with black. Told from immature Syrian Woodpecker by shorter moustachial stripe which does not reach bill. In mating season it has a distinct slow cry, 'gait-gait'. Does not drum as often as Great Spotted Woodpecker and drumming is weak.

LESSER SPOTTED WOODPECKER *Dendrocopos minor* L 15 Common in rather open deciduous and mixed woods, orchards and parks. Smallest of the European woodpeckers. Lacks white shoulder spots of Great Spotted, Syrian and Middle, but has boldly barred back. Usually stays well up among small branches of old trees. Sometimes mixes in flocks of tits. Call is a repetition of high-pitched 'kee' notes. Drums frequently, but a little less powerfully than Great Spotted, often weaker in the middle and usually longer (1.5 sec.). R

188

**Great
Spotted Woodpecker**

imm.

♀

♂

Syrian Woodpecker

imm.

♀

♂

**Middle
Spotted Woodpecker**

♀

♂

♀

♂

189

Lesser Spotted Woodpecker

WHITE-BACKED WOODPECKER *Dendrocopos leucotos* L 25 Rather uncommon in old deciduous forests and mixed woods with old, rotting trees. The largest of the *Dendrocopos* group, with a distinct white upper rump and lower back, and black upper back (diagnostic). The white back of the smaller Three-toed Woodpecker extends all the way to the neck. Bill is longer than that of any of the spotted woodpeckers. In flight the white lower back and upper rump are very distinctive. Female has a black instead of red crown; immatures have only a little red on the crown. Call is similar to that of Great Spotted Woodpecker. Drumming resembles Three-toed Woodpecker but becomes weaker and faster at the end.

THREE-TOED WOODPECKER *Picoïdes tridactylus* L 23 Rather uncommon, in coniferous and birch forests up to tree limit on mountains. Head is large and very dark, the male having yellow on crown. White back and upper rump are diagnostic. Flanks are barred. The white on the back of the much larger White-backed Woodpecker does not extend as far as on the Three-toed Woodpecker. Flight is stronger and faster than that of other woodpeckers. Less vocal and active than other woodpeckers, drumming infrequently. Call is rather similar to that of the Great Spotted Woodpecker. Drumming is stronger, slower and longer (1.5 sec.) than Great Spotted Woodpecker.

BLACK WOODPECKER *Dryocopus martius* L 4 Fairly common in old coniferous and deciduous forests particularly in mountain tracts. Largest of the European woodpeckers. Enormous size and uniform black plumage make this bird unmistakable. Male has a red crown, female only a red spot on the back of the head. Flight more straight than that of other woodpeckers, and heavier. Call is a far-reaching ringing 'kleoh'. Drums commonly and extremely loudly, drums lasting two to three seconds accelerating slightly towards the end.

WRYNECK *Jynx torquilla* L 18 Fairly common but retiring in parks and open land with plenty of bushes, trees and hedgerows. Does not resemble woodpeckers at all. Plumage is lilac and brown with a dark area down the neck, tail is long, and bill is short. Flight is undulating. Banded tail is distinctive when the bird is in flight. It often seen on the ground where it feeds on ants. Often turns its head at queer angles (hence name). Can hardly be mistaken for any other European bird. Call is a repetition of nasal crying 'gyeeh' notes. Does not drum. S

imm.

♂

Great Spotted
for comparison

♀

♂

White-
backed
Woodpecker

♂

♀

Three-toed Woodpecker

Black Woodpecker

♀ ♂

Wryneck

Crow for comparison

feeding on ground

191

Perching birds and songbirds (order

Passeriformes) form the largest order of birds both in number of species and individuals. Songbirds take advantage of all habitats from the seashore to the mountains and are met with more frequently than any other birds, except on the open sea. They are medium-sized to small and have feet well-adapted for perching, with three toes in front and one long one behind. Family identification is extremly important in this order with so many, often very similar, species. Bill shape, feather colours, and habits are most useful in family identification. The bill shape reflects feeding habits; generally the insectivorous species have thin, rather weak bills, whereas seed-eaters have strong, conical bills. Songs and calls are very important in identification.

Larks (family *Alaudidae*) are small or medium-sized with mostly brownish plumage. They walk on the ground. Often encountered in flocks, usually in open country. Heavier build than similarly coloured pipits. Nest on the ground. 11 species.   p. 194

Swallows (family *Hirundinidae*) are small, long-winged with forked tails and are perfect fliers, catching insects on the wing. They build characteristic nests. Some are colonial breeders. 5 species.   p. 200

Pipits and wagtails (family *Motacillidae*) resemble larks in terrestrial behaviour and pipits are brown, but both are smaller and more delicately built. Walk. Wagtails are brightly coloured with very long tails. Usually found in open country, sometimes in loose flocks. Nest on the ground. 13 species.   p. 202

Shrikes (family *Laniidae*) are medium-sized, brightly coloured, with hooked bills and long tails. Sit upright Found in bushy, semi-open landscapes. Nest in bushes 6 species.   p. 210

Orioles (family *Oriolidae*) are medium-sized, black and yellow, thrush-like woodland birds nesting in treetops 1 species.   p. 212

Starlings (family *Sturnidae*) are medium-sized, short-tailed and mainly black. Very sociable. Found in semi-open woodland and on open fields. Nest in cavities 3 species.   p. 212

Waxwings (family *Bombycillidae*) are medium-sized brownish, crested, berry-eating birds of woods and parkland. Sociable. Nest in trees. 1 species.   p. 213

Crows (family *Corvidae*) are large, rather strongly coloured with rounded wings. Omnivorous. Often sociable. Found in almost all habitats. Most nest in trees 12 species.   p. 214

Dippers (family *Cinclidae*) are medium-sized, plump brown and white birds of swift-running streams. Nest at water edges. 1 species.   p. 220

Wrens (family *Troglodytidae*) are very small, chubby brown birds of shrubbery and bushes, where they build domed nests 1 species   p. 220

Accentors (family *Prunellidae*) are small, grey and brown, sparrow-like birds with thin bills. Retiring in behaviour. Found in bushy and mountainous landscape. Nest in bushes and on the ground. 3 species.　　p. 220

Warblers and their allies (family *Muscicapidae*) form a very large family of insectivorous songbirds. Divided into a number of subfamilies:

Warblers (subfamily *Sylviinae*) are small, thin-billed, delicately built songsters. Many species are very similar and difficult to tell apart. Song is most important in field identification. In the hand, wing formula often most important. Found in dense vegetation from reed-beds to woods. Nest near ground in dense vegetation or bushes. 48 species.　　p. 222

Flycatchers (subfamily *Muscicapinae*) are small, thin-billed birds of parks and woods. Sit upright. Catch insects in flight. Nest in holes, 6 species.　　p. 248

Thrushes and their allies (subfamily *Turdinae*) are medium-sized to small, mainly insectivorous birds. Young and some adults have spotted plumage. Some adults brightly coloured. Includes wheatears, redstarts, robins, nightingales, thrushes and many others. Nest on the ground, in bushes or trees. Many use cavities. Good singers. 35 species.　　p. 250

Tits (family *Paridae*) are small, short-billed, active birds with characteristic facial patterns. Nuthatches (p. 272) are short-tailed, woodpecker-like relatives of tits. Wall-creeper is a small aberrant species (p. 274). Nest in tree cavities often using next boxes. Mostly found in woodland. 14 species.　　p. 266

Bearded Tits (family *Muscicapidae*, subfamily *Timaliinae*) are small, brown, long-tailed, tit-like birds of reed-beds. 1 species.　　p. 270

Penduline tits (family *Remizidae*) are small tit-like birds which build hanging nests. 1 species.　　p. 270

Treecreepers (family *Certhiidae*) are small, brown, with long, slightly decurved bills. Climb on tree trunks. Woodland birds. Nest in cracks of bark and trees. 2 species.　　p. 274

Weaver finches (family *Ploceidae*) are small brown, grey and black, seed-eating birds. Common in towns and farmlands. Nest in cavities, or build domed nests in trees or bushes. Social. 4 species.　　p. 276

Finches and their allies (family *Fringillidae*) have heavy, conical, seed-cracking bills. Many have striking colours. Male and female have different plumages. Outside breeding season sociable. Many found in woods or parkland. 23 species.　　p. 278

Buntings (family *Emberizidae*) are medium-sized brown, yellow and black birds with strong, conical bills. Most are found in open or semi-open country. In some, sexes differ in plumage. Somewhat sociable outside breeding season. Nest on the ground or in low bushes. 16 species.　　p. 288

Larks

(family *Alaudidae*) are rather dull-looking, small to medium-sized, brownish birds of open country. They sing in flight, sometimes high above the ground; outside the breeding season seen in loose flocks. Resemble pipits most but are chunkier with broader wings and shorter tails. Sexes are usually similar (except for Black Lark). Immatures resemble adults. Eat insects and small seeds. Nest on the ground. Clutch, 3–5 eggs.

DUPONT'S LARK *Chersophilus duponti* L 18 Very rare visitor from North Africa to western Mediterranean countries. Frequents dry steppes with scattered bushes. Rather long decurved bill and round head without trace of crest are diagnostic. Whitish eye-stripe is characteristic. No white on wings. Secretive in behaviour, hiding in vegetation. Runs quickly. When perched on the ground, stands more erect than other larks. Song, given in flight, contains rasping notes.

SHORT-TOED LARK *Calandrella brachydactyla* L 14 Common in open, dry country and on dried-out mudflats. Rather small and pale. Underside mainly unstreaked except for juvenile which has streaked breast. Dark patches on neck difficult to see. Centre of tail looks very dark in flight. Resembles Lesser Short-toed Lark closely but told from this by lack of striping of underparts, more rufous colours and, at short range, dark patches on neck. The tertials almost reach the end of the folded wing and cover all but one or two primaries. Usually flies low. Song is rather high-pitched, less varied than that of Skylark, given in flight as well as on the ground. The call has been described as a short 'tchirrup'.

LESSER SHORT-TOED LARK *Calandrella rufescens* L 14 Fairly common in dry, open country and on dried out mud-flats. Resembles Short-toed Lark closely, but has streaked upper breast and flanks and is darker, greyer and more uniform in colour. It also lacks the dark neck patches of the adult Short-toed Lark. The tertials are relatively shorter than in Short-toed Lark. Song, given in high circling flight, is rich and varied with characteristic short notes. The call has been described as a more protracted 'prrit'.

CALANDRA LARK *Melanocorypha calandra* L 2 Common in dry, open country. Very large with comparatively short tail and broad wings with white trailing edge. Bill thick. Large black neck patch sometimes difficult to see and less prominent in females. Flight usually low and undulating. Call is short and nasal. Song musical, resembling that of Skylark, usually uttered on the wing from a height.

bunting

thrush

pipit

Skylark

Meadow Pipit for comparison

Dupont's Lark

juv.

Short-toed Lark

Lesser Short-toed Lark

song-flights

Calandra Lark

195

WHITE-WINGED LARK *Melanocorypha leucoptera* L 19 Common in dry grasslands. Annual in eastern Europe, very rare in western Europe, mainly in winter, where it reaches as far as the British Isles. Similar to Calandra Lark, but large white wing patches, very prominent in flight, are diagnostic. Wings narrower than Calandra Lark's. Crown rich brown in male, more greyish in female. Song is loud, resembling Calandra Lark's. Usually does not rise as high as Calandra Lark during song-flight. V

BLACK LARK *Melanocorypha yeltoniensis* L 20 Fairly common on steppes, often near water. Rare winter visitor to central Europe, where it has reached as far west as Belgium. Male easily told from other larks by black plumage with brown feather margins. Female best told from Calandra Lark and White-winged Lark both of which also have heavy bill, by lack of black neck patch and lack of white wing patch. From other larks by heavy bill and plump build. Underwing is dark brown. Song resembles that of Calandra Lark.

CRESTED LARK *Galerida cristata* L 17 Common in dry open country with sparse vegetation, by roadsides, and in open spaces in towns. Crest is larger than that of any other lark except Thekla. Sandy edge of short tail characteristic in flight as are sandy underwings. Where range overlaps that of Thekla Lark (Iberian peninsula), identification is extremely difficult and probably only possible when direct comparison can be made. Tail is rather short, wings rounded compared with other larks. Immatures have less prominent crest and are more spotted above. Runs rapidly. Often very tame. Usually encountered in small groups. Call is a characteristic 'dee-dee-doo'. Song resembles that of Skylark but is shorter and less melodious. Usually delivered from the ground or from low perch on rock. V

Crested

THEKLA LARK *Galerida theklae* L 15 Common in dry open country with sparse vegetation, usually preferring rockier landscape and higher elevation than the Crested Lark, from which it can be distinguished only by direct comparison. Slightly smaller, with shorter and heavier bill. Greyer above and paler below with grey underside to wing. Breast spots clearer. Often perches on trees (which the Crested Lark rarely does), from which song resembling that of Crested Lark is given. This species and the preceding one show considerable geographical variation in darkness of plumage, further complicating identification.

Thekla

White-winged Lark

Black Lark

♀

running on
pavement

Crested Lark

Thekla Lark

197

SKYLARK *Alauda arvensis* L 18 Abundant in open cultivated and uncultivated country. Boldly striped with small crest and long white-edged tail. Told from Corn Bunting by characteristic lark-like undulating flight, horizontal posture when perched, brownish rather than greyish colours, white-edged tail and more slender bill. Told from rather similar Woodlark by longer tail with white edges and less conspicuous and striking stripe over eye. From Calandra Lark by longer tail, more slender bill, less triangular wing and lack of black spot on side of breast. Crest is much smaller and more rounded than that of Crested and Thekla Lark. Outside breeding season usually seen in loose flocks. Call is melodious 'treek-e'. Song, usually given from flight high-up, is liquid, varied and sustained. Often remains at the same spot in the air for long periods of time, sometimes beyond sight of the naked eye. RSWP

WOODLARK *Lullula arborea* L 15 Common in wood margins and clearings, heaths and mountains with scattered bushes. Resembles Skylark but has much shorter tail without white edges, and characteristic stripes over the eyes meeting on the nape. Small crest is much more rounded and less prominent than that of Crested and Thekla Lark. Has small dark spot on back of wing, but this is not nearly as obvious as the black spot on neck of Calandra Lark. Flight is more undulating than that of Skylark. Short tail is particularly noticeable in flight. Often perches on trees, bushes and even telephone wires. Outside breeding season sometimes mixes with Skylarks in the loose flocks so characteristic of larks, but more often seen in small unmixed groups. Call is a musical, liquid 'diedelie'. Skylark-like song, which is sometimes given from perch but more often in flight, is characterised by interspersed trilling 'lu-lu-lu-lu-lu'. Sometimes sings at night. RP

SHORE LARK *Eremophila alpestris* L 17 Fairly common, breeding on dry tundras above or north of the tree limit, wintering along shores and on fields with short vegetation. Facial pattern of black and sandy-yellow diagnostic, but can be somewhat obscured in winter, particularly on females and immatures, but it is always present to some degree. Outer tail-feathers are white. In winter usually encountered in small flocks, sometimes associated with Snow and Lapland Buntings. Flight is usually low and undulating. Call consists of faint pipit-like notes. Song, which is given from perch or in flight, is weak, high-pitched and repetitive. W

Skylark

flock over field

Skylark
song-flight

Woodlark

song-flight

Woodlark singing
from perch

juv.

Shore Lark

Swallows

(family *Hirundinidae*) have long pointed wings and all have more or less forked tails. Their flight is fast and elegant but wing action is not as stiff as that of rather similar swifts. Legs and bills are short, but mouths are wide for capturing flying insects. Commonly perch on wires, rarely on the ground. Often seen in large, mixed flocks. Outside breeding season often assemble in large roosts in reed-beds. Most nest in colonies. Eggs, 4–7, are white or spotted.

SAND MARTIN *Riparia riparia* L 13 Common near steep river-banks, sea cliffs and gravel pits, where they burrow their nest holes into the banks. Often seen near water. Brown breast-band diagnostic. Also told from Crag Martin by more deeply forked tail, narrower wings and lack of white spots on tail. Nests colonially. Call is a low, unmusical buzz.   S

CRAG MARTIN *Ptyonoprogne rupestris* L 15 Common but local in mountains and along rocky sea cliffs. Larger than Sand Martin, without breastband. Wings broader and tail less deeply forked. White spots on upper side of tail visible at short distance only. Nests colonially on cliffs. Call is high-pitched, weak 'tchnin', only rarely heard.

SWALLOW *Hirundo rustica* L 19 Very common in cultivated open country, where it builds an open mud nest on buildings. Tail very deeply forked. Red throat and front diagnostic. No white on upper rump. Flight extremly elegant. Nests singly and in small, loose colonies. Song is long and twittering.   S

RED-RUMPED SWALLOW *Hirundo daurica* L 18 Fairly common in open rocky country where it builds closed mud nest with tubular entrance under cliffs, bridges and buildings. Looks like Swallow, but notice light upper rump, light throat and less forked tail (rump looks long). Flight resembles that of Swallow but is not as elegant. Nests singly or in small, loose colonies. Song resembles that of Swallow.   V

HOUSE MARTIN *Delichon urbica* L 13 Common in cultivated country and in towns. White upper rump diagnostic. Tail shorter and less forked than in Swallow and Red-rumped Swallow. Wing action and flight stiffer than in Swallow. Often encountered in large flocks Builds closed nest. Breeds in colonies. Flight call sharp and high pitched. Song twittering.   S

Crag Martin on rock

Sand Martin

Swallow

Red-rumped Swallow

House Martin

Swift

Swallow

cliff-nesting Sand Martin colony

nest under rock

Sand Martin

Crag Martin

Swallow young and nest

Red-rumped Swallow nest

House Martin nest

Swallow

Red-rumped Swallow

House Martin

flock of Swallows on telephone wires

Pipits and wagtails (family *Motacillidae*) are sparrow-sized birds with slender bills; tails are dark with white outer feathers. They feed on the ground, walk leisurely, and wag their tails continually. They do not hop. Pipits are streaked but easily told from larks by more slender build and longer tails. Voice is important in identification. Wagtails have even longer tails. Clutch, 4–7 eggs, in a nest on the ground or in a bank.

TREE PIPIT *Anthus trivialis* L 15 Common in open woods, clearings, heath and more open landscapes with bushes and trees. Resembles Meadow Pipit from which it is told by unstriped upper rump, pink legs, short hind claw and stouter build, but best by voice. Call note is a characteristic coarse 'tzee'. Song, which is given from perch or more often in short song-flight with slow descent, is canary-like, ending with a repeated 'zeea'.

SP

OLIVE-BACKED PIPIT *Anthus hodgsoni* L 15 Common in its limited European range where it is found in the taiga. An extremely rare autumn visitor to north-western Europe. Resembles Tree Pipit closely but is slightly smaller, more olive-green above with less bold streaks, whereas underside is more boldly striped forming a gorget on buff breast. The belly is white. Eye-stripe more prominent and accentuated by black margins. Upper rump unstriped. Song, given from perch, is not as varied as that of the Tree Pipit and is higher pitched.

V

PECHORA PIPIT *Anthus gustavi* L 15 Common in scrubby and wooded tundras. A very rare autumn visitor to north-western Europe. Resembles Tree Pipit but has long hind claw, two pale stripes down the back, buffish (only rarely white) outer tail-feathers and more striped underside. Upper rump is striped. Call is a characteristic hard 'pipit', usually repeated three times. Song, given from perch or song-flight, consists of Wood-Warbler like phrase followed by low warble.

V

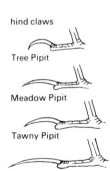

hind claws

Tree Pipit

Meadow Pipit

Tawny Pipit

Richards Pipit

RICHARD'S PIPIT *Anthus novaeseelandiae* L 18 A rare but probably annual, autumn (sometimes spring) visitor to Europe from Asiatic breeding grounds. Usually seen in open wet country near coasts. Large, long-legged with very long hind claw and boldly streaked plumage and prominent moustachial stripe. Has shorter, stouter bill, longer legs and more upright stance than immature Tawny Pipit which also has striped breast. Stands erect. Call is rather harsh 'r-reep'.

bunting   thrush   Skylark   pipit   wagtail

song-flight

Meadow Pipit for comparison

Tree Pipit

Olive-backed Pipit

Pechora Pipit

Richard's Pipit

203

MEADOW PIPIT *Anthus pratensis* L 15 Very common on moors, meadows, dunes and grasslands. Resembles Tree Pipit but is more white on breast and has brown legs and long hind claws. Upper rump is less striped than back, distinguishing it from Red-throated Pipit. Outside breeding season often encountered in loose flocks. Call is a thin 'zeep', very different from that of Tree Pipit and Red-throated Pipit. Song, usually given in song-flight, is weak, ending in a trill. RSWP

TAWNY PIPIT *Anthus campestris* L 17 Fairly common in open, dry and sandy country with sparse vegetation. Sandy colour, rather faint streaking and large size distinguish it from other pipits. Immatures in autumn are streaked like Richard's Pipit but distinguished by longer, more slender bill. Usually seen singly or in small groups. As in other pipits voice is of great importance in identification. Call is drawn out or of two notes. Song is a repeated 'tsili', given in flight or on the ground. V

RED-THROATED PIPIT *Anthus cervinus* L 15 Fairly common on tundra with low bushes. Uncommon visitor in west and central Europe. In summer easily distinguished from other pipits by rosy throat. In winter resembles Meadow Pipit but has more prominently streaked upper rump and more heavily streaked underside. Call is 'tseeh', quite different from that of Meadow and Tree Pipit. Song resembles that of Meadow Pipit and is given in flight. P

WATER PIPIT *Anthus spinoletta spinoletta* L 17 Common on mountains above the tree limit, in winter in open country of lower elevation. In summer greyish-brown upper side and unstreaked underside separate it from other pipits. In winter resembles Meadow Pipit but distinguished by black leg colour and darker plumage. Distinguished from very similar Rock Pipit by white, not grey, outer tail-feathers. Call and song more metallic than those of Meadow Pipit. WP

ROCK PIPIT *Anthus spinoletta* (*petrosus* group) L 17 Subspecies of Water Pipit. Common on coasts, particularly where rocky. Resembles winter plumage Water Pipit but is more olive on back and has greyish outer tail-feathers. Distinguished from other pipits by dark legs. Often found in association with Meadow Pipit outside the breeding season. Call and song similar to those of Water Pipit.

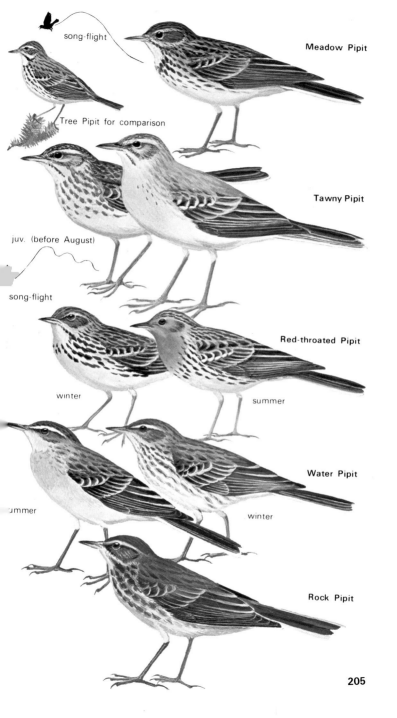

song-flight

Meadow Pipit

Tree Pipit for comparison

Tawny Pipit

juv. (before August)

song-flight

Red-throated Pipit

winter

summer

Water Pipit

summer

winter

Rock Pipit

YELLOW WAGTAIL *Motacilla flava* L 17 Very common in moist open areas. Long tail, yellow underside and green back distinguish it from all other species. Colour of head and neck variable according to race (see table). Flight undulating. Outside breeding season usually seen in loose flocks. Often associates with grazing cattle. Call is loud mellow 'tseep'. SP

Races of Yellow Wagtail

Race	Summer Plumage (male)	Summer Distribution
Blue-headed Wagtail. *M.f. flava*	Blue-grey head, yellow throat, with stripe over eye from bib to neck	Southern Scandinavia, western Europe except Great Britain and Iberian peninsula, and western part of east Europe
Yellow Wagtail. *M.f. flavissima*	Olive-yellow head, yellow throat, yellow stripe over eye	Great Britain and locally adjacent coasts of continent
Spanish Wagtail. *M.f. iberiae*	Grey head, white throat, white stripe over eye to neck	Iberian peninsula, south and south-west France, Balearic Islands
Ashy-headed Wagtail. *M.f. cinereocapilla*	Grey head, white throat, no stripe over eye	Italy, central Mediterranean islands, Albania
Sykes's Wagtail. *M.f. beema*	Pale grey head, white throat, white stripe over eye from bib to neck	South-east Russia
Kirghiz Steppes Wagtail. *M.f. lutea*	Yellow head, throat and stripe over eye	South-easternmost Russia (Lower Volga)
Grey-headed Wagtail. *M.f. thunbergi*	Grey head, yellow throat, no stripe over eye	Northern Scandinavia and Russia
Black-headed Wagtail. *M.f. feldegg*	Black head, yellow throat, no stripe over eye	Balkan and Black Sea coasts

Females and males in winter plumage are paler and difficult to distinguish. Within each subspecies, variations resembling other subspecies occur. In adjoining areas subspecies are less clearly defined and intermediate forms occur.

CITRINE WAGTAIL *Motacilla citreola* L 17 Fairl common in limited European range, usually in wet ope country. A very rare autumn visitor to north-wes Europe. Told in all plumages from Yellow Wagtail b grey back and two distinct white wing-bars particular noticeable in flight. Immature is very pale, whitish o underside, grey on upper side. Often associates wit Yellow Wagtail. Call shorter than that of Yellow Wagta described as a harsh 'dzeep'.

Subspecies of *Motacilla flava*

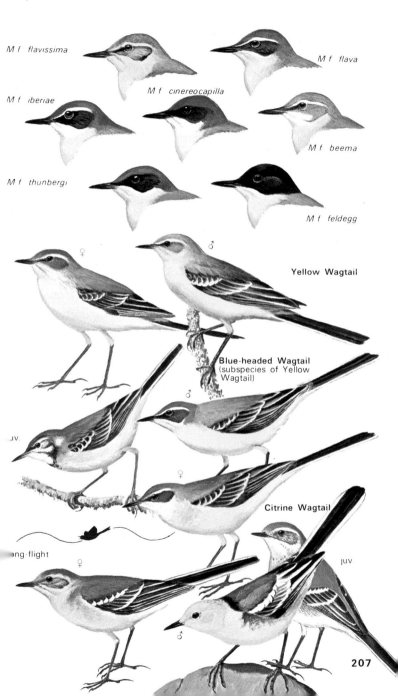

M f flavissima

M f flava

M f iberiae

M f cinereocapilla

M f beema

M f thunbergi

M f feldegg

♀ ♂

Yellow Wagtail

Blue-headed Wagtail
(subspecies of Yellow
Wagtail)

♂

juv.

♀

Citrine Wagtail

♀

song-flight

juv.

♂

207

Grey
Wagtail

White and Pied
Wagtails

See map above

GREY WAGTAIL *Motacilla cinerea* L 18 Common along mountain streams, in winter also frequenting sewage farms by water in lowlands, even in towns, and lakesides. Yellow underside, grey back and extremely long tail distinguish it in all plumages. Male in summer has black throat. Yellow underside distinguishes it from similar Pied and White Wagtails. Immatures have less yellow on underside and are more greyish-brown above but always have yellow under tail-coverts, distinguishing them from immature White and Pied Wagtail, which have pure white under tail-coverts and usually some black on breast. Usually seen singly but a few can associate at favourable feeding grounds. Call resembles that of Pied and White Wagtail, but is higher pitched and shorter. Song, seldom heard, is twittering.   R

WHITE WAGTAIL *Motacilla alba alba* L 18 Very common in open country, farms, villages, towns and rocky areas, usually near water. Nests on ledges or in open holes, usually low above the ground. Black, grey and white plumage and long, constantly-wagged tail distinguish it from all other birds except Pied Wagtail. Immature resembles immature Grey Wagtail, but has white (not yellow) under tail-coverts and a dark area on breast. Sometimes has greenish and yellowish areas on head. Male in spring has more extensive black than female, particularly on side of neck. On female grey back also extends further up. In winter both have white throat, but distinctive crescent-shaped black area on upper breast. Outside breeding season usually seen in small flocks but sometimes congregates in large roosts in reedbeds in winter. Tail-wagging and bobbing of head when walking are characteristic. Runs very fast. Lives on insects taken on the ground but will occasionally catch them in the air like the flycatchers. Flight very undulating. Call is two-syllable 'tsweep'. Song, which is seldom heard, is twittering.   F

PIED WAGTAIL *Motacilla alba yarrellii* L 18 Subspecies of White Wagtail limited to British Isles and sporadically on adjacent continental coasts. (Locally in Norway Germany, Holland, Belgium and north-western France) Habitat similar to that of White Wagtail. Adult bird easily told from White Wagtail by solid black back. Male told from female by more extensive black bib and side of neck. One year-olds resemble White Wagtails but upper rump is blackish, not grey. Immature resembles female White Wagtail in winter plumage closely but has whiter front and darker crown. Voice and behaviour similar to White Wagtail.   RSW

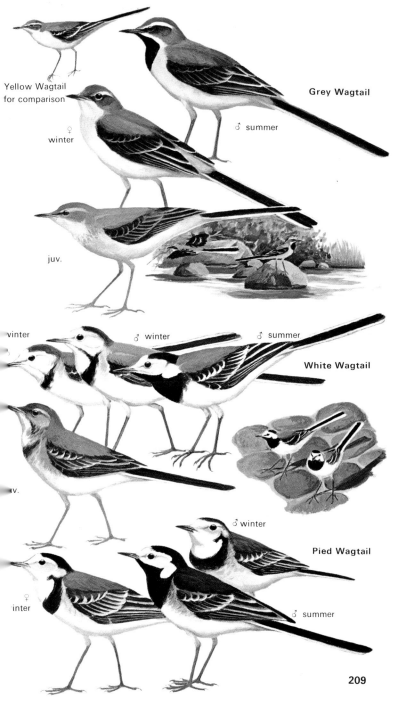

Yellow Wagtail
for comparison

Grey Wagtail

♀
winter

♂ summer

juv.

winter

♂ winter

♂ summer

White Wagtail

♀
juv.

Pied Wagtail

♂ winter

♀
inter

♂ summer

209

Shrikes

(family *Laniidae*) are medium-sized passerines with heavy hooked bills, striking colour patterns (except for Red-backed and Woodchat females and juveniles) and habit of pursuing insects, small birds and rodents, which they impale on thorn trees or barbed wire. They sometimes hover like Kestrels. Shrikes perch alone on treetops or wires in open country. Their flight is low and undulating. Bulky nests with 4–6 eggs are in thorny shrubs or well hidden in trees.

Declining as breeding species in Britain and north-west

RED-BACKED SHRIKE *Lanius collurio* L 18 Common in open country with bushes. Notice chestnut-red back and wings of male. Female and juvenile are brown with closely barred breast. Told from juvenile Woodchat by uniform colour of upper side. Call is grating 'chaek'. Song, seldom heard, is an attractive warbled medley. SP

ISABELLINE SHRIKE *Lanius isabellinus* L 18 A rare visitor to Great Britain, Germany and Sweden from Central Asiatic breeding grounds. It is pale greyish buff with a reddish tail and rump, white wing bars and black line through the eye. (Not illustrated) V

MASKED SHRIKE *Lanius nubicus* L 20 Common in open, dry country with trees and bushes. Notice largely black upper side and long tail. Immature is similar but much paler with less distinct markings. Call is harsh. Song is subdued and monotonous.

WOODCHAT SHRIKE *Lanius senator* L 18 Common in open, dry country with trees and bushes, sometimes in more wooded areas. Notice black upper side with white shoulder patches and upper rump and striking red neck patch. Juvenile resembles juvenile Red-backed but has lighter upper side with traces of white shoulder patches and upper rump. The head is more square in shape. Hides among foliage more often than other shrikes. Call is harsh. P

LESSER GREY SHRIKE *Lanius minor* L 20 Common in open country with scattered trees and bushes. Resembles Great Grey Shrike but is stouter with shorter tail, more prominent white markings, more extensive mask and the bill is shorter and deeper. Stands more upright than Great Grey Shrike. Juvenile is finely barred on head and has dark brown wings and tail with unbarred breast. Call is harsh 'chek'.

GREAT GREY SHRIKE *Lanius excubitor* L 24 Common in open country but prefers more well-wooded areas than most shrikes. Large size and pattern of black and white distinguish it. Compare with similar Lesser Grey Shrike. Often hovers. Call notes include shrill cries and rattles. Song is subdued with harsh notes interspersed. W

thrush Kestrel flycatcher shrike

Red-backed Shrike

juv.   ♀   ♂

Masked Shrike

♀   ♂

Woodchat Shrike

♀   ♂

juv.

Lesser Grey

juv.   ♂

Lesser Grey Shrike

Great Grey

juv.

Great Grey Shrike

Orioles

(family *Oriolidae*) are thrush-sized, colourful birds of woods and parks. Eggs, 3–5, are laid in a nest hanging basket-like from a high branch.

GOLDEN ORIOLE *Oriolus oriolus* L 24 Fairly common in parks and old woods. Male unmistakable. Female and juvenile difficult to see as they stay high in the canopy but once spotted cannot be confused with any other European bird. Solitary in behaviour. Flight undulating. The simple song is a flute-like calling of its name: 'or-i-ole'; and it utters harsh, cat-like cries. P

Starlings

(family *Sturnidae*) are medium-sized, short-tailed gregarious birds. Sexes similar. Eggs, 4–6, are laid in holes.

ROSE-COLOURED STARLING *Sturnus roseus* L 22 Common in open country. Irregular in west of breeding range. Rare vagrant to western Europe (particularly in late summer). Adult unmistakable. Juvenile resembles juvenile Starling but is paler, particularly on rump. Gregarious. Mixes with Starling, which it resembles closely in habits and call. V

STARLING *Sturnus vulgaris* L 22 Abundant, especially near human habitation. Nests in boxes and holes in trees, walls, cliffs, etc. Notice short tail, speckled plumage and long bill. Flight silhouette characteristic with short tail and pointed wings. Gregarious. Flies in tight flocks, often numbering thousands of birds. Congregates in large roosts outside breeding season. Song is long, varied, with much mimicry. Call and flight call are squeaky. RW

SPOTLESS STARLING *Sturnus unicolor* L 22 Replaces Starling in south-westernmost Europe. Resembles Starling, but blacker in all plumages, in summer without white spots. Nests colonially. Song resembles that of Starling but is more powerful.

Waxwings

(family *Bombycillidae*) are crested, gregarious, fruit-eating birds. In flight and flock formation resemble Starling. Sexes similar. Build open nest in bush. Clutch, 3–5 eggs.

WAXWING *Bombycilla garrulus* L 18 Common breeding in coniferous woods. In winter also in parks and gardens. Erratic in occurence, with mass movements in certain years. Unmistakable with large crest. Flocks compact. Resembles Starling in flight. Call is trilling 'shree'. W

thrush

Waxwing

Starling

Oriole

Golden Oriole

♀

♂

Rose-coloured Starling

juv.

Starling

juv.

summer

Spotless Starling

winter

summer

winter

Starlings

Waxwing

213

Crows and their allies

(family *Corvidae*) are medium-sized to large, gregarious, omnivorous passerines with heavy bills. Wings are rounded. Sexes are similar. Often chased by other birds. Songs are poor, mostly raucous. Eggs, 3–7, are usually coloured blue-green and speckled.

SIBERIAN JAY *Perisoreus infaustus* L 28 Fairly common. Almost exclusively confined to coniferous woods of the far north. Although resembling Jay in build, the longer tail, weaker bill and greyish-brown and rufous coloration distinguish it. The reddish colour of rump, tail and primaries is characteristic in flight. Flight silhouette resembles that of Jay but notice much longer, tapered tail. When searching for food in trees, movements resemble those of Great Tit. Call is loud, nasal 'pee-ach'.

JAY *Garrulus glandarius* L 36 Common. Prefers deciduous woods and parks. Notice white upper rump, and characteristic flight silhouette with weak, flapping flight on broad wings. Has habit of raising slight crest, giving head a square shape. Very restless, always on the move. Frequently jerks its tail. Usually encountered singly but in some winters in flocks. Often chased by smaller birds. Quite noisy, the call is an unmelodious 'skaaak'. RW

AZURE-WINGED MAGPIE *Cyanopica cyana* L 36 Common but very local in its limited range (which represents a relic population as the main distribution is in China). Found in park-like and wooded landscapes. Builds open nests in small colonies. Unmistakable with black hood, blue wings and long blue tail. Juveniles have short tail. Usually seen in small groups. Flight is like Magpie's but not as heavy. Call is unmelodious 'kree-eek'.

MAGPIE *Pica pica* L 46, tail 23 Very common. Prefers open and park-like landscapes, with scattered trees in which it builds its large domed nest. Often seen near human habitation but usually quite wary. The striking white and black colour pattern and extremely long tail are diagnostic. (Juveniles have short tails.) Flight is characteristic, with fast flapping followed by short glides. Usually seen in pairs; large flocks are rare and only seen at times of migration in northern part of range but may roost in numbers. Call is fast, harsh chatter. R

Siberian Jay

crest raised

Jay

Azure-winged Magpie

Magpie

juv.

NUTCRACKER *Nucifraga caryocatactes* L 33 Fairly common in coniferous forests in the mountainous areas of central Europe. Erratic in occurrence, as Siberian sub-species *N.c. macrorhynchos* (with thinner, longer bill) occasionally invades eastern, central and even western Europe in winters. Speckled plumage and characteristic flight silhouette with short tail and rounded wings make identification easy. Juveniles have fewer spots and are lighter brown. Notice broad black band on white under-side of tail. Flight is heavy. Outside breeding season usually seen in small flocks. Has preference for hazel nuts. Often perches in the open. Call is raucous 'grair'.

V

CHOUGH *Pyrrhocorax pyrrhocorax* L 38 Common in high mountains. Local along steep rocky coasts. Black with very rounded wings and square tail. Long decurved red bill distinguishes it from similar Alpine Chough, which has shorter, yellow bill. Juveniles have orange-red bill; otherwise similar to adult. Often seen in small parties and flocks. Flight strong and elegant and often soars. Nests colonially in crevices and caves. Call is high-pitched 'kiah' resembling Jackdaw, and other shrill, unmusical notes.

R

ALPINE CHOUGH *Pyrrhocorax graculus* L 38 Com-mon in high mountains to the snow limit, going into valleys in winter. Nests colonially in crevices and caves. In winter often seen in mountain villages. Closely resembles Chough but has shorter, yellow bill and shor-ter tail, and is less glossy. Juveniles have darker legs. Bill yellow (orange in Chough). Habits similar to those of Chough but soars more often. Calls include loud, weird trills.

JACKDAW *Corvus monedula* L 33 Very common in old open woods, in villages, towns and around farms. Black plumage, with grey nape and sides of face, distin-guishes it. Walks erect with bobbing movement of head. Head shape characteristic with high front. Flocks can in winter be mistaken for Pigeon flocks but notice slower wing-beats and more rounded wings of individual bird and more loose flock formation. Often soars and per-forms acrobatics in the air. Flight strong and agile. Social in behaviour. Flocks often mix with Rooks, Crows and Starlings in fields. Nests colonially in holes of trees or buildings. Call is rather high-pitched nasal 'jack', often repeated.

RSW

Nutcracker

juv.

Chough

Alpine Chough

Jackdaw

217

ROOK *Corvus frugilegus* L 46 Very common in cultivated fields with groups of trees or small woods. Glossy black plumage, with rather long straight bill and pale area around base of bill, distinguishes it from Carrion Crow. On ground, notice more loosely feathered thighs. Juveniles lack pale area around base of bill and have less prominent iridescence of plumage. Told from Carrion Crow by straighter, weaker bill and slimmer build. Usually seen in flocks. Wings narrower and wing-beats faster than those of Carrion Crow. Nests colonially in groves or wood edges. Social throughout the year and in winter Jackdaws, Starlings and Crows often associate in foraging flocks. In colonies, Jackdaws and sometimes Long-eared Owls are found nesting in unoccupied Rook nests. Call is more nasal but less harsh than Crow's.

RW

CARRION CROW *Corvus corone corone* L 46 Very common in all types of fairly open country, but also in cities. Black with only a little gloss. Best told from Rook by black base of bill (young Rooks also have this), heavier, more curved bill and much harsher crowing call. Generally more stout-looking than Rook and lacks characteristic 'thigh feathers' of this species. In flight broader wings and slower wing-beats distinguish it, even at a distance. Distinguished from Raven by smaller size, smaller bill and square tail. Forms flocks especially for roosting, but does not have same social organization as Rook, and pairs nest separately in trees or sea cliffs.

RW

HOODED CROW *Corvus corone cornix* L 46 Subspecies of Carrion Crow but unmistakable with grey and black plumage. In abundance, habitat and habits similar to Carrion Crow, with which it often mixes and interbreeds where ranges overlap. Birds intermediate between Hooded Crow and Carrion Crow are not uncommon in this zone. The light grey areas are then replaced with much darker colours.

RW

RAVEN *Corvus corax* L 64 Common only in remote mountains and other undisturbed areas. Nests singly on ledges or in trees. Often frequents garbage dumps of mountain villages. Largest passerine. All-black with large bill and long, wedge-shaped tail distinguishing it from Crows as well as birds of prey. It flaps less and soars more than Crow. Often performs acrobatics in flight. Wary. Usually seen singly, in pairs or, at favoured feeding grounds and around carcasses, in small groups. Call is very deep and hoarse croak.

RW

rookery

Rook

imm.

Carrion Crow

Hooded Crow

Raven

Dippers

(family *Cinclidae*) with their strong legs and special oil glands are well adapted to a watery habitat. Sexes similar. Solitary. Eggs, 4–6, are laid in a large, domed, moss nest.

DIPPER *Cinclus cinclus* L 18 Fairly common along swift-flowing mountain streams, in winter sometimes along shores. Notice short tail cocked slightly upward and large white breast patch. Constantly bobs up and down when perched (usually on rocks). Lies low in water when swimming. Flight low and direct. Call is short 'zirb'. Song, which can be heard even in winter, resembles that of Wren with grating notes. Continental populations lack chestnut on the underparts.   R

Wrens

(family *Troglodytidae*) are small, restless, brownish birds with narrow, finely barred, round tails which are often cocked upward. Sexes are similar. Eggs, 5–7, are laid in globular, domed nest.

WREN *Troglodytes troglodytes* L 10 Common among thick undergrowth in woods and gardens, but also found on remote islands and among rocks high in the hills. Small size, tail cocked upward and brown plumage identify it. Keeps low, well in cover. Call is harsh and grating. Song is rapid succession of very high, clear notes and trills.   R

Accentors

(family *Prunellidae*) are small grey and brown thin-billed birds of retiring habits. Solitary ground-feeders. Sexes similar. Clutch of 4–6 blue-green eggs is laid in nest placed in low bush or among rocks.

ALPINE ACCENTOR *Prunella collaris* L 18 Common in high mountains above tree limit. Resembles Dunnock but notice spotted white throat and brown spots on flanks. Call is a short vibrating trill. Warbling song is given from ground or in song-flight.   V

SIBERIAN ACCENTOR *Prunella montanella* L 18 A very rare visitor from Asia to eastern Europe. Notice prominent ochreous stripe over eye.

BLACK-THROATED ACCENTOR *Prunella atrogullaris* L 18 Breeds in Urals. Plumage similar to Siberian Accentor, with black throat.

RADDE'S ACCENTOR *Prunella ocularis* L 15 Breeds in Caucasus. Plumage similar to Siberian Accentor, but lacks rufous flanks and has less cinnamon (greyer) back.

Black-throated Accentor

DUNNOCK *Prunella modularis* L 15 Common in gardens and woods with thick undergrowth but also on scrub-clad hills. Notice slate-coloured head and breast and striped, brown back. Song is short, high-pitched tinkling usually from exposed perch.   RF

Dipper

juv.

swimming

Wren

Alpine Accentor

Siberian Accentor

Dunnock

Warblers and their allies

(family *Muscicapidae*) are divided because of their great variety into subfamilies:

warbler

flycatcher

Warblers (subfamily *Sylviinae*) (pp. 222–47) small, very active, mainly dull-coloured.

Flycatchers (subfamily *Muscicapinae*) (pp. 248–9), small, soft-billed, catch insects in flight.

Thrushes and their allies (subfamily *Turdinae*) (pp. 250–65), small to medium-sized, vary in looks but all juveniles more or less spotted. Divided into small, more uniform groups: wheatears (pp. 250–3), small, mainly grey, black and white birds of open country; Whinchat and Stonechat (pp. 254–5), also of open country; and the rock thrushes (pp. 254–5), larger, brightly coloured, found in mountains. Redstarts (pp. 256–7), warbler-like with red, constantly flicking tails, found in woods, gardens. Bluethroat, Robin and Red-flanked Bluetail (pp. 256–9), small, brightly coloured, found in gardens, bushy and wooded country. The nightingales (pp. 258–9), excellent songsters, rather uniformly brown, found in dense, damp shrubbery. Siberian Rubythroat is closely related. The thrushes (pp. 260–5), medium-sized, usually spotted birds of garden and woods, unlike other *Muscicapidae* gregarious outside breeding season; their songs are mellow.

Bearded Tit (subfamily *Timaliinae*) (pp. 270–1), tit-like bird in its own subfamily, found in reed-beds. Differs from other *Muscicapidae*.

Warblers

(family *Muscicapidae,* subfamily *Sylviinae*), small, very active, mainly dull-coloured songbirds with slender, soft, straight pointed bills. In most species, sexes differ little in plumage making field identification hard. Songs distinctive often very different even between closely related species. Some species only positively identified by song; or in the hand, where wing formulae (relative length and shape of primaries) are important. Mostly solitary in habitats with dense vegetation. Most are insectivorous and migratory migrating mainly at night.

thrush

Warblers are conveniently grouped in genera, those in the same genus usually being similar in habits and habitat as well as in plumage and structure. The number of European species is given after each genus name.

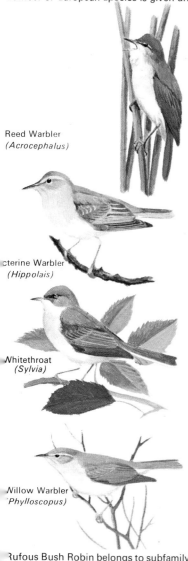

Reed Warbler
(*Acrocephalus*)

cterine Warbler
(*Hippolais*)

Whitethroat
(*Sylvia*)

Willow Warbler
(*Phylloscopus*)

Genus *Cettia* (1 species), Cetti's Warbler. Characteristic large, rounded tail; otherwise like *Acrocephalus*.

Genus *Locustella* (5 species). Characteristic well-graduated tails, brownish colour, mechanical-sounding songs. Live in dense reeds, herbage, thickets.

Genus *Acrocephalus* (9 species) are all brown. Head shape characteristic with high crown, sloping front. Mostly found in reed-beds, marshes. Less skulking than other genera of same habitat. Songs strong, musical, repetitious. Several are good mimics. Moustached Warbler has characteristic habit of cocking tail.

Genus *Cisticola* (1 species), Fantailed Warbler. Brown, striped, with rounded tail. Found in marshes.

Genus *Hippolais* (5 species). Greenish or brownish above, yellow or whitish below. Bill long and straight, crown high with sloping front. Movements slower, more deliberate than in following genera. Found in gardens, parks, woods. Songs very musical, liquid. Perch more upright than other warblers of similar habitat.

Genus *Sylvia* (14 species). More colourful than other warblers; sexes differ in plumage in several species. Bill short but strong, head well rounded. Mostly skulking, usually found in scrub, gardens, parks. Songs liquid, often thrush-like.

Genus *Phylloscopus* (11 species). Small, greenish with short thin bills. Adults have orange or yellow and black pattern on crown.

Genus *Regulus* (2 species). Very small, greenish with orange or bright yellow crown.

Rufous Bush Robin belongs to subfamily *Muscicapinae*.

Some divide warblers into 5 groups corresponding roughly to one or more genera: swamp warblers (*Cettia, Lusciniola, Acrocephalus, Cisticola*); tree warblers (*Hippolais*); scrub warblers (*Sylvia*); leaf warblers (*Phylloscopus*); goldcrests (*Regulus*).

CETTI'S WARBLER *Cettia cetti* L 14 Common in dense low vegetation of ditches, streams and swamps where it stays well hidden and is difficult to see. Notice unstriped, dark, rich chestnut-brown upper side, greyish white underside and white stripe over eye which distinguishes it from all related species. There is a small whitish area below the eyes. Tail wide and rounded, rather untidy-looking. Wings are short and rounded. Flicks tail downward. Bill is thin and pointed. Sexes similar. More often heard than seen. Call is a short 'teck'. Song, which starts and ends abruptly, is very loud and consists of repeated variations of 'cheeweewee', given from well-hidden perch.   V

SAVI'S WARBLER *Locustella luscinioides* L 14 Common but local in dense reed-beds and swamps with scattered bushes. Unstriped reddish olive-brown above, whitish below with pale reddish-brown flanks and poorly pronounced stripe over eye. Darker than the other swamp warblers. Tail long, wide and rounded. Call is a subdued 'tsek'. Song resembles that of Grasshopper Warbler but is shorter, deeper and with a much higher frequency. Song is more monotonous than that of River Warbler, which is broken up into short sections. Song often starts slowly. Sings from exposed perch in reeds or bushes.   S

RIVER WARBLER *Locustella fluviatilis* L 13 Common among dense bushes and other vegetation in moist areas of woods and clearings. Unstriped olive-brown above with warmer brown tail, whitish below with faint spotting on throat, breast and flanks. Has whitish stripe above the eye. Tail wide and rounded. Under tail-coverts are brownish with white tips. Stays well hidden in dense vegetation. Call is harsh. Song, which is given from exposed low perch, is trilling, resembling Grasshopper Warbler, but with individual notes clearly separated. Less monotonous, more broken, than that of Grasshopper and Savi's Warblers. Sings mostly at dusk, even at night.
                                                        V

PADDYFIELD WARBLER *Acrocephalus agricola* L 13 Common in dense vegetation of swamps and lakesides. A very rare autumn visitor to western Europe. Resembles Reed Warbler closely but is paler brown, with more pronounced stripe over eye. Rump and upperparts more rust-coloured than in other *Acrocephalus* species. Wings shorter and more rounded (2nd primary shorter than in Marsh and Reed Warbler) and tail longer. The bill is shorter and stouter than especially similar Blyth's Reed Warbler. Call is described as 'schick'. Song resembles that of Marsh Warbler.   V

singing hidden in vegetation

Cetti's Warbler

cocking tail downwards

Savi's Warbler

singing from top of reeds

River Warbler

singing from top of bush (under tree)

Paddyfield Warbler

Reed Warbler
for comparison

225

tail from above

PALLAS'S GRASSHOPPER WARBLER *Locustella certhiola* L 13 A very rare autumn visitor to north-western Europe from Asia. Found in swamps, marshes and meadows with dense vegetation. Told from Sedge Warbler by less pronounced stripe over eye, darker upper side and dark tail contrasting with lighter rump and lighter underside, usually with a few breast spots. Leg colour is pink but this is difficult to see. Told from Grasshopper Warbler by having reddish, unstreaked rump and greyish tail becoming gradually darker towards the tip, which has narrow whitish vein (difficult to see and not always present). Immatures have less pronounced stripe over eye but more often streaks on breast. Habits resemble those of Grasshopper Warbler; keeps well hidden in dense vegetation. Sharp two-note call. V

GRASSHOPPER WARBLER *Locustella naevia* L 13 Fairly common in dry as well as moist open land with thick vegetation and scattered bushes. Main coloration somewhat varied. Striped olive-brown upper side, faint stripe over eye, whitish underside with a few indistinct breast-spots, and characteristically graduated tail distinguish it. The less distinct stripe over eye in combination with the strongly striped back is best field mark when seen, but best identification feature is song. Very secretive in habits, staying well hidden in dense vegetation and only reluctantly takes to the wing when flushed. Call is short 'tirk'. Song, given mostly at dusk and dawn, from low perch which it leaves at the least disturbance, is a characteristic high-pitched, fast trilling sustained for very long periods, often appearing to vary in volume as the bird turns its head. Savi's Warbler has somewhat similar song, but it is shorter, deeper in tone and of higher frequency. Song of River Warbler is not as monotonous as it is broken up into short sections. S

LANCEOLATED WARBLER *Locustella lanceolata* L 12 Fairly common in dense vegetation of marshes, swamps and the edges of lakes. A rare autumn visitor, to north-western European islands in particular. Resembles Grasshopper Warbler, but is smaller, more densely striped on upper side and has characteristic streaking on breast. Some streaks on flanks and sometimes on throat. Stripe over eye poorly pronounced. As in Grasshopper Warbler, colours are somewhat variable. Habits and voice resemble those of Grasshopper Warbler and the bird stays well hidden among vegetation. It is more skulking and often seen on the ground. Can sometimes be approached very closely.

Pallas's
Grasshopper Warbler

skulking in thick vegetation

imm.

Grasshopper Warbler

adult whitish underparts

adult yellowish underparts

Sedge Warbler for comparison

Lanceolated Warbler

MOUSTACHED WARBLER *Acrocephalus melano-pogon* L 13 Common in reed-beds and swamps with dense vegetation, often together with Sedge Warblers. Resembles Sedge Warbler but is darker brown above especially on the crown with white and more pronounced stripe over eye and white throat. Cocks tail frequently, a habit not seen in any similar species. Sings from perch in high reeds with tail depressed. Song is rapid and varied, resembling that of Sedge Warbler, but includes Nightingale-like 'too-too-too-too' notes, which are not present in song of Sedge Warbler.   V

AQUATIC WARBLER *Acrocephalus paludicola* L 13 Fairly common in dense vegetation of low height and limited extent near open water. Resembles Sedge Warbler but is paler, and has striped head. Stripe over eye is buffish, not white. Stripes on back extend down onto rump. Indistinct stripes on breast and flanks. Tail is more rounded than that of Sedge Warbler. More secretive than Sedge Warbler, staying well hidden in dense vegetation. Song, which resembles that of Sedge Warbler, is also given in short song-flight.   V

SEDGE WARBLER *Acrocephalus schoenobaenus* L 13 Very common in reed-beds, swamps and other dense vegetation along banks of lakes and rivers. Striped upper side and distinct (but not pure white) stripe over eye distinguish it. Is most easily confused with Moustached Warbler (but is paler) and Aquatic Warbler (but stripe on crown of juvenile never pronounced, and never stripes on upper rump). Told from Grasshopper Warbler by more pronounced stripe over eye and less mottled back. Tail is more square than on any of these three species. Juveniles can have faintly spotted breast. It is never streaked on lower rump or upper tail-coverts. Song, which is delivered from perch or almost vertical song-flight, is varied (more so than that of Reed Warbler), repetitive, rapid, and interspersed with many harsh notes.   S

FAN-TAILED WARBLER *Cisticola juncidis* L 10 Fairly common in dense vegetation, usually in wet open country but also in drier localities. Varies considerably in abundance from year to year. Small size, pronounced stripes on crown and upper side, and very short tail with black and white tip distinguish it. Very secretive in behaviour, keeping well hidden except in short undulating song-flight, which is performed even in the middle of the day in the middle of summer when few other birds sing. Song consists of weak repeated 'zit' uttered in flight.   V

Moustached Warbler

bobbing tail

Aquatic Warbler

Sedge Warbler

singing in song-flight
and from top of reeds

Fan-tailed Warbler

song-flight

229

BLYTH'S REED WARBLER *Acrocephalus dumetorum* L 13 Fairly common in swampy scrub, edges of woods and clearings with dense shrubbery. A very rare autumn visitor to north-western Europe. Resembles Marsh Warbler but slightly greyer above; shorter and more rounded wings (2nd primary shorter than that of Marsh Warbler) identify it with certainty. Bill looks longer than Marsh Warbler's. In flight looks short-winged and long-tailed. Tail often flicked. Song resembles Marsh Warbler's but is even more musical and often given from high perch. It is delivered at a more leisurely pace than that of Marsh Warbler. Like the Marsh Warbler it is an expert mimic.   V

MARSH WARBLER *Acrocephalus palustris* L 13 Common in dense, low shrubbery in swamps and other wet locations. Closely resembles Reed Warbler but has pale pink legs and is much more greyish-olive above with cleaner white underparts. Also distinguished by habitat (not in reeds), less secretive behaviour and more musical song, which lacks the harsh notes interspersed in the song of Reed Warbler. An expert mimic. Practically indistinguishable from Blyth's Reed Warbler in field except for faster delivery of song, warmer brown colours and shorter bill. In the hand, told by more pointed wing (2nd primary longer than that of Blyth's Reed Warbler). Sings from low perch.   S

REED WARBLER *Acrocephalus scirpaceus* L 13 Very common in reed-beds and other water edges with dense vegetation. Unstreaked brownish upper side and lack of stripe over eye distinguish it from Sedge Warbler found in similar habitat. More rufous on upper side and more buff on underparts than Marsh Warbler and usually has dark brown legs. In flight the tail is spread out. In the hand, 2nd primary is the same length as that of Marsh Warbler but is more pointed. Song is varied and musical, with repetition of same notes several times, but contains harsh chattering notes. It is not as rapid and varied as that of the Sedge Warbler. Like others of the *Acrocephalus* group it imitates other bird-songs. Sings normally from perch.   S

GREAT REED WARBLER *Acrocephalus arundinaceus* L19 Common but local in reed-beds and in reeds along the edge of lakes. Very large warbler with long bill and thin stripe over eye. Resembles Reed Warbler most but is much larger and the thin eye-stripe is more pronounced and well defined. Less secretive in behaviour than other *Acrocephali*. Perches in the open. Fans tail in flight. Song loud and strident with characteristic 'car' and 'cier' notes. Sings from exposed perch on reed.   V

Wing formulae

Blyth's Reed Warbler

2 5 6

Blyth's Reed

Marsh Warbler

2 3 8 7

Marsh

Marsh Warbler singing

from reed

Reed Warbler

2 4 8 10

eed

Great Reed Warbler

nest

ICTERINE WARBLER *Hippolais icterina* L 13 Common in deciduous woods with undergrowth, parks and gardens. Greenish-grey upper side and usually bright yellow underside, including belly, distinguish it from all other warblers except the very similar Melodious Warbler, which replaces it in south-western Europe. Very long-winged. Legs bluish. Sits more upright than the *Phylloscopi* and is less active. When excited, often raises crown feathers. Call is short metallic 'teck'. Song is varied and sustained but includes many discordant notes. Song perch usually in open. Bill is wide open and points upward when singing.   P

MELODIOUS WARBLER *Hippolais polyglotta* L 13 Common in open deciduous woods with rich undergrowth, parks and gardens, riparian scrub. Resembles Icterine Warbler closely but has shorter wings (tips do not protrude beyond upper tail-coverts) more rounded crown, brownish legs and less prominent wing patch. Head shape differs in having slightly more rounded crown and more angled front. Habits like those of Icterine Warbler. Song is faster, with fewer discordant notes than that of Icterine.   P

OLIVE-TREE WARBLER *Hippolais olivetorum* L 15 Fairly common in olive groves, open oak woods and taller scrub. Large size, brownish-grey upper side, whitish underside, striped wings and long pointed bill distinguish it from all other warblers. The wings are longer than in any other *Hippolais* species. Resembles Icterine Warbler in habits but keeps itself better hidden. Song is loud and slow, resembling that of Great Reed Warbler, and is thrush-like in quality.

OLIVACEOUS WARBLER *Hippolais pallida* L 13 Common in open, damp woods, parks and gardens. Notice brownish-grey upper side with darker wings and tail and whitish underside. Best told from similarly coloured Garden Warbler by typical *Hippolais* build with long, wide bill, angled forehead and short under tail-coverts. Habits resemble those of Icterine Warbler. Song resembles that of Sedge Warbler, rapid with grating notes.   V

BOOTED WARBLER *Hippolais caligata* L 11 Common in bushes and scrub. A rare autumn visitor to western Europe. Resembles Olivaceous but is smaller, has brown upper side, rather pronounced creamy stripe over eye, much shorter bill and buffish wash on sides and flanks. Sometimes has pale tips on tail-feathers. Song resembles that of Sedge Warbler.   V

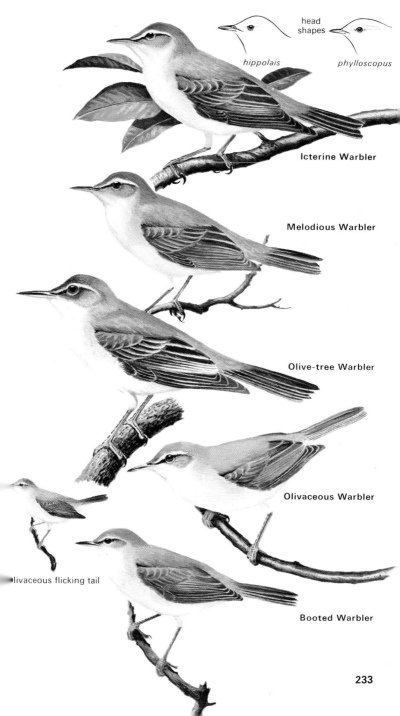

head shapes

hippolais *phylloscopus*

Icterine Warbler

Melodious Warbler

Olive-tree Warbler

Olivaceous Warbler

Olivaceous flicking tail

Booted Warbler

233

BARRED WARBLER *Sylvia nisoria* L 15 Fairly common in open country with shrubs and hedges, wood edges and clearings. Often nests close to Red-backed Shrike. Barring and pale eye easily distinguish adult. The barring is less pronounced in the female, which has grey rather than yellow (male) eye. Juvenile resembles Garden Warbler but is larger, stockier with longer tail and wings, more grey and shows wing-bars, and has dark brown or grey eyes. Keeps well hidden. Call is grating 'tack' resembling that of Garden Warbler, as does song which is given in short song-flight. The characteristic grating call note is included in the song.   P

ORPHEAN WARBLER *Sylvia hortensis* L15 Common in open woods, groves and parks. Large, with dull black hood, distinctly light-coloured iris, white outer tail-feathers and white underside. Somewhat similarly coloured Sardinian Warbler is much smaller. Juvenile resembles juvenile Barred Warbler but.has comparatively shorter tail and bill and less distinct wing-bars. Call is sharp 'tack'. Song is loud, thrush-like in the south-eastern European subspecies *S.h. crassirostris.* In the south-western European subspecies *S.h. hortensis* the song is much more monotonous, consisting of alternating high and low notes.   V

GARDEN WARBLER *Sylvia borin* L 14 Common in gardens, parks and open woods with plentiful undergrowth. Brown upper side and greyish-white underside; legs grey-brown. Has no specific characteristics. Most easily confused with Olivaceous, Booted and juvenile Barred Warbler. Notice the very rounded shape of head distinguishing from most other brown warblers. Stays well hidden in foliage even when singing. Song is musical, mellow and liquid, resembling that of Blackcap but longer and more subdued. Call is sharp 'tack'.   SP

BLACKCAP *Sylvia atricapilla* L 14 Common in parks and woods with rich undergrowth. Small black cap of male and reddish brown cap of female diagnostic. Juveniles resemble female. Has no white on tail. Less secretive in behaviour than Garden Warbler, but often stays well hidden. Sturdy and able to endure quite severe cold. Often eats berries. Sings from well covered perch. Song is a short, mellow musical warble of rising strength, less subdued and uniformly liquid than that of Garden Warbler. Call is short mechanical 'tack'.   SW

song-flight

imm.

Barred Warbler

Orphean Warbler

singing from
middle of bush

imm.

Garden Warbler

singing from undergrowth

♂

♀

Blackcap

singing from
middle of bush

WHITETHROAT *Sylvia communis* L 14 Very common in scrub, hedges, bushy edges and clearings of woods and gardens. White throat, grey (male) or brown (female and juvenile) hood, light brown wings and rather long tail with white outer edges and pale legs characterize it. Best told from Lesser Whitethroat by longer tail and brownish wings. Very active, constantly on the move in bushes and shrubbery. Call is rasping 'tze'. Song, which is usually given in characteristic low song-flight but also from covered perch, is a fast, short, rather high-pitched warble. Usually sings longer into the summer than most other warblers. SP

LESSER WHITETHROAT *Sylvia curruca* L 13 Common and very local in thorny bushes in mainly rocky woods and gardens. Resembles Whitethroat but is slightly smaller with shorter tail, grey-brown above with grey-brown wings, dark ear-coverts and dark legs. The dark ear-coverts can give it a hooded appearance, but this is not nearly as apparent as that of the Sardinian and Rüppell's Warbler. Breast is whitish, not pink as in Spectacled Warbler. Usually stays well hidden in bushes and foliage of trees. Call is a short 'tack'. Song, which is given from hidden perch or while moving about, consists of two parts. First a subdued warble, then a fast, rattling repetition of 'chik-ke' notes. SP

RÜPPELL'S WARBLER *Sylvia ruepelli* L 14 Uncommon and very local in thorny bushes in mainly rocky areas. Male easily distinguished by pitch-black cap and throat with narrow white separating line, grey upper side and white outer tail-feathers. Female lacks black throat but has underside of black cap strongly demarked by white line. Brilliantly red eye and leg are obvious in both male and female. Call is a loud 'chat' repeated several times. Song resembles that of Sardinian Warbler but is not as hurried, although faster than that of the Dartford Warbler. It is delivered from a perch or very high song-flight somewhat similar to that of Tree Pipit but more twisting.

SARDINIAN WARBLER *Sylvia melanocephala* L 13 Very common in shrubs and bushes in open and mountainous country, but also in woods with undergrowth. Solid black cap of male, and easily visible red eye-ring of male and female are characteristic. Orphean Warbler is much larger. Very active. Fans tail in flight. Call consists of loud chattering notes. Song, which is usually given in Whitethroat-like song-flight, is long, hurried and musical interspersed with chattering notes. V

song-flight

singing from perch

♂

♀

Whitethroat

Lesser Whitethroat

singing in hedgerow

♂

♀

song in flight
and perched

Rüppell's Warbler

♂

♀

song in flight
and perched

Sardinian Warbler

juv.

237

MÉNÉTRIES' WARBLER *Sylvia mystacea* L 13 Common in shrubs (tamarisk), often in rocky areas but also in river valleys. Not recorded in western Europe. Greyish-brown upper side. Male has black cap blending into dark back. Eye is dark red with yellow eye-ring. Underside whitish with buffish breast and wash on flanks. Tail rounded. Female is more brown on upper parts. Very active, keeping well hidden in bushes. In flight tail is carried high. Call is a sharp repeated 'tart'. Song resembles that of Whitethroat but is more musical and variable.

SUBALPINE WARBLER *Sylvia cantillans* L 13 Common in low bushes of dry scrubland, and in wood clearings. Grey above, with orange throat, breast and flanks clearly separated by white moustachial stripe. Throat and breast of female paler and browner. Resembles Spectacled Warbler but underside more orange and wings grey rather than light brown. Juveniles similar to female. Best distinguished from juvenile Sardinian Warbler by paler colours and from juvenile Spectacled Warbler by the lack of the conspicuous brown wing patch characteristic of that species. Skulking in behaviour, keeping well hidden in the bushes. Characteristically raises and spreads tail. Call is short, sharp 'teck'. Song, often given in song-flight, is very musical, resembling that of Whitethroat without the harsh notes. Not as fast as that of Sardinian Warbler.   V

DESERT WARBLER *Sylvia nana* L 11 Common in bushy steppes and deserts. A very rare autumn visitor to western Europe. Resembles Garden Warbler but is much lighter in colour. Sexes similar. Very small, sandy-coloured upper side with more rufous rump and tail, whitish underside with no distinguishing marks other than rather prominent, white outer tail-feathers. Stays well hidden in bushes and flies low over the ground from one patch of scrub to the next. Call is short trill. Song is a low series of repeated 'tee' notes.   V

SPECTACLED WARBLER *Sylvia conspicillata* L 13 Common in open dry localities with shrubs. Resembles small Whitethroat but has narrow white eye-ring and darker, more reddish breast and paler legs. Told from Subalpine Warbler by conspicuous brown area on wings and by buffish rather than orange breast. Females told by conspicuous brown area on wing. Legs are paler than those of any other *Sylvia* species. Secretive in behaviour. Call is rattling. Song is a short high-pitched, rather monotonous and deliberate warble given from exposed perch or long song-flight.   V

Ménétries' Warbler

♀

♂

Subalpine Warbler

♂

♀

Desert Warbler

♂

song in flight
and perched

♀

Spectacled Warbler

239

DARTFORD WARBLER *Sylvia undata* L 13 Fairly common in dry, bushy localities in Mediterranean region, rarer on heaths with scrub, especially gorse, in north-western Europe. Long-tailed, very dark brown above, reddish brown below. Male has richer tints than female. Keeps well hidden. Darker than any other warbler except for similar Marmora's Warbler which has a dark grey, not reddish breast. In winter sometimes found in small flocks. Usually holds tail cocked upwards and flicks it frequently. Flight low and weak with characteristic movements of tail. Wing-beats fast. Call consists of hard and loud 'chir' and 'tuck' notes. Song resembles that of Whitethroat but is feebler and includes fewer rasping notes. It consists of short phrases interrupted by pauses of varying length. Can be heard singing throughout the year. Song is not as rapid as that of Sardinian Warbler. Often given in short song-flight. In very hard winters it suffers great losses in numbers, particularly in the north of its range where it is less common. In southern England it almost disappeared completely in the severe winter of 1962/63. R

MARMORA'S WARBLER *Sylvia sarda* L 13 Fairly common in dry bushy localities, often in rocky country. Resembles Dartford Warbler but has grey, not brown-red underside. Female is browner on upper side with lighter underside. Juveniles are similar to females except for even lighter underside. Long tail and dark colours distinguish it from all other warblers. In habits it resembles Dartford Warbler. Extremely difficult to catch sight of as it stays well hidden in the scrub. Call is short 'tick'. Song, which is given in short song-flight, does not resemble that of Dartford Warbler, being more mellow, weaker and slurred.

RUFOUS BUSH ROBIN *Cercotrichas galactotes* L 15 Comparatively rare in open, dry, bushy localities: vineyards, hedges and gardens in southern Spain, particularly cactus hedges. Two distinct subspecies occur in Europe. *C.g. galactotes* of south-western Europe has reddish-brown crown, neck and back, which in the south-eastern European *C.g. syriacus* are much paler sandy coloured. Characterizing both subspecies is the long tail with striking black and white markings at tip. Less secretive than other warblers, often seen perched in the open with tail raised and fanned, showing the characteristic pattern. Often seen on the ground. Call is a sharp 'tack'. Song consists of clear flute-like ascending notes given in an even rhythm. Given from open perch or song-flight. Sings persistently.

song in flight

Dartford Warbler

imm.

and perched

Marmora's Warbler

imm.

Rufous Bush Robin

western
(red back)

song in flight

eastern
(brown back)

d perched on telephone wire

WILLOW WARBLER *Phylloscopus trochilus* L 11 Abundant in open woods, usually deciduous but also coniferous, with heavy undergrowth, and in tree-clad heathland, parks and large gardens. Plain greenish above, without wing-bars, but some individuals are browner, resembling Chiffchaff. Juveniles have more yellow underside. Usually has lighter leg colour than Chiffchaff. In hand, lack of margination of 6th primary distinguishes it from Chiffchaff. Like the other *Phylloscopi* it is very active and restless. Call is plaintive 'fooeed'. Song is a musical, liquid and soft, descending warble.   SP

CHIFFCHAFF *Phylloscopus collybita* L 11 Very common in deciduous and coniferous woods with undergrowth, and woodland edges. Prefers higher trees than Willow Warbler. Resembles Willow Warbler closely but is browner, usually has blackish legs (but they can be light) and in the hand notice margination of 6th primary. Call is plaintive 'hooeed'. Song is rather monotonous repeated 'chiff-chaff', combined in various ways, sometimes with grating introductory notes. Very active, often flicking wings. The most sturdy *Phylloscopus,* arriving at breeding grounds before the others. RSP

WOOD WARBLER *Phylloscopus sibilatrix* L 13 Common in mature deciduous and mixed woods. Bright yellow throat and breast and yellow area on wings distinguish it. Underside is white. Very active. Call is liquid 'diu'. Song, often given in song-flight, is characteristic series of 'sip' notes repeated at an accelerating rate. Second song, often combined with the trill, is a series of lengthened call-notes.   S

GREEN WARBLER *Phylloscopus nitidus* L 11 Common in mountainous woods in the Caucasus. Very rarely observed elsewhere in Europe. Resembles Arctic and Greenish Warblers but has white underside with yellow suffusion on breast. Upper side is more green (less yellow). Song resembles Willow Warbler's. Call is not as mellow as Willow Warbler's.

DUSKY WARBLER *Phylloscopus fuscatus* L 11 Very rare Asiatic autumn visitor, resembles Radde's Warbler very closely but has more slender bill, darker upper side and more rusty colour at rear end of stripe over eye and on flanks. Usually found in damp areas with rich undergrowth. Skulking in behaviour. Call is described as 'tak'.

RADDE'S WARBLER *Phylloscopus schwarzi* L 13 Very rare autumn visitor to western Europe from Asiatic breeding grounds. Found in scrub and trees. Olive-brown upper side, yellow-brown flanks, stout bill and prominent stripe over eye, whiter behind the eye.

Willow Warbler

Willow Warbler

2 5 6

Chiffchaff

Chiffchaff

7 8

Wood Warbler

Green Warbler

Dusky Warbler

Radde's Warbler

243

BONELLI'S WARBLER *Phylloscopus bonelli* L 11
Common in mountainous mixed and coniferous woods,
but also sometimes found in similar habitats of lower
elevation. A rare autumn visitor to north-western Europe.
Pale greenish-brown upper side with greyish head and
mantle and silky yellowish patch on wings and rump,
and white underside are characteristic. Juveniles have
less contrast between back and rump than adults. Active,
usually keeping well hidden in foliage. Call is a rather
plaintive 'hoo-eet'. Song resembles trill of Wood Warbler
but is not accelerated. It consists of two different phrases
of different pitch and length.   V

YELLOW-BROWED WARBLER *Phylloscopus inor-
natus* L 10 Rare but regular autumn visitor to north-
western Europe from Asiatic range. On migration found
in woods as well as bushes. Very small with green upper
side, white underside, pale yellow stripe over eye and two
distinct wing-bars. Sometimes has faint yellow stripe
through crown. Sometimes shows conspicuous yellow
patch on primaries. Resembles Willow Warbler in habits,
and often associates itself with other migrating *Phylloscopus* species and tits. Call resembles that of Willow
Warbler but is more high-pitched and sharp, sometimes
consisting of two syllables: 'weeesp'.   P

ARCTIC WARBLER *Phylloscopus borealis* L 12
Common in damp birch and mixed woods and scrub. A
very rare autumn visitor to western Europe. Rather large
but slim *Phylloscopus* with one wing bar well-defined, a
second hardly visible, well-marked and long yellowish
stripe over eye, white underside and pale legs. Juveniles
are not as bright green as adults. The bill is long. Arctic
can be confused with Greenish Warbler but notice
distinct stripe over eye and pale legs. Very active, flicking
wings in the manner of Willow Warbler. Usually keeps
well hidden in the canopy. Call is a metallic 'zick'. Song is
short, high trill.   V

GREENISH WARBLER *Phylloscopus trochiloides*
L 11 Common in deciduous and mixed woods, particularly near hedges and clearings, parks and gardens.
Resembles Willow Warbler and Chiffchaff but has more
distinct stripe over eye and a narrow (sometimes invisi-
ble) wing-bar. Arctic Warbler also has one wing-bar but
has paler legs and more pronounced stripe over eye. Very
active, but usually keeps well hidden in the foliage. Call
is a high-pitched 'tsi-lee'. Song is short and loud, starting
with a few calls, then merging with a trill followed by a
short high-pitched warble.   V

Bonelli's Warbler

Willow Warbler
for comparison

Yellow-browed Warbler

Arctic Warbler

Greenish Warbler

245

PALLAS'S WARBLER *Phylloscopus proregulus* L 9
Very rare, late autumn (October and November) visitor
to north-western Europe from Asiatic breeding grounds.
Mainly found in coniferous and mixed woods, but also
in bushes and scrub. Very small, resembling Firecrest,
but with more black on head and prominent, bright
yellow upper rump (diagnostic). Yellow crown stripe is
not always visible but is evident when the bird is seen
head on. Yellow rump is particularly prominent in flight,
especially when the bird hovers briefly to pick insects off
leaves as is its habit. Best told from somewhat similar
Yellow-browed Warbler by yellow rump and more
prominent yellow crown stripe (a pale stripe is sometimes present on Yellow-browed Warbler). Sometimes
associates with foraging flocks of goldcrests and tits.
Habits resemble those of Goldcrest, including fluttering
among the foliage for insects. Call is a high-pitched
'tweet', quite unlike any call of Goldcrest or Firecrest.

V

GOLDCREST *Regulus regulus* L 9 Very common in
coniferous and mixed woods, outside breeding season
also in hedges and scrub. Smallest European bird. Generally green colours distinghish it from small tits. Adult
has black edge to yellow and orange (male only) crown.
Juvenile lacks characteristic crown pattern. In all plumages told from Firecrest by lack of stripes over and
through eye. Juvenile told from *Phylloscopus* warblers
by small size, rather plump body and very small, thin bill.
Very active, usually keeping high in trees and constantly
fluttering among the branches. Outside breeding season
usually seen in small flocks, sometimes together with
tits. Wing action very rapid, flight weak. Call is extremely
thin and high-pitched. Song is of similar quality ending
in short warble. Basket nest of moss hangs from branch,
usually of conifer.   RP

FIRECREST *Regulus ignicapillus* L 9 Common in
deciduous, coniferous and mixed woods and parks.
Resembles Goldcrest but in all plumages told from it by
pronounced white stripe over eye and black eye-stripe.
Colour generally looks clearer than in Goldcrest. Told
from Pallas' Warbler by the lack of the yellow rump.
Habits resemble those of Goldcrest. Call is less high-
pitched than that of Goldcrest and song is a monotonous, accelerating repetition of 'zis' notes. Nest is
similar to that of Goldcrest, built in coniferous or deciduous trees, but also sometimes in bushes or tall creepers.
RW

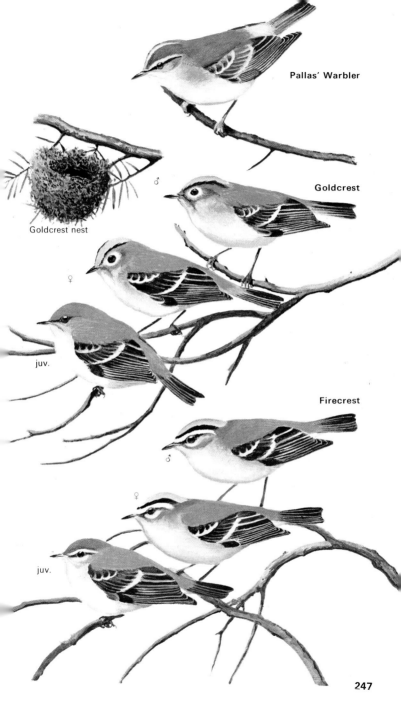

Pallas' Warbler

Goldcrest

Goldcrest nest

♂

♀

juv.

Firecrest

♂

♀

juv.

247

Flycatchers

(family *Muscicapidae,* subfamily *Muscicapinae*) are small, slender-billed, with prominent bristles by the gape. Perch in an upright position, usually in the open and catch insects in a fast swoop, often returning to same perch. Build in holes or on ledges. Lay 4–9 blue or spotted eggs.

PIED FLYCATCHER *Ficedula hypoleuca* L 13 Common in open, usually deciduous or mixed, woodland and park-like habitats with little undergrowth. Females have brown and white plumage almost indistinguishable from female Collared Flycatcher but are usually more brown above. Collared males have more white on wing, while black and white Pied male lacks pale collar. Typical flycatcher in habits but does not usually return to same perch after aerial sally. Call a short 'wit', emphasised when alarmed. Song rather unmelodious but variable stream of 'cher' notes. SP

COLLARED FLYCATCHER *Ficedula albicollis* L 13 Common in open woods, parks and gardens. Male has white neck-band and pale upper rump. Grey-brown female almost indistinguishable from Pied. Song is a repeated 'zoet'. Call is a hard 'teck'. V

SEMI-COLLARED FLYCATCHER *Ficedula semi-torquata* L 13 Breeds less commonly in the Balkans, on Crimea, and in the Caucasus. Closely related to the Collared Flycatcher (calls similar) and females inseparable in the field. Male on the other hand resembles Pied but has more white in the wing (white-tipped median wing-coverts) and often more white on sides of neck.

RED-BREASTED FLYCATCHER *Ficedula parva* L 12 Common in woods and parks, mainly deciduous. Prominent white patches on tail-feathers of brownish bird distinguish it. Male has bright orange throat throughout the year. Cocks and flicks tail very frequently. Much more warbler- than flycatcher-like in habits. Call is chattering but soft. Song is loud and trilling, reminiscent of Willow Warbler's. P

SPOTTED FLYCATCHER *Muscicapa striata* L 14 Common in open woods, parks and gardens. Brownish-grey with striped breast. Sexes similar. Typical flycatcher in stance and behaviour. Flicks tail frequently. Call is a sharp 'zit'. Song is a repetition of three or four call notes, mainly heard soon after arrival in spring. SF

BROWN FLYCATCHER *Muscicapa latirostris* L 12 Very rare autumn visitor to north-western Europe from Asia. Typical flycatcher without tail, wing or breast markings and with a narrow white ring around eye. Sexes similar. Keeps more hidden than other flycatchers. V

pipit

shrike

warbler

flycatcher

Pied catching insects

♂

Semi-collared Flycatcher

ed flicking tail up

ollared lycatcher

♂

♀

Pied Flycatcher

Red-breasted Flycatcher

♂

♀

tching insects m ground

Brown Flycatcher

Spotted Flycatcher

Wheatears

Wheatears are small terrestrial birds found in bare, open country. Varying degrees of white on tail characterize the different species. Male more brightly coloured than female. Often perches on rocks or low bushes. Bows and flicks tail frequently. Very active. Sometimes catches insects flycatcher-style. Clutch of 4–6 bluish eggs in nest built in hole in ground or among rocks.

European wheatears can be confusing, especially the females. The characteristic distribution of black and white on tail (ratio between length of black on edge of tail to black on centre of tail) is given below together with the general characteristics of male and female and their distribution in summer.

	Male	Female	Ratio between length of black on edge and centre of tail	Distribution
Wheatear (*O.oenanthe*)	Black ear-coverts, grey back	Prototype	1:2	All of Europe
Isabelline Wheatear (*O.isabellina*)	As female	Large, pale	1:1$\frac{1}{3}$	N.E. Greece and Turkey
Pied Wheatear (*O.pleschanka*)	Black breast, black back	As Black-eared	1:3	Eastern Black Sea coast
Black-eared Wheatear (*O.hispanica*)	Dimorphic: black ear-coverts (and throat), buff back	Dark wings	1:4	Mediterranean countries
Desert Wheatear (*O.deserti*)	Black throat, sandy back	As Black-eared	1:1	Vagrant
Black Wheatear (*O.leucura*)	Black	Brownish black	1:2	Iberian peninsula, S. France

WHEATEAR *Oenanthe oenanthe* L 15 Common in open country, preferring areas with sparse vegetation. The most widespread and numerous of the wheatears. Tail in all plumages has evenly cut black tip with long black central feathers. Male distinguished by a steel-grey back and crown in summer. Females resemble other female wheatears but have characteristic tail pattern and more pronounced white stripe over eye. Juveniles resemble females but are spotted. Greenland subspecies *Oenanthe oenanthe leucorrhoa,* which migrates through western Europe, is slightly larger with brighter colours. Call is a hard 'tack'. Song, given from perch or short song-flight, is a short warble of lark-like quality. SP

ISABELLINE WHEATEAR *Oenanthe isabellina* L 16 Common in open steppes and low hills. Large, uniform sandy colour with less contrasting wings than other wheatears. Tail pattern resembles Wheatear's, but dark parts paler. Facial pattern not pronounced. Rather inactive. Call is loud, metallic, piping 'wheet'. Song contains whistling notes. Often imitates other birds. V

wagtail

pipit

Whinchat

Wheatear

Wheatear

♂

♀

juv.

winter

Isabelline Wheatear

♂

PIED WHEATEAR *Oenanthe pleschanka* L 15 Common but irregular on stony steppes, and along sea and river cliffs. Black back clearly distinguishes the male from Black-eared Wheatear male. Outer part of white on tail is bordered with black. Females resemble Black-eared females closely but are more earth-brown on back. Often perches high, dropping to the ground like a shrike to obtain insects. Very lively. Not found as much on flat ground as Wheatear. Call is hard 'tack'. Song is lark-like with whistling notes, given in phrases of varying length, usually from perch or song-flight.　　　　　　　　　　V

BLACK-EARED WHEATEAR *Oenanthe hispanica* L 15 Very common in open rocky and sandy habitats. In all plumages it has a little more white on tail than Wheatear. Males have two forms, a black-throated and a white-throated. Black-throated form distinguished from Pied Wheatear by buff back; from male Desert Wheatear by richer buff colour of back and extent of white along edges of tail. Females told from Wheatear by darker ear-coverts and paler back with contrasting darker wings. Female of south-eastern European subspecies more earth-brown on back and practically indistinguishable from Pied Wheatear female. Call consists of hard 'tack', usually followed by a whistling note. Song, which is given from perch or song-flight and rather more often than Wheatear's, resembles Wheatear's but is louder and higher-pitched. Sometimes imitates the song of other species.　　　　　　　　　　V

Finsch's Wheatear

FINSCH'S WHEATEAR *Oenanthe finschii* L 13 Breeds in deserts of Caucasian region. Resembles black-throated form of Black-eared Wheatear, but has pale grey upperparts and more black on throat.

Red-tailed Wheatear

RED-TAILED WHEATEAR *Oenanthe xanthoprymna* L 14 Breeds on western shore of Caspian Sea. Differs from other wheatears by dark brown crown, nape and back and rufous rump.

DESERT WHEATEAR *Oenanthe deserti* L 15 Very rare autumn visitor from African and Asiatic breeding grounds. Frequents dry open habitats. Resembles black-throated form of Black-eared Wheatear, but only rump is white and wings are not as solid black. Back is more sandy coloured, not as rich buff. Female resembles female Black-eared and Pied Wheatear but has no white on edge of tail. Call is a hoarse whistle.　　　　　V

BLACK WHEATEAR *Oenanthe leucura* L 18 Common in dry rocky mountains and seashores. Largest of the wheatears, in all plumages uniformly black or blackish except for white rump and part of outer tail-feathers. Flight is heavy. Call is a high-pitched 'pee-pee-pee-pee'. Song is a rich, short warble resembling that of Blue Rock Thrush but not as loud.　　　　　V

Pied Wheatear

Black-eared Wheatear

black-throated form

Desert Wheatear

Black Wheatear

253

WHINCHAT *Saxicola rubetra* L 13 Common in open heaths and grassland with bushes, and occasionally in fields. Notice prominent stripe over eye of male. In all plumages told from Stonechat by white base of outer tail-feathers (prominent in flight). This white area is much smaller than that of the Red-breasted Flycatcher, which is quite different in build and habits. Perches upright, usually on top of a low bush, thistle or other exposed perch. Often bobs tail. Call starts with a musical 'due', continuing with hard 'teck, teck'. Song, which is given from perch or song-flight, is a short, high-pitched warble, often with some notes imitating other birds. SP

STONECHAT *Saxicola torquata* L 13 Common in open heaths and grassland with bushes, usually preferring rougher country than Whinchat. Black hood of male diagnostic. Has no white on tail, distinguishing females and juveniles from generally paler Whinchat. Streaked white rump only on male. Stockier-looking and more upright when perched than Whinchat, which it resembles in habits. Head seems large and very rounded. Call consists of sharp 'teck' notes. Song, which is given from perch or in song-flight, consists of short, repeated, rather high-pitched notes. RS

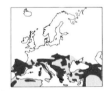

ROCK THRUSH *Monticola saxatilis* L 19 Common in rocky and mountainous areas with or without scattered trees usually at high altitudes but sometimes lower. Male unmistakable with blue, white and red pattern. Female is strongly mottled all over and may have a suggestion of white on the back. Colours of winter male are mostly obscured. In all plumages distinguished by orange-red tail. Retiring in habits, often hiding among rocks. Usually seen singly or in pairs. Call is a short 'tack'. Song, which is given from open perch or in song-flight, is a musical, fluting warble, but is very variable. V

BLUE ROCK THRUSH *Monticola solitarius* L 20 Common in sunny, rough mountains with sparse vegetation, more often at lower altitudes than Rock Thrush. Male unmistakable with dark blue plumage. In winter looks blacker. Female barred, resembling female Rock Thrush but with dark brown, not chestnut, tail. Shy and retiring in habits. Like Rock Thrush it typically dives among rocks when approached. Usually seen singly or in pairs. Call is a hard 'tick'. Song is loud, musical and thrush-like. It is usually given from perch on rock or song-flight.

juv.

Whinchat

♀

♂

Stonechat

♀

juv.

♂

Rock Thrush

♂

♀

Blue Rock Thrush

♂

♀

255

REDSTART *Phoenicurus phoenicurus* L 14 Common in parks, gardens and open deciduous and mixed woods, rarely in coniferous. Male unmistakable. Female is grey-brown above, buff below. Juvenile like young Robin. In all plumages reddish tail, constantly jerked, distinguishes it from all but much darker Black Redstart. Active, often catches insects in flycatcher fashion. Nests in holes or on ledges. Call is plaintive 'fu-et'. Song is short, melodious, Robin-like warble ending in a short twitter.   SP

GÜLDENSTÄDT'S REDSTART *Phoenicurus erythrogaster* L 18 Resident of the Caucasus, found in the high mountains in summer, lower in winter. Nests in rock crevices. Resembles Redstart, but male has black back, creamy crown and white wing patch. Female resembles Redstart female but is considerably larger.

BLACK REDSTART *Phoenicurus ochruros* L 14 Common in mountains, towns, villages and along rocky coasts. Very dark plumage, with reddish tail, distinguishes male from all other species. Females and immatures resemble Redstart but are much darker with greyish underparts. Resembles Redstart in habits. Nests in holes. In England nests in crevices in old buildings and bomb-sites. Call is a series of 'tic' notes. Song, usually given from perch on building or rock, is a short, fast, simple edition of that of Redstart, often ending with a peculiar rattle.   RSWP

BLUETHROAT *Luscinia svecica* L 14 Fairly common in scrub along edges of swamps, lakes and streams and on heaths. In all plumages distinguished by reddish patches at base of tail, conspicuously shown by frequent flicking and cocking of tail. Northern subspecies *Luscinia svecica svecica*, nesting in Scandinavia and Russia, has red centre of blue bib whereas southern subspecies *L.s. cyanecula* has white centre. Stays well hidden. Call is a short 'tack'. Song, often given in song-flight, is varied, gentle, musical warbling, rather high-pitched.   P

ROBIN *Erithacus rubecula* L 14 Very common in woods with undergrowth, parks and gardens. Adults told by orange breast and brown tail. Told from Red-breasted Flycatcher male by more extensive and well-defined red breast and lack of white on tail. Mottled juvenile told by dark brown tail. Juvenile Nightingale is similarly mottled but has longer tail, slimmer build. Spends much time on the ground. Visits bird feeders. Often flicks wings and tail. Often very tame. Call is series of 'tic' notes. Song, given from low perch, is series of fast, rather high-pitched, warbling notes, usually starting subdued.   RSWP

catching
insect in
flight

flicking
tail

Redstart

♂

Black Redstart

♀

♂

Bluethroat

♂
white-
spotted
form

juv.

red-spotted
form

♀

♂

Robin

juv

257

RED-FLANKED BLUETAIL *Tarsiger cyanurus* L 14
Fairly common in deep, swampy, coniferous woods and thickets. A very rare autumn visitor to north-western Europe. In all plumages has bluish-grey rump and tail. Female and immatures have white throat contrasting with greyish breast. No other European bird of its size has blue tail. Adults have prominent orange flanks somewhat paler in female than male. Immature heavily spotted but also has blue tail. In habits resembles Redstart but is seen more on the ground. Secretive, keeping well hidden in scrub. Sings from exposed perch. Call is a short 'teck teck'. Song is very loud, musical and thrush-like.   V

NIGHTINGALE *Luscinia megarhynchos* L 17 Common in swampy thickets, wet undergrowth of woods and parks. Sometimes in drier thickets and woods. Uniformly brown with more chestnut tail in all plumages, including mottled juvenile. This distinguishes juvenile from similarly mottled juvenile Robin which has shorter, darker tail and is less slim. Rather large and long-tailed. Almost indistinguishable in the field from Thrush Nightingale but has more clean brown back, redder tail, and never has barring on breast; in the hand, told by short 1st primary but long 2nd primary. Very secretive, keeping well hidden in bushes. Much more often heard than seen. Call is a liquid 'hu-eet'. Song is very loud and musical with characteristic series of deep 'jug' notes and drawn-out 'pins'. Sings from depth of thickets, often at night.   S

THRUSH NIGHTINGALE *Luscinia luscinia* L 17 Common in swampy thickets and wet undergrowth of woods and parks. Resembles Nightingale closely but can sometimes be identified by greyer back and tail and finely barred breast (difficult to see). In the hand told from Nightingale by long 1st primary, but shorter 2nd primary (2nd shorter than 4th in Thrush Nightingale; longer in Nightingale). Song resembles that of Nightingale and is even louder, but less musical. Sings from well-hidden perch, often at night.   V

WHITE-THROATED ROBIN *Irania gutturalis* L 16 Breeds in rocky scrubs in Caucasus. Male dark above (almost black) with white supercilium and throat and rufous underparts. Female paler and less rufous.

White-throated Robin

SIBERIAN RUBYTHROAT *Luscinia calliope* L 14 Common in coniferous woods with rich undergrowth. A very rare straggler to south-western Europe. Builds covered nest on the ground. Facial pattern of male unmistakable with bright red throat, white stripe over eye and moustachial stripe. Female told from other brownish soft-billed non-warblers by pronounced whitish stripe over eye and white throat. Juvenile resembles female but is more spotted. Distinguished from juvenile Bluethroat by lack of chestnut in tail. In behaviour resembles Robin. Song is loud and musical.   V

Red-flanked Bluetail

juv

Nightingale

Nightingale

2 5 6

Thrush Nightingale

Thrush
Nightingale

2 4

Siberian Rubythroat

Thrushes

form a homogeneous group within the subfamily *Turdinae*. Three genera comprise this group: *Zoothera*, with two European species: White's Thrush and Siberian Thrush; *Catharus*, to which belong three vagrants from North America, Grey-cheeked Thrush, Swainson's Thrush and Hermit Thrush; and the largest, *Turdus*, to which the rest of our thrushes belong.

Thrushes are medium-sized birds with rather slender bills, long wings and tails. All are spotted as juveniles, most also in adult plumage. They are often seen standing or running on the ground. They all eat worms, insects and fruit. Most thrushes migrate at night. Outside the breeding season many occur in loose flocks. They build open, cup-shaped nests in trees or bushes. Clutch, 3–6 eggs.

GREY-CHEEKED THRUSH *Catharus minimus* L 19
A very rare autumn visitor to western Europe from North America. Small, greyish brown, with grey face and without distinct eye-ring. Call is a rather nasal 'vee-a'. V

SWAINSON'S THRUSH *Catharus ustulatus* L 18
A rare visitor to western Europe from North America. Small, greyish brown, with buffish face and rather distinct buffish eye-ring. Call is a high-pitched 'whit'.
V

HERMIT THRUSH *Catharus guttatus* L 17 Very rare visitor from North America. Resembles Swainson's Thrush, but has clearly rusty tail which is slowly raised and lowered.

EYE-BROWED THRUSH *Turdus obscurus* L 19
A rare autumn visitor to Europe from Asia. Male has grey head, neck and breast with distinct white stripe over eye, olive-brown back and buff flanks. Female is browner, with spots on flanks. Call resembles that of Song Thrush.
V

DUSKY THRUSH *Turdus naumanni eunomus* L 24
A rare autumn visitor to Europe from Asia. Very dark with conspicuous stripe over eye, rusty area on wings (both sides) and rump, and boldly barred or spotted breast and flanks. Call resembles that of Fieldfare. V

NAUMANN'S THRUSH *Turdus naumanni naumanni* L 24 Same species as Dusky Thrush. A rare autumn visitor to Europe from Asia. Grey-brown plumage above, with buffish stripe over eye and reddish breast and tail, distinguishes male. Female is brown with more spotted breast. Call resembles that of Fieldfare.

shrike

Skylark

Starling

thrush

Grey-cheeked Thrush

Swainson's Thrush

Eye-browed Thrush

Dusky Thrush

Naumann's Thrush

261

RING OUZEL *Turdus torquatus* L 24 Fairly common in rocky country with bushes or scattered trees. White crescent-shaped breast-band identifies adult male. Also notice less pitch-black appearance (scaled with white) than Blackbird, with lighter, silvery area on wing. Juvenile more spotted than juvenile Blackbird. On migration mixes with other thrushes. Has clacking call and, when flushed, gives Blackbird-like alarm. Song, given from exposed perch, is usually a ringing 'tew, tew, tew', but sometimes resembles that of Song Thrush, though more monotonous and interspersed with short chuckling.   SP

BLACKBIRD *Turdus merula* L 25 Abundant in gardens, parks and woods. Male unmistakable with pitch-black plumage and bright yellow bill. Uniform brownish colour of female and dark spotted appearance of juvenile identify them easily. Juveniles are lighter in colour and more heavily spotted than females. They are not as spotted as juvenile Ring Ouzel, which is also more greyish and has whitish markings on wings. Feeds openly on the ground. In winter may occur in flocks though mainly solitary in behaviour. Call is repeated 'chack'. Song is a musical, fluting warble. Sings from open perch mostly at dusk and dawn.   RW

BLACK-THROATED THRUSH *Turdus ruficollis atrogularis* L 24 Common in clearings and edges of coniferous forests; in winter in more open country. Rare visitor to western Europe. Dark breast, grey upper side distinguishes male. Female and juvenile brown with closely spotted breasts, pale panel on closed wing and paler rump. Asiatic subspecies Red-throated Thrush (*Turdus ruficollis ruficollis*) male has reddish breast and reddish tail in all plumages and is an even rarer vagrant to western Europe. Both subspecies have rusty underwing. In behaviour both resemble Fieldfare. Song resembles Song Thrush's.

SIBERIAN THRUSH *Zoothera sibiricus* L 23 Rare autumn visitor to Europe from Asia. Male very dark with white stripe over eye, characteristic underwing pattern, white spots on tail; female like scaly Song Thrush, but like the male, has white spots on tail and characteristic underwing pattern. Juveniles resemble females but are more heavily spotted. Shy and skulking in behaviour. Call resembles that of Song Thrush.   V

AMERICAN ROBIN *Turdus migratorius* L 25 Rare autumn and winter visitor to western Europe from North America. Unmistakable. Juveniles have spotted, not clear, red breast. Behaviour and voice resemble those of Blackbird.   V

juv.

Ring Ouzel

♂

♀

Blackbird

juv.

Black-
throated
Thrush

♀

♂

♂ red-
throated
form

Siberian Thrush

♀

♂

American Robin

263

REDWING *Turdus iliacus* L 20 Common in birch woods and parks, sometimes in towns. Outside breeding season in other deciduous woods and fields. Prominent stripe over eye, speckled underside and red flanks diagnostic. Gregarious outside breeding season, often associating with Fieldfares. Icelandic subspecies *T. i. coburni*, visiting Britain in winter, has more heavily streaked breast and is slightly larger than continental subspecies. Call is penetrating, prolonged high-pitched 'zee-up'. Song is short repetition of flute-like notes followed by low, rather unmusical warble, but is very variable. RW

SONG THRUSH *Turdus philomelos* L 23 Very common in woods, parks and gardens, though not as numerous as Blackbird. Uniform brown above, spotted below, and buff underwing distinguish it from all other thrushes. Solitary except during migration. 'Workshops' of broken snail shells around stones are often found in woods and gardens. Call is thin, short 'seep'. Song is flute-like and varied, tending to repeat short sections. RSWP

MISTLE THRUSH *Turdus viscivorus* L 28 Common in mature woods and the edge of woodlands. Sometimes, usually outside breeding season, found in open country. In some areas also in gardens in towns and villages. Large, heavily spotted below with white underwing and uniformly grey-brown above; pale outer tailfeathers. Occurs in small flocks outside breeding season. Stands more erect on the ground than other thrushes. Flight characteristic with alternating flapping and closing of wings. Call is characteristic dry rattling chatter with pauses between bursts. Song resembles Blackbird's but is briefer and less flute-like. RSW

FIELDFARE *Turdus pilaris* L 25 (variable). Common in open woods. Nests in colonies, sometimes in gardens and parks of towns and villages. Can also nest singly. Outside breeding season found on fields and pastures in large flocks, often accompanied by Redwings. Large, with grey head and rump, darker tail, chestnut-brown back and spotted underside. Varies considerably in size and colour, but general pattern is maintained. Travels in long undulating 'bands'. Flight characteristic with alternating flapping and short closing of wings. Call is loud 'schack, schack'. Song is twittering and often given in flight. WP

WHITE'S THRUSH *Zoothera dauma* L 28 Common in woods with undergrowth. Rare winter visitor to western Europe. Large, covered with prominent, black, crescent-shaped spots. Bold black and white underwing. Flight undulating. Wary. Call piping. V

Redwing

Song Thrush

Song Thrush
breaking snails

Mistle Thrush

Fieldfares

Fieldfare

White's Thrush

265

Tits (family *Paridae*)

are small, short-billed, acrobatic birds, tame or indifferent to man. They usually have striking colour patterns, but some are plain, with dark caps and bibs. Sexes are similar and juveniles resemble adults. Outside breeding season they often occur in mixed flocks, sometimes including Lesser Spotted Woodpeckers, Nuthatches and Goldcrests. Most nest in tree cavities, will use nest boxes readily and are attracted to bird tables. Their clutches vary from 5 to 16 eggs, white with reddish spots.

MARSH TIT *Parus palustris* L 11 Common in deciduous wood with undergrowth, thickets and parks. Resembles Willow Tit but has shorter black bib, glossy cap and uniformly coloured wing. Juveniles cannot with certainty be distinguished from juvenile Willow Tits. In the hand note that all tail-feathers are same length, whereas tail of Willow Tit is rounded (outside feathers a little shorter than central feathers). Best distinguished from Willow Tit by voice. Typical calls are loud 'pitchu' and repeated, scolding 'tzee'. Usual song, a repeated 'tschuppi'. R

WILLOW TIT *Parus montanus* L 11 Common in deciduous, mixed and coniferous woods with stronger affinity for wet situations than Marsh Tit. Most striking characteristic of the northern subspecies *Parus montanus borealis,* found in Scandinavia and northern Russia, is the pure white cheek. In rest of Europe resembles Marsh Tit more but has larger bib, no gloss on cap, and light area on wing. Juveniles cannot safely be distinguished from juvenile Marsh Tit. Call is a repeated nasal 'tchay'. Usual song is drawn-out 'tew tew tew', but there is also an unexpected warbling song, seldom heard in some areas. R

SOMBRE TIT *Parus lugubris* L 14 Fairly common in deciduous and mixed woods and thickets in rocky country. Large, with long bill and bib. Has much less brown in plumage than Marsh, Willow or Siberian Tit. Not social in behaviour and more wary than most tits. Call resembles that of Great Tit.

SIBERIAN TIT *Parus cinctus* L 13 Common in coniferous and mixed woods. Large tit, with brown cap and large black bib which is not sharply delineated from the buffish underside. Plumage more loose than that of other tits giving it a rather untidy look. Call resembles that of Willow Tit but is even more drawn out.

flycatcher

finch

warbler

tit

Great Tit at nest box

Marsh, Blue and Great Tits at bird table

Marsh Tit

Willow Tit

Willow Tit Scandinavian subspecies

Sombre Tit

Siberian Tit

267

CRESTED TIT *Parus cristatus* L 11 Common in coniferous and mixed woods. Prominent crest diagnostic. Greyish. Black facial markings characteristic, also of the juvenile which has smaller crest. Sometimes associated with Coal Tit, which it resembles in habits, but is less sociable than most tits. Rarely uses nest boxes. Call is characteristic purring trill. R

BLUE TIT *Parus caeruleus* L 11 Very common in all kinds of woods, parks and gardens. Outside breeding season frequently found in reed-beds. Blue cap diagnostic. Juvenile has yellow cheek and is greenish-brown above. Characteristically explores branches and trunks of trees and bushes, less often coming to the ground than Great Tit. Quite aggressive in behaviour. Call varied, but most commonly a high-pitched 'zee', often repeated several times and sometimes introducing trilling song. RP

AZURE TIT *Parus cyanus* L 13 Common in deciduous and mixed woods around lakes and streams where it nests in holes in dead trees. Very rare visitor to central and western Europe. White head and blue back diagnostic. Rather long-billed. Much more blue than Blue Tit. Juvenile is greyer above and on the crown. Two white wing-bars are prominent, particularly in flight. Call 'tseerr'. Song is loud and trilling.

COAL TIT *Parus ater* L 11 Common in coniferous and mixed woods. Outside breeding season sometimes associated with Crested Tit, more often in unmixed flocks or mixed with other tits. Black head, with white on cheek and nape of neck, and buffish white underside are diagnostic. Short-tailed. Often feeds near trunk of trees but also in the outermost branches of evergreens. Call is a thin 'tset', more plaintive than that of other tits. Song is a repeated 'weetse'. R

GREAT TIT *Parus major* L 14 Very common in all kinds of woods, parks and gardens. Large size and black central stripe through yellow underside diagnostic. Stripe broader in male than female. Often seen in flocks mixed with other tits, when its larger size distinguishes it at a glance, but less gregarious than most species. Often searches for food in low bushes and even on the ground. Calls numerous, and usually stronger than those of other tits. Song is a very characteristic penetrating, metallic series of 'zee-de' notes. RP

nest site
in pine stump

Crested Tit

Blue Tit

Azure Tit

Coal Tit

flock of tits and
Nuthatch

Great Tit

269

LONG-TAILED TIT *Aegithalos caudatus* L 14 Common in undergrowth in woods, thickets, parks and gardens. In winter often seen with other tits. Small size, black and white plumage with very long tail distinguish it from other tits. Northern subspecies *Aegithalos caudatus caudatus* has completely white head and is found in Scandinavia, Baltic states and northern Russia. Southern subspecies *A.c. rosaceus* has wide black stripe above the eye. Intermediates found in central Europe. Resembles other tits in habits but rarely feeds at bird tables. Nest is domed, lichen-covered and built in bushes or forks of trees. Call is a repeated trilling 'tsimp' and thin 'see-see-see'. Song, rarely heard, is a mixture of these notes.   R

Bearded Tits (family *Muscicapidae*, subfamily *Timaliinae*) resemble tits in looks and habits although they belong to a different family. Eggs, 5–7, are laid in open nest placed in reeds.

BEARDED TIT *Panurus biarmicus* L 16 Very local, but numerous where it occurs, in extensive reed-beds, along streams or lakes or in swamps. Brownish colours and very long tail distinguish it. Male has distinctive black moustachial stripe and black under tail-coverts. These features are missing in female and juvenile. Very active, climbing about in reeds with jerky movement. Flight weak, with very rapid wing action and characteristic tail movements, usually low over reeds. Outside breeding season occurs almost exclusively in flocks. Call is a hard 'tink-tink' like stones knocked together. Song twittering.   RW

Penduline Tits (family *Remizidae*) are small tit-like birds with longer and more pointed bills. Sexes similar. Nest is delicately woven and domed, with a funnel shaped entrance at the top and is usually suspended under branches above water. Clutch, 6–8 white eggs.

PENDULINE TIT *Remiz pendulinus* L 11 Locally common in riparian bushes and thickets. Sporadic in occurrence, extending its range towards the north-west. Black mask on generally brown bird distinguishes adult. Juvenile lacks the black mask and is more greyish brown but is easily told from juvenile Bearded Tit by much shorter tail. Habits somewhat resemble those of tits. Call is a drawn-out, sweet 'zee-eh'. Song is twittering, but it is quiet and only heard for a short time. The suspended nest is a peculiar ovoid shape with a funnel-like entrance built in the outer twigs of a bush, sometimes in reeds.   V

southern form

Long-tailed Tit

nest

northern form

Bearded Tit

♀

♂

juv.

nest

juv.

Penduline Tit

nest

271

Nuthatches

(family *Paridae*, subfamily *Sittinae*) are large-headed, short-tailed, short-legged, tree-climbing birds. They pick insects from the bark of trees with their long, straight bills. Very acrobatic, climbing up, around or down tree trunks, often head first (woodpeckers cannot do this). Outside breeding season often found in flocks with tits. Flight is jerky and undulating. Sexes similar. Nest in holes. Clutch, 5–7 eggs, white with reddish spots.

NUTHATCH *Sitta europaea* L 14 Common in mature deciduous and mixed woods, parks and gardens. Besides woodpecker-like silhouette, distinguished by bluish-grey upper side and chestnut-coloured flanks. Juvenile is similar to adult but lacks chestnut on flanks. Colour of underside in adults varies from white in *Sitta europaea europaea,* found in Scandinavia and northern Russia, to clear buff in *Sitta europaea caesia* of western Europe. Intermediates occur. Best told from very similar Rock Nuthatch by habitat, stronger colours and white spots on tail. Calls are tit-like. Typical song is a characteristic, repeated, musical 'tueeh'. Does not drum like woodpeckers, but hammering on nuts of various sorts to open them can often be heard. Nests in tree holes, often reducing size of entrance hole with mud. Will also use nestboxes. R

CORSICAN NUTHATCH *Sitta whiteheadi* L 11 Fairly common in mountain woods and groves. Resembles small Nuthatch but notice distinct head pattern, with black crown and distinct white line over the eye. Female and juveniles are duller in colours, but pattern is distinctive. Underside is clean white. Habits resemble those of Nuthatch, but more retiring. Excavates its own nest in trees. Call is much more nasal and quieter than that of Nuthatch. Song consists of two phrases of different pitch.

ROCK NUTHATCH *Sitta neumayer* L 14 Common on rocky slopes and mountains with scattered bushes. Resembles Nuthatch closely but colours are paler and it lacks white spots on tail. Very active, darting among the rocks. In movements and stance it is very similar to Nuthatch except that it climbs rocks instead of trees. Nests in crevices and holes in rocks, adding funnel-shaped entrance of mud. Very noisy, with loud and high-pitched calls, less musical than those of Nuthatch. It has a large variety of calls. Song is a loud, descending trill.

Krüper's Nuthatch

KRÜPER'S NUTHATCH *Sitta krueperi* L 13 Breeds in coniferous forests of Asia Minor, the Caucasus and south-eastern Greece (Lesbos). Resembles Corsican Nuthatch but has reddish-brown breast band. Call is a soft 'twit'.

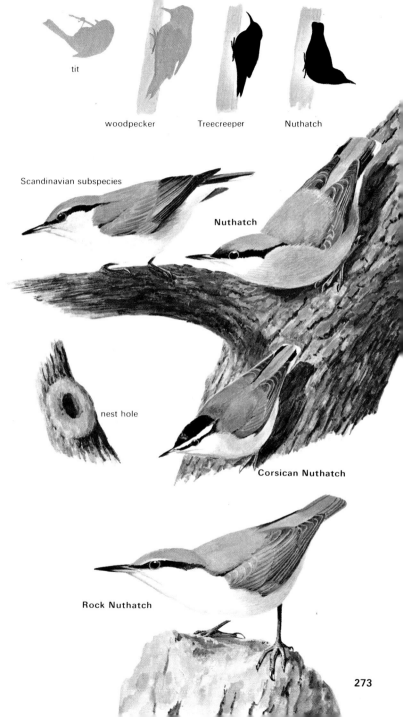

tit

woodpecker Treecreeper Nuthatch

Scandinavian subspecies

Nuthatch

nest hole

Corsican Nuthatch

Rock Nuthatch

273

Wallcreepers

(family *Paridae,* subfamily *Tichodromadinae*) are most closely related to the nuthatches, but with long decurved bill and creeping habits resemble the treecreepers most. Builds bulky nest in rock crevice. Eggs, 4–5, are white with reddish spots.

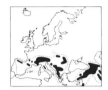

WALLCREEPER *Tichodroma muraria* L 17 Uncommon and local in high mountains to snow limit, moving further down in winter. A very rare visitor outside its normal range in autumn, winter and spring, when it also occurs on buildings and ruins. Characterized by long, decurved bill, greyish upper parts and in summer black, in winter whitish, underside. Most striking are the wide, rounded wings with large red areas and white spots. Flight characteristically fluttering. Climbs on rocks looking for insects, but can also be seen perched in trees. Call is thin and piping. Song is a repeated, accelerated and rising, high-pitched 'zee-zee-zee-tui'.   V

Treecreepers

(family *Certhiidae*) are small, short-legged, brown-backed birds with thin decurved bills. Creep spirally up trees searching for insects, dropping down to the bottom of another tree when one is explored. Usually seen singly. Very active. Oval nest is in cracks or behind bark. Eggs, 5–7, are white with reddish spots.

TREECREEPER *Certhia familiaris* L 13 Common in mature woods, parks and gardens, both coniferous and deciduous. In southern Europe where occurring with Short-toed Treecreeper, shows greater preference for coniferous woods at higher elevations. Inconspicuous but easily told from other birds except Short-toed Treecreeper from which it is distinguished by more distinct stripe over eye, lack of buffish brown on flank and more contrasting reddish rump. Call is a single very high note. Song is high, faint and accelerated.   R

SHORT-TOED TREECREEPER *Certhia brachydactyla* L 13 Common in mature deciduous woods, parks and gardens, usually at lower elevations than Treecreeper, particularly in southern part of its range. Resembles Treecreeper closely but has less distinct stripe over eye and has buffish brown flanks. The rump is not as rusty as that of the Treecreeper. In the hand it can be distinguished by its shorter toes. Bill is a little longer than that of Treecreeper. Habits like Treecreeper's. Call is a firm 'zeet'. Song is more plaintive than that of Treecreeper, and may be delivered from exposed perch.

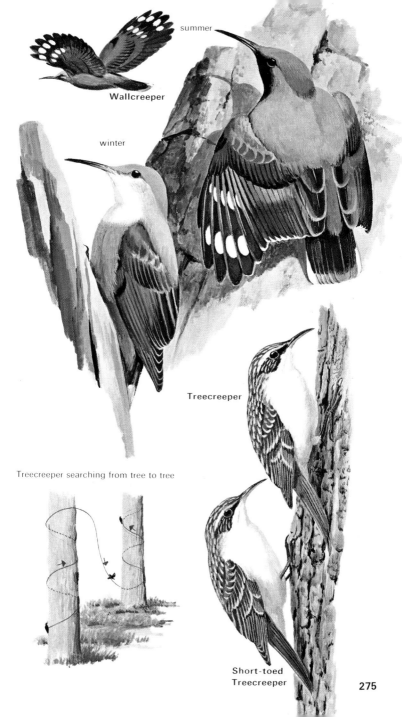

summer

Wallcreeper

winter

Treecreeper

Treecreeper searching from tree to tree

Short-toed
Treecreeper

275

Weaver finches

(family *Ploceidae*) are small, thick-billed, rather short-legged, more compact than most other passerines. In some, sexes are similar. Gregarious: most breed in small colonies. Feed on the ground. Build in holes or bulky domed nests. Eggs, 4–6, are bluish, spotted or white. Calls are unmusical chirps. Snow Finch, belonging to this family, is treated on p. 296.

HOUSE SPARROW *Passer domesticus* L 15 Abundant on farms, in towns and villages. Closely associated with man. Male has grey crown, black bib. Female and juvenile much more uniformly coloured with unstreaked breast, striped back and buffish stripe over eye. Gregarious. Nests under roofs, in holes, nest boxes or builds bulky domed nests in bushes and trees. Calls and song consist of monotonous chirps. Italian Sparrow *P.d. italiae*, male distinguished by chestnut crown and clear white cheeks, found on Italian peninsula, Corsica and Crete. RWP

SPANISH SPARROW *Passer hispaniolensis* L 15 Common but local near fields. Less closely associated with human habitation than House Sparrow. Male easily distinguished from male House Sparrow by larger black bib, black stripes on flanks and back, and chestnut crown. Extent of black is variable, but always more than on House Sparrow male. Females and juveniles told with difficulty by lighter throat, darker back and faint dark stripes on flanks. Nests colonially in the open, in thickets, nests of large birds or trees. Calls resemble House Sparrow's but are richer. V

TREE SPARROW *Passer montanus* L 14 Common in cultivated areas with trees. Less closely associated with human habitation than House Sparrow. Smaller, more delicately built than House Sparrow, with which it often mixes. Note chestnut crown, small bib and black spot on white cheek. Sexes similar. Nests in holes, mainly in trees. Uses nest boxes. Calls resemble House Sparrow's but are higher-pitched and sharper. RWP

ROCK SPARROW *Petronia petronia* L 14 Common but local in rocky country, uncultivated or cultivated. Very pale with striped crown and prominent white spots on tail. More active than House Sparrow with which it sometimes associates. Sometimes runs. Usually seen in small flocks looser than those of House Sparrows. Many calls resemble House Sparrow's but has characteristic 'dui-ee' call.

PALE ROCK SPARROW *Petronia brachydactyla* L 14. Breeds in desert areas of Middle East into Caucasus. Resembles very pale Rock Sparrow lacking yellow breast spot and distinctive pattern on head and crown. Tail dark with pale tips. Often in flocks.

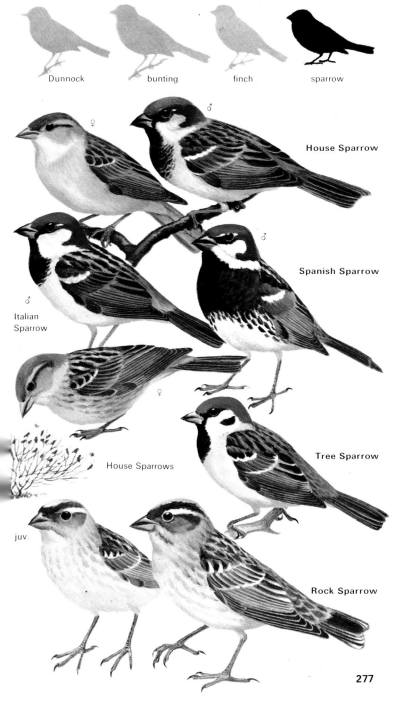

Dunnock   bunting   finch   sparrow

♀ ♂ House Sparrow

♂ Spanish Sparrow

Italian Sparrow

♀

House Sparrows

Tree Sparrow

juv.

Rock Sparrow

Finches

(family *Fringillidae*) are small to medium-sized, with short heavy bills well-adapted for eating seeds. Usually brightly coloured, the male more so than the female. Outside breeding season most occur in flocks. Nest in trees, shrubs, weeds and on the ground. Clutch, 3–6 eggs.

CHAFFINCH *Fringilla coelebs* L 15 One of the most common European birds. Nests in woods, deciduous and coniferous, gardens and parks. In winter also found in flocks in more open country. Notice distinct white wing-bars, white on outer tail-feathers, blue and red plumage of male, and greenish plumage of female and juvenile. Outside breeding season often seen in flocks varying in size from a dozen to thousands. Flocks may consist mainly of individuals of the same sex. Often mixes with Bramblings. Seeks food on the ground. Song, given from rather exposed perch, is melodious, short rattling with many geographic variations. Flight call is a short 'juep juep', and usual call a ringing 'pink'.   RWP

BRAMBLING *Fringilla montifringilla* L 15 Common but variable in numbers. Nests in woods and semi-open country. In winter found in woods, parks, gardens and fields, usually in flocks. Notice distinct white upper rump, black back and white wing-bar. Flocks often mixed with Chaffinches. In years of irruption flocks can number thousands, even millions of birds. Seeks food on the ground. Song is rather monotonous repetition of Greenfinch-like calls, given from an exposed perch. Flight call is nasal 'tjaek, tjaek' or 'chup-chup'.   WP

BULLFINCH *Pyrrhula pyrrhula* L 15 Rather common, in deciduous and coniferous woods, parks and gardens. Notice white rump, black and grey upper parts, red underside and short heavy bill of male, more subdued brownish colours of female. In winter often seen in small flocks. Movement very slow and deliberate. Feeds mainly in trees and bushes on berries, buds and seeds. Flight slow and undulating. Song, not well developed, is low, piping warble, but will learn to sing in captivity. Call is soft, melancholy 'peu, peu'.   RWP

HAWFINCH *Coccothraustes coccothraustes* L 18 Uncommon. Often missed as it is wary, spending most of its time among the foliage of the treetops. Almost exclusively found in deciduous woods. Notice extremely large, heavy bill, short tail and characteristic colour pattern; also white pattern on wings, characteristic in flight. Usually seen singly, in pairs or family groups. Song is low and twittering, rarely heard. Call is metallic 'tpik'.   R

warbler

bunting

sparrow

finch

♀ ♂

♂ winter

♀

Chaffinch
♂ summer

♀

♂ winter

Brambling
♂ summer

♂

winter

♀

♂

Bullfinch

♂

♀

adult

Hawfinch

♂

juv.

CITRIL FINCH *Serinus citrinella* L 11 Common in mountains with open coniferous woods. In winter moves to lower altitudes. Unstreaked greenish-yellow underside and rump, yellow wing-bars and grey neck distinguish adult. Juvenile is brownish and heavily striped. It lacks the yellow wing-band of Goldfinch juvenile and is considerably more heavily striped, particularly above, than any other finch. Flight undulating, resembling that of Goldfinch. Usually seen in flocks. Call is a plaintive but characteristic 'sit'. Song, often given in song-flight, resembles that of Serin. V

SERIN *Serinus serinus* L 11 Common in open woodland, parks and gardens. Streaked plumage, yellow underside and rump distinguish it. Immatures are less yellow, more streaked. Sociable, usually seen in small flocks. Often feeds on the ground. Flight undulating. Call is a varied twittering 'chirlit'. Song, which is given from high open perch or in song-flight, is a jingling, sibilant twitter. Very vocal. V

RED-FRONTED SERIN *Serinus pusillus* L 11 A resident of the high mountains of the Caucasus. Resembles Serin but has black head and breast with red front. These features are present but paler in the female.

GREENFINCH *Carduelis chloris* L 14 Very common in rather open, cultivated country, gardens and parks. Greenish or brownish with distinct yellow spots on tail and wings. Females and juveniles are easily told from other brownish finches by their heavy build and wing and tail pattern. Bill and head large. Usually encountered in pairs or small flocks, in winter sometimes mixing with sparrows and other finches. Flight undulating. Calls include a rapid trilling 'chick, chick, chick', and more nasal 'twee-ee'. Song, which is given from high open perch or in butterfly-like song-flight, is a twittering mixture of calls. RSWP

SISKIN *Carduelis spinus* L 11 Common. Nests in coniferous and mixed woods. Outside breeding season seen typically in birch and alder, but also in other types of woods. Streaked, greenish with yellow areas on sides of tail, and yellow wing-bars are characteristic. It is much smaller and more streaked than Greenfinch. Outside breeding season in flocks, sometimes with Redpolls. Makes compact flocks in flight. Wheezy call diagnostic. Song, delivered from high perch or in song-flight, is twittering. RW

juv.

Citril Finch

adult

Serin feeding on ground

Serin

♀

♂

Greenfinch display flight

♀

♂ Greenfinch

Siskin

♀

♂

281

GOLDFINCH *Carduelis carduelis* L 12 Common in all kinds of open country with scattered trees and bushes, in parks and gardens. In winter also open fields. Adult unmistakable. Sexes very similar but female can be told by slightly less extensive red on the face. Juvenile brownish and streaked. In all plumages the wide yellow wing-bar is diagnostic and especially striking in flight. Gregarious outside breeding season, usually occurring in small flocks, sometimes mixed with other finches. Often seeks its food (seeds) in thistles and similar plants, climbing nimbly over them. Usually perches in the open. Flight is markedly undulating. Call is a characteristic, liquid 'deedelit', often repeated. Song, delivered from an exposed perch, is a similarly liquid twittering. RS

LINNET *Carduelis cannabina* L 13 Very common on heaths and in open country with hedges and bushes, in parks and gardens. In winter usually found in open country. Male characteristic with greyish head and dark brown back. In summer, red on breast and front, part of which can be retained in winter plumage. Female and juvenile resemble Twite but have much more pronounced white wing and tail patches. Bill is dark, also in winter. In all plumages it has a whitish, streaked throat whereas Twite has a buffish unstriped throat and Redpoll a small black bib. Gregarious outside breeding season, flocks often associated with other finches. Flight undulating but less so than Goldfinch's. Call 'tsweet'; twitters in flight. Song, usually given from open perch, is a pleasant, varied twitter. RSW

TWITE *Carduelis flavirostris* L 13 Common in moorland and cultivated open country with or without low bushes in summer. In winter frequents completely open land, often along seashores like Snow Bunting and Shore Lark. Rather nondescript, brownish, striped plumage. Like Linnet it has white patches on wings and tail, but these are less distinct. Male has pinkish rump. Female has greyish-brown, spotted rump. In winter bill is yellow (Linnet's bill is dark) but in summer it is dark. Upper side generally darker and breast richer yellow-brown than Linnet's. Throat is unstriped buffish (whitish and streaked in Linnet). Gregarious outside breeding season. Flight undulating but less so than Goldfinch. Flocks in flight rather close. Nests in loose colonies. Call is a nasal, metallic 'tweeh'. Song, delivered from perch or in song flight, resembles that of Linnet but is slower and harder. RW

juv

Goldfinch

adult

undulating flight

♀

♂

Linnet

flock in
field in winter

♂ winter

♂ summer

♀

♂

Twite

283

REDPOLL *Carduelis flammea* L 13 Fairly common in birch and mixed woods. Red forehead and small black chin-spot distinguish it from all other species except Arctic Redpoll. Told from this by more streaked rump and underside and less distinct white areas. Several subspecies of varying sizes and shades of darkness occur. The Lesser Redpoll *(C.f. cabaret),* found in the British Isles and the Alps, is smaller and darker than the Mealy Redpoll *(C.f. flammea)* of Scandinavia. Greater Redpoll *(C.f. rostrata)* from Greenland is dark and the largest. Gregarious, often nesting in colonies. Flocks are compact. Actively searches trees and bushes for food (seeds). Flight undulating. Call is a hoarse 'chi-chi-chit'. Song, given from perch or in song-flight, is a trilling twitter.

RWP

ARCTIC REDPOLL *Carduelis hornemanni* L 13 Fairly common in more open tundra. In winter as Redpoll, from which it is told by unstreaked white rump, fewer streaks on underside and more clear white areas, particularly on head. This is particularly evident in the Greenland subspecies, Hornemann's Redpoll *(C.h. hornemanni),* whereas the Scandinavian subspecies, Coues's Redpoll *(C.h. exilipes)* resembles the Redpoll more. Often occurs with Redpoll. Habits and voice as those of Redpoll. V

TRUMPETER FINCH *Bucanetes githaginea* L 14 A very rare visitor to Mediterranean countries from north African breeding grounds. Male in summer unmistakable. In winter plumage resembles female and juvenile more. Notice very short bill. Terrestrial in habits. Call is short and nasal.

SCARLET ROSEFINCH *Carpodacus erythrinus* L 14 Common in damp bushy areas. Rare autumn visitor to western Europe. Male unmistakable. Female and juvenile streaked greyish brown, with distinct wing-bars. Characteristically holds head tucked between shoulders. Call is soft repeated 'screet'. Song is piping and trilling. Call is a loud whistle. V

PALLAS'S ROSEFINCH *Carpodacus roseus* L 15 Rare visitor to eastern Europe from Asia. It resembles Scarlet Grosbeak, but slightly larger with red areas paler.

GREAT ROSEFINCH *Carpodacus rubicilla* L 20 A resident of the Caucasus. It resembles Scarlet Grosbeak, but is larger and is more pink (entire underside) with the bill of both sexes straw-coloured. Female greyish-brown with boldly streaked underside.

PINE GROSBEAK *Pinicola enucleator* L 20 Fairly common in coniferous and mixed woods. Very large. Male red, female green, immature more grey, all with two distinct wing-bars. Outside breeding season in flocks. Usually tame. Call consists of three high whistles. Song is a loud warble. V

in winter

Greater Redpoll ♂

Mealy Redpoll ♂

Redpoll

Lesser Redpoll ♂

♀ ♂ Arctic Redpoll

♀ ♂ winter

Trumpeter Finch

♂ summer

♀ ♂ Scarlet Rosefinch

♀ Pine Grosbeak ♂

285

Crossbills

(family *Fringillidae*, genus *Loxia*) are closely related to the other finches but have very characteristic bills in which the hooked tips of upper and lower mandibles cross each other, a special adaptation for opening conifer cones and extracting the seeds. They are very irregular in their occurrence. Gregarious, usually seen in small closely-knit flocks. Males are red, females green, juveniles grey. Nesting season very long, starting in winter. Clutch, 4 spotted eggs.

CROSSBILL *Loxia curvirostra* L 17 Common in coniferous forests. Crossing of bill not always noticeable. Told from Parrot Crossbill by smaller (not as deep) bill and head, and less stocky appearance; and from Two-barred Crossbill by lack of wing-bars. May nest in almost any season but mostly from January to April. Usually seen in small flocks. Climbs on outer branches of conifers acrobatically, tearing cone scales to get at seeds. Occurs in varying numbers mainly depending on local crop of cones. Sometimes makes large-scale invasions, during which it can reach any part of Europe and often settles to nest for one or more seasons if conditions are favourable. Call is unmistakable 'kip, kip, kip' given with great emphasis. Song is twittering, with characteristic calls interspersed. R

SCOTTISH CROSSBILL *Loxia scotica* L 17 Bill is intermediate between Crossbill and Parrot Crossbill. The face is broader than that of Crossbill. Like Parrot Crossbill it prefers pine and is limited in distribution to northern and eastern Scotland. Its call is louder and deeper than that of the Crossbill and it has a characteristic alarm call: 'toop, toop', which is lacking in the Crossbill.

PARROT CROSSBILL *Loxia pytyopsittacus* L 17 Fairly common in coniferous and mixed woods with preference for pine (Crossbill prefers spruce). Resembles Crossbill, but is more plump with larger head and bill. Outside breeding season may mix with Crossbills but more usually found in 'clean' flocks. Habits resemble Crossbill's. Irregular in winter occurrence south of its range. Call deeper and louder than Crossbill's. V

TWO-BARRED CROSSBILL *Loxia leucoptera* L 15 Uncommon in coniferous woods with preference for larch. Smaller than Crossbill with weaker bill and two distinct, white wing-bars. Habits resemble those of Crossbill but more irregular in occurrence. In some years some birds reach most western European countries, but never in as large numbers as Crossbill. Call consists of three to four redpoll-like notes, higher and decidedly different from call of Crossbill. Song is long and canary like. V

juv.

Crossbill

Crossbill

Scottish
Crossbill

Parrot
Crossbill

♂

Parrot Crossbill

Two-barred Crossbill

juv.

Buntings

(family *Emberizidae*) are sparrow-sized birds with short, thick bills. They are found in open country with bushes. Males are usually more brightly coloured than females and juveniles usually resemble the female (see pp. 298–9 for comparison of females). In some the sexes are similar. Look rather compact, large-headed. Outside breeding season some are seen in flocks. The food, which is mainly seeds, is most often taken on the ground. Nest in low bushes or on the ground. Songs short and characteristic. Eggs, 3–6, are blotched or scribbled.

CORN BUNTING *Miliaria calandra* L 18 Very common but often local in open country with only few bushes. Greyish brown, heavily streaked without distinctive features. Sexes similar. Heavy-looking. Some show dark spot in centre of breast. Outside breeding season in flocks, often mixed with other buntings and finches. Flight heavy (easily told from larks even at a long distance), often with legs dangling. Some males are polygamous. Call is short and harsh 'tsrip'. Characteristic song, which is usually given from exposed perch (often from wires), is monotonous, jingling.   R

LITTLE BUNTING *Emberiza pusilla* L 13 Uncommon in wet, fairly open tundra; on passage also found in marshes and on hills. A rare autumn visitor to western Europe. Chestnut and black on head in summer diagnostic. In other plumages, without distinct field characters but combination of small size, streaked and spotted plumage with rusty cheeks distinguishes it. Most easily confused with Reed and Rustic Bunting females and juveniles, but is much smaller with paler colours and finer black streaking of breast and flanks. The bill has straight or even concave upper-mandible. Call is a sharp 'tick'. Song is short and melodious, of same quality as Robin's.   P

RUSTIC BUNTING *Emberiza rustica* L 15 Fairly common on edges of moist woods and thickets. Outside breeding season also in more open situations. A rare spring and autumn visitor to western Europe. Black and white patterned head, rusty nape, breast, flank and rump and very white underside of summer male diagnostic. In other plumages best told from other buntings by rusty breast-band and flanks and brown pattern on head. Most easily confused with female and juvenile Reed Buntings, but these have blackish spots on breast and flanks, not rusty. Moustachial streak is less conspicuous in Rustic Bunting female and juvenile. Often raises crown feathers. Call is a short, sharp 'tick'. Song varied, but usually rather short with a Dunnock-like quality.   V

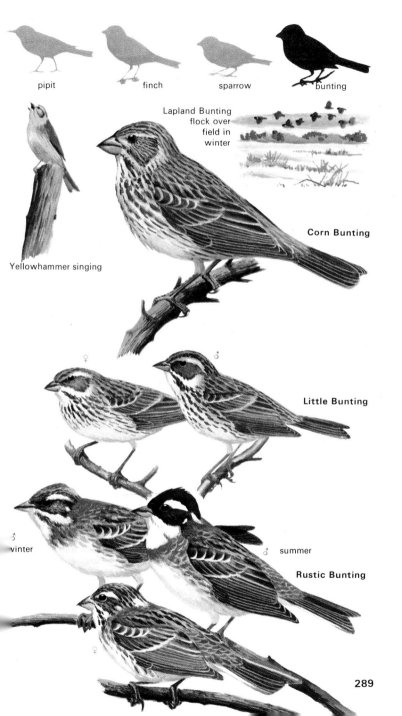

pipit finch sparrow bunting

Lapland Bunting
flock over
field in
winter

Corn Bunting

Yellowhammer singing

♀ ♂

Little Bunting

♂
winter

♂ summer

Rustic Bunting

♀

ROCK BUNTING *Emberiza cia* L 16 Fairly common in mountains with bushes and scattered trees and vineyards, in winter moving to lower altitudes. Grey and black head pattern distinguishes male. Female much duller but has grey throat (no other European bunting has this). Immatures resemble immature Yellowhammer in general colours and chestnut-coloured rump but are separated by reddish underside. Also told from immature Cretzschmar's and Ortolan Buntings by chestnut rump and dark bill. White outer tail-feathers displayed as it flicks its tail. Often seen on the ground, but also perches freely in trees. Call is a thin, sharp 'zeet'. Song, which is usually given from high, open perch, is a high-pitched series of 'zee' notes, somewhat varied in sequence.   V

ORTOLAN BUNTING *Emberiza hortulana* L 17 Common in rather open, dry country with scattered bushes and trees. Sometimes gardens. Outside breeding season also in more exposed areas and cultivated fields. Adult male told from other buntings except Cretzschmar's by greenish-grey unmarked head and rusty-brown underside. From Cretzschmar's by yellow (not orange) throat and greenish-grey (rather than grey) head and neck. Female has yellow throat (rusty in Cretzschmar's). Head is greenish-grey with streaks. Juveniles rather indistinctly streaked brown, with brown (not chestnut as in Yellowhammer and Rock Bunting) streaked rump. At short range narrow eye-ring and light colour of bill noticeable. Less buffish on underside than juvenile Cretzschmar's. Call is a high-pitched soft 'tsee'. It is a rather secretive bird keeping well hidden. Song resembles that of Yellowhammer but has a 'ringing' quality and is much slower. The last notes are of a lower pitch than the preceding ones.   P

Grey-necked Bunting

CRETZSCHMAR'S BUNTING *Emberiza caesia* L 17 Common in dry, rocky country with scattered bushes but also found in gardens and lowlands. Resembles Ortolan Bunting in all plumages, but male has grey (not greenish) head and rather orange (not yellow) throat. Females have rusty (not yellow) throat. The head is bluish-grey with some streaks. Juveniles are slightly more buff below but not safely distinguished in the field from juvenile Ortolan. Told from juvenile Rock Bunting by more brown (not chestnut) rump and flesh-coloured (not black) bill. Usually seen on the ground. Call is harder and sharper than Ortolan's and more penetrating. Song is a short twitter resembling that of Ortolan.   V

GREY-NECKED BUNTING *Emberiza buchanani* L 15 Breeds in dry rocky areas in Caucasus eastwards. Resembles Cretzschmar's Bunting but head is all grey and breast and throat pinkish.

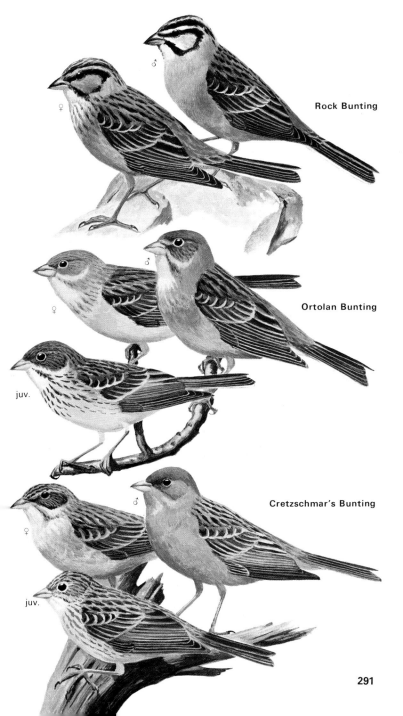

Rock Bunting

Ortolan Bunting

Cretzschmar's Bunting

291

RED-HEADED BUNTING *Emberiza bruniceps* L 15
Common in rather open, bushy country, often near water,
even in reed-beds. A rare visitor to western Europe,
usually in cultivated fields. Many of the records are
probably escaped cage birds as it is popular as such.
Male unmistakable with red head and breast. Female
most resembles female Black-headed Bunting, but
whereas Black-headed Bunting female has some chestnut on back, this is lacking in the Red-headed Bunting,
which is more green. Red-headed also has whitish
rather than yellow under tail-coverts. Juveniles not
safely separable from juvenile Black-headed Bunting.
Habits resemble those of Black-headed Bunting. Call is
a series of harsh notes. Song is a short, fast, monotonous
warble.   V

PINE BUNTING *Emberiza leucocephalos* L 16 Common in rather open, bushy country and open mixed and
coniferous woods. A rare autumn visitor to western
Europe, usually occurring in cultivated areas. Male
unmistakable with white and brown pattern on head.
Female has indistinct brown breast-band and white
throat, but white crown, when present is diagnostic.
Juveniles most closely resemble juvenile Rustic Bunting
in having chestnut rump, but have less chestnut on wing
and breast. Gregarious outside breeding season.
Resembles Yellowhammer in habits. Call resembles that
of Yellowhammer, of which it may be a subspecies. Song
somewhat similar to that of Chaffinch with an ascending
pitch.   V

CINEREOUS BUNTING *Emberiza cineracea* L 17
Very rare and local, breeding on island of Lesbos in the
Aegean Sea. Present from March to August. Prefers
barren, rocky country. Colours greyish, male with
unmarked yellow head, female and juvenile with less
yellow and more stripes on head and throat. Song is
simple, bunting-like.

REED BUNTING *Emberiza schoeniclus* L 15 Common
in and near reed-beds, in winter also resorting to cultivated areas, sometimes in the company of other buntings
and finches. Male in summer plumage unmistakable
with white collar, black hood and bib. Female has
strongly patterned head, and white throat surrounded by
dark streaks. White outer tail-feathers show as bird flicks
tail. Can be confused with Rustic Bunting female and
juvenile but has black streaks on breast and flank, not
rusty. Much larger than Little Bunting, which is lighter
with finer streaks. Upper-mandible is convex. Outside
breeding season often in small flocks. Call is a loud
'zeek'. Song, which is usually given from open perch, is
short and monotonous 'chi-chi-chi-chitty'.   RWP

Red-headed
Bunting

Pine Bunting

Cinereous Bunting

Reed Bunting
winter

summer

YELLOWHAMMER *Emberiza citrinella* L 17 Very common in rather open country with bushes, edges and clearings of woods, in winter also on open cultivated fields. Streaked yellow head, chestnut-brown rump and white outer tail-feathers. Females and immatures less boldly coloured and generally more heavily streaked, most easily confused with female and juvenile Cirl Bunting, but have chestnut, not brown, rump. Outside breeding season found in flocks, often with other buntings and finches. Feeds on ground. Call is sharp 'tjip'. Song, uttered from exposed perch, is monotonous 'little bit of bread and no——cheese'. RW

YELLOW-BREASTED BUNTING *Emberiza aureola* L 14 Common in moist thickets and birch woods. In winter also in more open country. Rare autumn visitor to western Europe. Male unmistakable with black head, chestnut breast-band on yellow underside and distinct white wing-bars, which are also present in winter plumage. Female resembles Yellowhammer but is darker above with characteristic yellow crown-stripe and supercilium. Juveniles resemble female but are less distinct in pattern. Told from Yellowhammer by yellow-brown rump; from Cirl Bunting by streaked under tail-coverts and paler colours. Appears slim and rather pipit-like in flight. Gregarious, nests in loose colonies. In winter found in flocks. Call is short 'tick'. Song resembles Ortolan's but is louder and faster. V

CIRL BUNTING *Emberiza cirlus* L 17 Common in open country with bushes, trees, hedges. In winter also in more open fields. Facial pattern distinguishes male. Told from Yellowhammer by brown, not chestnut, rump; from Yellow-breasted Bunting by unstreaked under tail-coverts and darker colours; from Ortolan Bunting by more pronounced facial pattern and dark, not flesh-coloured, bill. Outside breeding season in flocks, often with other buntings and finches. Call is repeated 'sip'. Song, given from exposed perch, is vibrating repetition of metallic notes. R

BLACK-HEADED BUNTING *Emberiza melano-cephala* L 17 Fairly common in rather open country with scattered bushes and trees. Male unmistakable with solid black hood. Adults told from other buntings by unstreaked yellow or white underside and lack of white on tail. Female resembles Red-headed female but has chestnut on back, and yellow (not white) under tail-coverts. Juveniles are not safely separated from juvenile Red-headed. Red-headed may be subspecies of Black-headed. Resembles Yellowhammer in habits. Call is short 'sit'. Song starts with a few similar short notes ending in short, pleasant warble. Usually given from exposed perch. V

juv.

♂

♀

Yellowhammer

♀

♂

Yellow-breasted Bunting

♀

♂

Cirl Bunting

♂

♀

Black-headed Bunting

295

LAPLAND BUNTING *Calcarius lapponicus* L 15 Common in open and fairly open Arctic tundra; in high mountains in southern part of range. In winter rather uncommon in fields and open areas near seashores. Summer male has black head and throat with buffish stripe over eye, and unstreaked chestnut neck-band, distinguishing it from Rustic and Reed Bunting males. Winter male, female and juvenile much less distinct with streaked brown plumage. Usually shows some chestnut on wing (adults also on nape) and has indistinct buffish central stripe on head, distinguishing it from very similar Reed Bunting female. More compact and short-tailed than most buntings. Has long hind claw. Gregarious, often mixing with flocks of other buntings, finches and larks. Terrestrial, running on the ground. Call is short trill. Song, usually given in song-flight, has same quality as Skylark's, but is shorter.   WP

SNOW BUNTING *Plectrophenax nivalis* L 16 Common in open rocky country reaching high up into mountains, but in the northern part of range also found at sea level. In winter frequents open coastal areas but also found on open high ground inland and on fields. Black and white summer plumage identifies male. Winter male, female and juvenile paler than any other buntings; large white wing patches particularly noticeable in adult birds, less so in immatures. Males have black back, females and juveniles brown back. Gregarious outside breeding season, when usually seen in flocks, occasionally with other buntings, finches and larks. Rarely perches in trees. Sometimes flicks tail. Flight undulating. Call is short descending whistle: 'seeoo'. Song, given from rocky perch or song-flight, is a loud, short, lark-like warble.   RW

Snow Bunting juv.

Weaver finches (family *Ploceidae*) are described on p. 276, except for the Snow Finch, which is treated here for identification purposes.

SNOW FINCH *Montifringilla nivalis* L 18 Common in high mountains above tree limit and below snow limit, moving to lower altitudes in winter. Often found near human habitations. In all plumages easily told from Snow Bunting by grey head. Note large white wing patches and tail-feathers. Females more brownish with less extensive white areas than males. Juveniles resemble females. Bill colour changes from yellow in winter to black in spring. Less compactly built than buntings. Perches more upright. Often jerks tail. Outside breeding season often found in small flocks. Nests in crevices or under rocks. Call is rather harsh 'zjeeh'. Song, given from rocky perch or song-flight, is twittering.

Lapland Bunting

♂ winter

♀

♂ summer

juv.

♂ summer

Snow Bunting

♂

♂ winter

♀

♀

♀

♂

♂

Snow Finch

Immature and female buntings

Corn
♂♀

Little

Ortolan juv.

Cretzchmar's juv

Reed
♀

Yellowhammer juv

Cirl
♀

♀

Black headed

Rustic

♀

Rock juv.

Red-headed

♀

♀

Pine

♀

Cinereous

♀

Yellow-breasted

Lapland juv.

♀

Snow

299

Vagrant North American Passerines

Red-eyed Vireo *Vireo olivaceus* L 15 Autumn visitor. Warbler-like, but with heavier bill and more sluggish behaviour. Immatures have brown iris. V

Parula Warbler *Parula americana* L 11 Autumn visitor. Double wing bars, broken eye-ring, yellow breast and yellow patch on bluish black characteristic. The male also has a narrow black and chestnut band across the breast. V

American Redstart *Setophaga ruticilla* L 13 Autumn visitor. Tail pattern, habit of flicking and fanning tail and flycatching behaviour characteristic. Female and immature have white underparts, grey-brown head and back and a distinct eye-ring. V

Blackpoll Warbler *Dendroica striata* L 13 Autumn visitor. Notice streaked back, double wing bar and white undertail coverts and spots on undertail. The stripes on breast are more distinct in autumn male and female. Spring male white underside and cheeks, black cap and whiskers. V

Yellow-rumped Warbler *Dendroica coronata* L 14 Autumn visitor. Note white eye-ring, yellow or orange side-patches and yellow rump. Yellow crown absent in immatures. The male has similar, but more distinct pattern. V

Northern Waterthrush *Seirus noveboracensis* L 14 Autumn visitor. Pipit-like. Walks with bobbing motion like Common Sandpiper. Throat often faintly streaked. Feeds on ground near water. V

Increasing interest and expertise in the identification of birds has meant that an increasing number of vagrants from North America have been recorded in western Europe, in Great Britain and Ireland in particular. The more frequent visitors are described below. North American Thrushes are described on p. 260 to 263.

Bobolink *Dolichonyx oryzivorus* L 19 Autumn visitor. Male in autumn plumage resembles female with characteristic streaked crown, buffy breast and narrow, pointed tail feathers. In spring male has black underparts and face.   V

Northern Oriole *Icterus galbula* L 19 Autumn and spring visitor. Females and immatures resemble Golden Oriole female but colours are more orange with prominent wing bars.   V

White-throated Sparrow *Zonotrichia albicollis* L 16 Spring and autumn visitor. Notice well defined white throat and yellow spot at bill. Striped crown pattern variable in definition according to age and sex. V

Fox Sparrow *Passerella iliaca* L 18 Spring visitor. Notice heavily streaked underparts with a rather large breast spot and rufous rump and tail   V

Song Sparrow *Melospiza melodia* L 15 Spring visitor. Notice heavily streaked breast with small breast spot and greyish-brown upper parts. Tail is characteristically 'pumped' in flight.

Slate-coloured Junco *Junco hyemalis* L 15 Spring visitor. Notice slaty colour with light pink bill and prominent white outer tail-feathers. V

Rose-breasted Grosbeak *Pheucticus ludovicianus* L 20 Autumn visitor. Adult male unmistakable. Female and immature have striped crown, very heavy bill and orange-yellow wing linings. Male in spring has black throat and head.   V

winter

Accidentals

**VERY RARE SPECIES ON THE EUROPEAN LIST
NOT DEALT WITH IN THE MAIN SECTION OF THE BOOK**

COMMON NAME	SCIENTIFIC NAME	ORIGIN	OBSERVED
Yellow-nosed Albatross	*Diomedea chlororhynchos*	South Seas	Iceland
Grey-headed Albatross	*Diomedea chrysostoma*	South Seas	Norway
Light-mantled Sooty Albatross	*Phoebetria palpebrata*	South Seas	France
Capped Petrel	*Pterodroma hasitata*	America	Great Britain, France
Magnificent Frigate-bird	*Fregata magnificens*	South Seas	Great Britain, France, Denmark, Holland
Green Heron	*Butorides striatus*	America	Great Britain
Schrenck's Bittern	*Ixobrychus eurhythmus*	Asia	Italy, Germany
Least Bittern	*Ixobrychus exilis*	America	Iceland
West African Reef Heron	*Egretta gularis*	Africa	Spain
Bald Ibis	*Geronticus eremita*	Africa	Spain
Lesser Flamingo	*Phoenicopterus minor*	Africa	Spain
Black Duck	*Anas rubripes*	America	Great Britain, Ireland, Sweden
Bufflehead	*Bucephala albeola*	America	Great Britain, Iceland, Czechoslovakia
Hooded Merganser	*Mergus cucullatus*	America	Great Britain, Ireland, Germany
Chanting Goshawk	*Melierax metabates*	Africa	Spain
American Kestrel	*Falco sparverius*	America	Denmark, Russia
Sandhill Crane	*Grus canadensis*	America	Ireland
Sora Rail	*Porzana carolina*	America	Great Britain, Ireland, France, Sweden
Green-backed Gallinule	*Porphyrio madagascariensis*	Africa	Italy
American Purple Gallinule	*Porphyrula martinica*	America	Great Britain, Norway
American Coot	*Fulica americana*	America	Greece
Western Sandpiper	*Calidris mauri*	America	Great Britain, Ireland
Red-necked Sandpiper	*Calidris ruficollis*	Asia	Germany
Eskimo Curlew	*Numenius borealis*	America	Great Britain, Ireland, Norway
Willet	*Catoptrophorus semipalmatus*	America	France, Yugoslavia
Franklin's Gull	*Larus pipixcan*	America	Great Britain, Faeroe Isles
White-eyed Gull	*Larus leucophthalmus*	Africa	Greece
Grey-headed Gull	*Larus cirrocephalus*	Africa	Spain
Lesser Crested Tern	*Sterna bengalensis*	Africa	Spain, France, Switzerland, Italy
Royal Tern	*Sterna maxima*	America, Africa	Great Britain, Ireland Spain
Forster's Tern	*Sterna forsteri*	America	Iceland
Bridled Tern	*Sterna anaethetus*	America, Africa	Great Britain, Ireland
Noddy	*Anous stolidus*	South Seas	Germany
Crested Auklet	*Aethia cristatella*	North Pacific	Iceland
Parakeet Auklet	*Cyclorrhynchus psittacula*	North Pacific	Sweden
Spotted Sandgrouse	*Pterocles senegallus*	Africa, Asia	Italy
Chestnut-bellied Sandgrouse	*Pterocles exustus*	Africa	Hungary
Eastern Stock Dove	*Columba eversmanni*	Asia	Russia
American Nighthawk	*Chordeiles minor*	America	Great Britain, Finland Iceland, Faeroe Isles, Yugoslavia
Belted Kingfisher	*Ceryle alcyon*	America	Iceland, Holland
Smyrna Kingfisher	*Halcyon smyrnernsis*	Asia	Greece
Needle-tailed Swift	*Hirundapus caudacutus*	Asia	Great Britain, Ireland, Italy, Malta, Finland, Norway
Yellow-bellied Sapsucker	*Sphyrapicus varius*	America	Great Britain, Iceland
Acadian Flycatcher	*Empidonax virescens*	America	Iceland
Desert Lark	*Ammomanes deserti*	Africa, Asia	Spain
Bar-tailed Desert Lark	*Ammomanes cincturus*	Africa, Asia	Malta
Hoopoe Lark	*Alaemon alaudipes*	Africa, Asia	Malta

COMMON NAME	SCIENTIFIC NAME	ORIGIN	OBSERVED
Indian Sand Lark	*Calandrella raytal*	Asia	Spain
Bimaculated Lark	*Melanocorypha bimaculata*	Asia	Great Britain, Italy, Finland
Common Bulbul	*Pycnonotus barbatus*	Africa, Asia	Spain
Brown Thrasher	*Toxostoma rufum*	America	Great Britain, Germany
Catbird	*Dumetella carolinensis*	America	Germany
Daurian Jackdaw	*Corvus dauuricus*	Asia	Finland
Gray's Grasshopper Warbler	*Locustella fasciolata*	Asia	France, Denmark
Thick-billed Reed Warbler	*Acrocephalus aedon*	Asia	Great Britain
White-crowned Black Wheatear	*Oenanthe leucopyga*	Africa, Asia	Malta
Moussier's Redstart	*Phoenicurus moussieri*	Africa	Italy, Malta
Veery	*Catharus fuscescens*	America	Great Britain
Wood Thrush	*Hylocichla mustelina*	America	Iceland
Tickell's Thrush	*Turdus unicolor*	Asia	Germany
Narcissus Flycatcher	*Ficedula narcissina*	Asia	France
Mugimaki Flycatcher	*Ficedula mugimaki*	Asia	Italy
Red-breasted Nuthatch	*Sitta canadensis*	America	Iceland
Black-and-white Warbler	*Mniotilta varia*	America	Great Britain
Tennessee Warbler	*Vermivora peregrina*	America	Iceland, Great Britain
Yellow Warbler	*Dendroica petechia*	America	Great Britain
Black-throated Green Warbler	*Dendroica virens*	America	Germany
Hooded Warbler	*Wilsonia citrina*	America	Great Britain
Yellowthroat	*Geothlypis trichas*	America	Great Britain
Ovenbird	*Seiurus aurocapillus*	America	Great Britain
Yellow-headed Blackbird	*Xanthocephalus xanthocephalus*	America	Denmark, Sweden
Summer Tanager	*Piranga rubra*	America	Great Britain
Scarlet Tanager	*Piranga olivacea*	America	Great Britain
White-crowned Sparrow	*Zonotrichia leucophrys*	America	France
Evening Grosbeak	*Hesperiphona vespertina*	America	Great Britain, Norway
Rufous-sided Towhee	*Pipilo erythrophthalmus*	America	Great Britain
Indigo Bunting	*Passerina cyanea*	America	Iceland, Great Britain
Lazuli Bunting	*Passerina amoena*	America	Great Britain
Siberian Meadow Bunting	*Emberiza cioides*	Asia	Italy
Yellow-browed Bunting	*Emberiza chrysophrys*	Asia	Belgium, France
Chestnut Bunting	*Emberiza rutila*	Asia	Holland, Norway
Black-faced Bunting	*Emberiza spodocephala*	Asia	Germany
Pallas's Reed Bunting	*Emberiza pallasi*	Asia	Denmark, Russia

Bibliography

Hundreds of books on birds are published every year. Each country has its own extensive literature and a complete listing of books on European birds alone would take up more space than this entire volume. But some books are of special interest and below you will find a short list of the most important works on European birds and neighbouring regions. Besides the books on birds of a certain geographical region, many monographs treat individual birds or groups of birds, and the largest series of this kind are Collins' *New Naturalist* and Ziemsen's *Die Neue Brehm-bucherei*.

Bannerman, D. A. and W. M. *Handbook of The Birds of Cyprus and migrants of the Middle East.* Edinburgh, 1971

Bannerman, D. A. and Lodge, G. E. *The Birds of the British Isles.* 12 vol. London, 1953–63.

Bauer, K. and Rokitansky, G. *Die Vögel Österreichs, Kritische Ümbersicht der bisher fur Österreich nachgewiesenen Vogelarten und Rassen.* Neusiedl, 1951.

Bauer, W. et al. *Catalogus Faunae Graeciae.* Aves. Thessaloniki, 1969.

Bernis, F. *Prontuario de la Avifauna Española (Incluyendo Aves de Portugal, Baleares y Canarias).* Madrid, 1954.

Blaedel, N. et al. *Nordens fåglar i färg.* 7 vol. Malmö 1959–67.

British Ornithologists' Union. *The Status of Birds in Britain and Ireland.* Oxford, 1971.

Bruun, B. *The Concise Encyclopedia of Birds.* London, 1974.

Campbell, B. and Ferguson-Lees, J. *A Field Guide to Birds' Nests.* London, 1972.

Cerný, W. et al. *Fauna CSSR – Ptaci (Vogel).* Prague.

Commissie voor de Nederlandse Avifauna. *Avifauna van Nederland.* Leiden, 1970.

Commission pour l'Avifaune Belge. *Avifaune de Belgique.* Brussels, 1967.

Cramp, S. and Simmons, K. E. L. (eds.) *Handbook of the Birds of Europe, the Middle East and North Africa; The Birds of the Western Palaearctic.* Vol. 1, London, 1977.

Curry-Lindahl, K. (ed.) et al. *Våra fåglar i Norden.* 4 vol. Stockholm 1959–62.

Delacour, J. and Scott, P. *The Waterfowl of the World.* 4 vol. London, 1954–64.

Dementiev, G. P., Gladkov, N. A. et al. *Birds of the Soviet Union.* 6 vol. Moscow, 1951–54. (Israel Progr. for Sci. Transl., Jerusalem, 1966–70).

Etchécopar, R. D. and Hue, F. *Les oiseaux du Nord e l'Afrique.* Paris, 1964. (English edition, *The Birds of North Africa,* Edinburgh, 1967).

Ferguson-Lees, J., Hockliffe, Q. and Zweeres, K. A. *A Guide to Bird Watching in Europe.* London, 1975.

Fisher, J. *Thorburn's Birds.* London, 1967.

Frieling, H. *Was fliegt denn da?* Stuttgart, 1958.

Géroudet, P. *La Vie des Oiseaux.* 6 vol. Neuchatel and Paris, 1947–57.

Glutz von Blotzheim, U.N. et al. *Die Brutvögel der Schweiz.* Aarau, 1962.

Glutz von Blotzheim, U.N. et al. *Handbuch der Vögel Mitteleuropas.* Frankfurt 1966. (Under publication, 7 vols. published.)

Gooders, J. *Where to Watch Birds in Europe.* London, 1970.

Haftorn, S. *Norges fugler.* Trondhjem, 1971.

Harrison, C. *A Field Guide to the Nests, Eggs and Nestlings of British and European Birds.* London, 1975.

Hartert, E. *Die Vögel der Paläarktischen Fauna.* Berlin, 1910–1922. (Suppl. 1923, 1932–36.)

Heinzel, H., Fitter, R. and Parslow, J. *The Birds of Britain and Europe with Nort Africa and the Middle East.* London, 1972.

Hollom, P. A. D. *The Popular Handbook of British Birds.* London, 1962.

Hollom, P. A. D. *The Popular Handbook of Rarer British Birds.* London, 1960.

Hortling, I. *Ornitologisk handbok.* Helsinki, 1929–32.

Hulten, M. and Wassenich, V. *Die Vogelfauna Luxemburgs.* Luxembourg, 1960–61.

Hüe, F. and Etchécopar, R. D. *Les oiseaux du Proche et du Moyen Orient de la Mediterranée aux contreforts de l'Himalaya.* Paris, 1971.

Ivanov, A. I., Portenko, L. A. et al. *Ptitsy SSSR.* Moscow, 1951–60.

Kennedy, P. G. et al. *The Birds of Ireland.* Edinburgh and London, 1954.

Keve, A. *Nomenclator Avium Hungariae.* Budapest, 1960.

King, B. F. and E. C. Dickinson. *A Field Guide to the Birds of South-East Asia.* Boston, 1975.

Lövenskiold, H. L. *Avifauna Svalbardensis.* Oslo, 1964.

Makatsch, W. *Die Vogelwelt Macedoniens.* Leipzig, 1950.

Makatsch, W. *Verzeichnis der Vögel Deutschlands.* Radebeul and Berlin, 1957.

Makatsch, W. *Wir bestimmen die Vögel Europas.* Leipzig, 1969.

Matvejev, S. D. and Vasic, V. F. *Catalogus Faunae Jugoslaviae.* IV/3. Aves. Ljublijana, 1973.

Mayaud, N. et al. *Inventaire des Oiseaux de France.* Paris, 1936. (Suppl. in Alauda, 1953: Liste des Oiseaux de France.)

Merikallio, E. *Finnish Birds.* Helsinki, 1958.

Niethammer, G. *Handbuch der Deutschen Vogelkunde.* 3 vol. Leipzig, 1937–42.

Niethammer, G. et al. *Die Vögel Deutschlands: Artenliste.* Frankfurt on Main, 1964.

Parslow, J. *Breeding Birds of Britain and Ireland.* London, 1973.

Patett, P. *The Birds of Bulgaria.* Sofia, 1950

Peterson, R. T. et al. *A Field Guide to the Birds of Britain and Europe.* London, 1966.

Peterson, R. T. *A Field Guide to the Birds.* Boston, 1947.

Porter, R. F. et al. *Flight Identification of European Raptors.* Berkhamsted, 1974.

Robbins, C. S., Bruun, B. and Zim, H. *Birds of North America.* New York, 1966.

Rosenberg, E. *Fåglar i Sverige.* Stockholm, 1972.

Salomonsen, F. *Oversigt over Danmarks Fugle.* Copenhagen, 1963.

Scott, P. *A Coloured Key to the Wildfowl of the World.* London, 1968.

Sharrock, J. T. R. *The Atlas of Breeding Birds in Britain and Ireland.* London, 1976.

Stresemann, E., Portenko, L. A. et al. *Atlas der Verbreitung palaearktischer Vögel.* Berlin, 1960. (Series under publication.)

Sveriges Ornitologiska Förening. *Förteckning över Sveriges fåglar.* 6th ed. Stockholm, 1970.

Tait, W. C. *Birds of Portugal.* London, 1924.

Thomson, A. Landsborough. *A New Dictionary of Birds.* London, 1964.

Timmermann, G. *Die Vögel Islands.* Reykjavik, 1938–49.

Tomailojć, L. *Ptaki Polski.* Warsaw, 1972.

Vaurie, C. *The Birds of the Palearctic Fauna.* 2 vol. London, 1959, 1965.

Verheyen, R. *La Vie des Oiseaux.* 8 vol. Brussels, 1943–51.

Voous, K. H. *Atlas of European Birds.* London, 1960.

Witherby, H. F. et al. *The Handbook of British Birds.* 5 vol. London, 1949.

Ornithological magazines

Magazines treating the various aspects of bird life are published in hundreds every year. Almost every country in the world and certainly most countries in Europe have several magazines of varying content and importance. Most are published by ornithological societies, some are published by museums and universities, and some are private publishing ventures. The most important European publications on ornithological subjects are listed below together with the society or institute publishing them. Where no such society or institute is mentioned, the publishing is commercial.

Austria	Egretta (Vogelkundische Nachrichten aus Österreich)	Österreichischen Vogelwarte
Belgium	Gerfaut	Société Ornithologique de la Belgique
Denmark	Dansk Ornithologisk Forenings Tidsskrift, Feltornithologen	Dansk Ornithologisk Forening
East Germany	Beiträge zur Vogel-kunde Der Falke	
Finland	Ornis Fennica	Suomen lintutieteellinen yhdistys
France	L'Oiseau	Société Ornithologique de France
	Alauda	
Germany	Journal für Ornithologie	Deutsche Ornithologeu-Gesellschaft
	Die Vogewarte	D.O.G. (Bird Stations on Heligoland and at Radolfzell)
Great Britain and Ireland	British Birds	
	Ibis	British Ornithologists' Union
	Bird Study	British Trust for Ornithology
	Irish Bird Report	Irish Ornithologists' Club
	Annual Report	The Wildfowl Trust
	Birds	The Royal Society for the Protection of Birds
	Scottish Birds	Scottish Ornithologists' Club
	Zoological Record : Aves	Zoological Society of London
Hungary	Aquila	Institutus Ornithologicus Hungaricus
Italy	Rivista Italiana di Ornitologia	
	Avocetta	Associazione Ornitologica Italiana
Netherlands	Ardea	Nederlandse Ornithologische Vereenigung
	Limosa	Club van Nederlandsche Vogelkundigen
Norway	Vår Fuglefauna	Norsk Ornitologisk Forening
	Sterna	Stavanger Museum
Poland	Acta Ornithologica	Musei Zoologici Polonici
	The Ring	
Scandinavia	Ornis Scandinavica	Skandinavisk Ornithologisk Union
Spain	Ardeola	Sociedad Española de Ornithologia
Switzerland	Nos Oiseaux	Société Romande pour l'Etude et la Protection des Oiseaux
	Der Ornithologische Beobachter	Schweizerische Gesellschaft Für Vogelkunde und Vogelschutz
Sweden	Vår Fågelvärld	Sveriges Ornitologiska Förening
	Fauna och Flora	Naturhistoriska Riksmuseet
	Anser	Skånes Ornitologiska Förening
	Calidris	Ölands Ornitologiska Förening
Yugoslavia	Larus	Institute of Biology, University of Zagreb

Recordings

Records of bird-songs and of calls are becoming increasingly popular. They are extremely useful as an aid in identification besides being a pleasure to listen to. The most important European series are listed below. Many other valuable records are available, but the ones listed cover a large number of species in a more or less systematic order.

Bondesen, P. *Fuglesangen. En Verden Af Musik.* Rhodos. Copenhagen.

Chappuis, C. *Oiseaux de France.* Chappuis. Rouen.

Conder et al. *British Garden Birds.* Record Books. London.

Fentaloff, C., Thielcke, G. and Tretzel, E. *Stimmen Einheimischer Vögel.* Kosmos. Stuttgart.

Kellogg, P. P. et al. *A Field Guide to the Bird Songs of Eastern and Central North America.* Houghton Mifflin. Boston.

Kirby, J. *Listen . . . the Birds.* European Phono Club. Amsterdam.

Lewis, V. *Bird Recognition : An Aural Index.* H.M.V. London.

North, M. E. W. and Simms, E. *Witherby's Sound Guide to British Birds.* H. F. and G. Witherby Ltd, London.

Paatela, J. *Laulava lintukirja.* WSOY Helsinki.

Palmer, S. *Radions fågelskivor.* Sveriges Radio. Stockholm.

Palmer, S. and Boswall, J. *A Field Guide to the Songs of Britain and Europe.* Sveriges Radio. Stockholm.

Reisinger, H., *Die Singvögel, Europas.* Kosmos, Stuttgart.

Roché, J. C. *Oiseaux en Camargue.* Pacific. Neuilly.

Roché, J. C. *Oiseaux en Bretagne.* Pacific. Neuilly.

Roché, J. C. *A Sound Guide to the Birds of Europe* (three volumes). International Centre for Ornithological Sound Publications. Aubenas-les-Alpes.

Shove, J. C. et al. *British Bird Series.* London.

Thielcke, G. *Zimmerleute des Waldes.* Kosmos. Stuttgart.

Veprintsev, B. *The Voices of Birds in Wild Nature.* Union Studio of Disc Recording. Moscow.

Wahlström, S. *Våra svenska fåglar i ton.* AB Svensk Litteratur. Stockholm.

Index

This index contains the common and scientific names of species. (The pages dealing with groups of birds can be conveniently found by using the table of contents.) The page reference is to the text page, and the illustration appears on the opposite page. A number of commonly used alternative names have been indexed and cross-referenced to the names used in this book.